· BORN TO KVETCH ·

ALSO BY MICHAEL WEX

Shlepping the Exile
Die Abenteuer des Micah Mushmelon,
Kindlicher Talmudist

· BORN TO KVETCH ·

YIDDISH LANGUAGE AND CULTURE IN ALL ITS MOODS

Michael Wex

ST. MARTIN'S PRESS

NEW YORK

www.stmartins.com

Library of Congress Cataloging-in-Publication Data

Wex, Michael.
    Born to kvetch : Yiddish language and culture in all its moods / Michael Wex.—1st U.S. ed.
        p. cm.
    ISBN 0-312-30741-1
    EAN 978-0-312-30741-7
    1. Yiddish language—History. 2. Yiddish language—Social aspects. 3. Yiddish wit and humor. 4. Jews—Civilization. I. Title.

PJ5113.W482005
439'.109—dc22

2005046589

10 9 8 7 6

Sabinae Filiae
Nunc scio quid sit amor

CONTENTS

Acknowledgments

It's impossible to thank everybody who contributed to this book. Many of the phrases and expressions that follow first came to my attention as responses to my impertinent questions and youthful misbehavior by people whose names I never knew. They—and my long-suffering family—can at least look down from wherever they are now and know that I was listening to their admonitions, even if I never acted upon them.

Far more direct thanks are due my friend Seth Rogovoy, who hooked me up with my agent, Gareth Esersky. Jane Rosenman accepted the project on behalf of St. Martin's Press and then passed it into the more-than-capable hands of Ethan Friedman, whose patience I have tried on more than one occasion.

Thanks are also due to Henry Sapoznik and Hy Goldman for giving me the opportunity to develop much of the material here as lectures at Klezkamp and Klezkanada, respectively. Also to Michael Alpert, who first came up with the brilliant idea of hiring me to teach "language and ethos" in West Virginia many years ago. Eleanor Levine, Helen Zukerman, and Abe Goldstein have both done more than their share to help this project see the light of day, while Heiko Lehmann has taken care of business in Berlin.

Finally, my daughter, Sabina, has been a source of endless love and trust, silly fun and complete delight. My wife, Marilla, has made our home a much larger and brighter and happier place. She came looking for romance and got a snootful of Yiddish; without her, this book would not be here. Her love is on every page and *zi hot gehat,* as they'd say, *a sakh oystsushteyn.*

INTRODUCTION

The material presented in this book does not always correspond to the way in which Yiddish is sometimes portrayed in the more popular English-language media. Together with what we've come to see as typical Yiddish earthiness and typical Yiddish humor, there is a good deal here that is neither pretty nor politically correct—and there's almost nothing that could be described as naïve. Like the Talmud, which lies at the root of so many Yiddish attitudes, Yiddish is a lot of things, but innocent isn't one of them. As a definitive cultural phenomenon—as the main language of a whole society—Yiddish can be said to have flourished from the First Crusade to the end of World War II, give or take a few years on either end. As far as attitude and influence are concerned, it is entirely fair to say that we'll be looking at a language and culture that were born in one massacre and died in another.

Since a historical approach to such material could easily prove depressing, I've chosen to present a portrait rather than a biography—a series of portraits, to be strictly accurate: here's Yiddish talking about food; here's Yiddish dealing with sex and death; here's Yiddish posing with some relatives. Enough background will be provided for the reader to grasp the words and idioms in the same way that someone living in a Yiddish-speaking world would have. Some portraits might take the form of X-rays, but that doesn't make them any the less portraits.

In order to frame things properly, though, we have to start with a look at Judaism in general, and those features of Jewish life and faith that were crucial to the development of Yiddish. If the first chapter seems to talk more about the Bible and Talmud than *bupkes* and *tukhes,* it's because the Bible and Talmud are to Yiddish what plantations are to the blues. The only difference is that blues left the plantations behind, while Yiddish—try as it still sometimes does—never escaped from the Talmud.

A Note on Transliteration, Translations, and Sources

The Yiddish that appears in this book has been transliterated according to the system of YIVO, the Yidisher Visnshaftlikher Institut. It's the only system in general academic and scholarly use, and has been adopted by virtually all libraries that hold Yiddish-language materials. The main points to watch out for are:

1. The letter *e* at the end of a word is *not* silent; it's pronounced like a very short English "e." For example, *kashe* has two syllables, *ka-* and *-she.* It rhymes with Sasha.

2. The hard "h" sound—as in the first syllable of Chanuka—is rendered with *kh.* The YIVO version of the holiday comes out as *khanike.*

3. *Ey* in this system is pronounced like the Canadian "eh?" *Kley,* which means "glue," sounds just like the English "clay."

4. *Ay* is the same as the English long *y. Fray,* the Yiddish for "free," sounds just like the English "fry."

I've diverged from the YIVO system when using well-known Yiddish words in the English text. So Rosh Hashana, Yom Kippur, kvetch, and bar mitzvah all look like this when mentioned in English. When used in Yiddish, they're transcribed according to the rules above: *rosheshone, yom kipper, kvetsh, bar-mitsve.*

All other translations not otherwise credited are my own.

Standard biblical translations are based on the Revised Standard and Jewish Publication Society versions.

In a book of this sort, aimed at a general audience, there isn't much point in providing a bibliography when virtually all sources are in Yiddish. Still, mention has to be made of four seminal works that I have used no less than anyone else working in Yiddish: Uriel Weinreich's *Modern English-Yiddish Yiddish-English Dictionary;* Alexander Harkavy's *Yiddish-English-Hebrew Dictionary;* Nokhem Stutchkoff's *Oyster fun der Yidisher Shprakh (Thesaurus of the Yiddish Language);* and Max Weinreich's *Geshikhte fun der Yidisher Shprakh,* available in English as *History of the Yiddish Language* (Chicago, 1980).

· BORN TO KVETCH ·

ONE

Kvetch Que C'est?

THE ORIGINS OF YIDDISH

I

A man boards a Chicago-bound train in Grand Central Station and sits down across from an old man reading a Yiddish newspaper. Half an hour after the train has left the station, the old man puts down his paper and starts to whine like a frightened child. "Oy, am I thirsty. . . . Oy, am I thirsty. . . . Oy, am I *thirsty*. . . ."

The other man is at the end of his rope inside of five minutes. He makes his way to the water cooler at the far end of the car, fills a cup with water, and starts walking back to his seat. He pauses after a few steps, goes back to the cooler, fills a second cup with water and walks gingerly down the aisle, trying to keep the cups from spilling. He stops in front the old man and clears his throat. The old man looks up in mid*oy*, his eyes beam with gratitude as he drains the first cup in a single gulp. Before he can say or do anything else, the man hands him the second cup, then sits back down and closes his eyes, hoping to catch a bit of a nap. As he sits back, the old man allows himself a sigh of thanks. He leans into his own seat, tilts his forehead toward the ceiling, and says, just as loudly as before, "Oy, was I thirsty. . . ."

II

If you can understand this joke, you'll have no trouble learning Yiddish. It contains virtually every important element of the

Yiddish-speaking mind-set in easily accessible form: the constant tension between the Jewish and the non-Jewish; the faux naïveté that allows the old man to pretend that he isn't disturbing anyone; the deflation of the other passenger's hopes, the disappointment of all his expectations after he has watered the Jew; and most importantly of all, the underlying assumption, the fundamental idea that kvetching—complaining—is not only a pastime, not only a response to adverse or imperfect circumstance, but a way of life that has nothing to do with the fulfillment or frustration of desire. Kvetching can be applied indifferently to hunger or satiety, satisfaction or disappointment: it is a way of knowing, a means of apprehension that sees the world through cataract-colored glasses.

The old man's initial kvetches are a means to an end. He's thirsty, he's lazy, he figures that if he yells loudly enough he's going to get what he wants. But these first few *oys* are only the setup; the quintessentially Yiddish aspect—what Yiddish would call *dos pintele yidish*, the essence of Yiddish—appears only in the joke's last line. The old man knows what's happening; he knows that he could have died of thirst for all that his seatmate cared, as long as he did so quietly. He knows that the water is a sign of contempt, not a gesture of mercy, and he also knows that in a world where indifference is the *best* that can be expected, the principle of *aftselakhis* (very literally, "in order to provoke anger"), the impulse to do things only because someone else doesn't want you to, is sometimes essential to the world's moral balance. And the old man understands how *aftselakhis* works: alone in the history of the world, Yiddish-speaking Jews long ago broke the satisfaction barrier and figured out how to express contentment by means of complaint: kvetching becomes a way of exercising some small measure of control over an otherwise hostile environment. If the Stones's "(I Can't Get No) Satisfaction" had been written in Yiddish, it would have been called "(I Love to Keep Telling You that I Can't Get No) Satisfaction (Because Telling You that I'm Not Satisfied Is All that Can Satisfy Me)."

III

Like so much of Jewish culture, kvetching has its roots in the Bible, which devotes a great deal of time to the nonstop grumbling of the Israelites, who find fault with everything under the sun. They kvetch about their problems and they kvetch about the solutions. They kvetch in Egypt and they kvetch in the desert. No matter what God does, it's wrong; whatever favors He bestows, they're never enough.

So, for example, the Israelites are on the edge of the Red Sea, with Pharaoh and his hosts closing fast behind them. God has been plaguing the Egyptians left and right and has just finished killing every one of their firstborn males. The Israelites are understandably nervous, but there's a big difference between being slightly apprehensive and insulting the agent of your deliverance: "And they said to Moses: 'What? There's no graves in Egypt, you had to take us into the *desert* to die. . . . What did we tell you in Egypt? Get off our backs and let us serve the Egyptians, because serving the Egyptians is better than dying in the desert'" (Exod. 14:11–12).

This sort of thing constitutes what might be called the basic kvetch, the initial declaration of unhappiness that identifies the general area of complaint. Had Isaac Newton been struck by a potato kugel instead of an apple, the whole world would now know that for every basic kvetch there is also an equal and opposite counterkvetch, a retaliation in kind provoked by the original complaint. Such counterkvetching also appears in the Bible, most notably when God decides to answer the Israelites' complaints about the food in the desert by giving them something to kvetch about.

The Jews want meat instead of the manna that they've been getting? Moses tells them:

> God's going to give you meat and you're going to eat it.
> Not one day
>   Or two days;
>   Not *five* days
>   Or *ten* days
>   Or *twenty* days.
> *But for a month* you're going to eat it, until it's coming out of your
> noses (Num. 11:19–20).

They get meat, all right—quails, hundreds and hundreds of
quails—and for dessert they get a plague. Thus ends the eleventh
chapter of the Book of Numbers. In the first sentence of Chapter
Twelve we are told that, "Miriam and Aaron spoke against
Moses"—kvetching is to the Jewish soul as breathing is to the
Jewish body.

This sort of antiphonal grousing pervades the Old Testament—
what is Hebrew prophecy but kvetching in the name of God?—
and forms the basis of much of the Jewish worldview. Not only do
Judaism in general and Yiddish in particular place an unusual emphasis on complaint, but Yiddish also allows considerable scope for
complaining about the complaining of others, more often than not
to the others who are doing the complaining. While answering
one complaint with another is usually considered a little excessive
in English, Yiddish tends to take a homeopathic approach to
kvetching: like cures like and kvetch cures kvetch. The best response to a complaint is another complaint, an antiseptic counterkvetch that makes further whining impossible for anybody but
you.

Yet the entry for *kvetshn* (the verbal form) in Uriel Weinreich's *Modern English-Yiddish Yiddish-English Dictionary* reads simply: "press, squeeze, pinch; strain." There is no mention of grumbling or complaint. You can kvetch an orange to get juice, kvetch a buzzer for service, or *kvetsh mit di pleytses,* shrug your shoulders, when no one responds to the buzzer that you kvetched. All perfectly good, perfectly common uses of the verb *kvetshn,* none of which appears to have the remotest connection with the idea of whining or complaining. The link is found in Weinreich's "strain," which he uses to define *kvetshn zikh,* to press or squeeze oneself, the reflexive form of the verb. Alexander Harkavy's 1928 *Yiddish-English-Hebrew Dictionary* helps make Weinreich's meaning clearer. It isn't simply to strain, but "to strain," as Harkavy has it, "at stool," to have trouble doing what, if you'd eaten your prunes the way you were supposed to, you wouldn't have any trouble with at all. The connection with complaint lies, of course, in the tone of voice: someone who's kvetching sounds like someone who's paying the price for not having taken his castor oil—and he has just as eager an audience. A really good kvetch has a visceral quality, a sense that the kvetcher won't be completely comfortable, completely satisfied, until it's all come out. Go ahead and ask someone how they're feeling; if they tell you, "Don't ask," just remember that you already have. The twenty-minute litany of *tsuris* is nobody's fault but your own.

Along with cursing and deflating the expectations of others, which is just kvetching about things that have not been allowed to happen, complaining seems to be Yiddish's major claim to fame among Jews and non-Jews alike. Where, at least since Hegel, the standard Western view of the nature of things is one of thesis, antithesis, and synthesis; the Jewish view is somewhat different. Look at the biblical quotations above. The thesis is that we're going to die in the desert. The antithesis is that we're going to eat ourselves to death in the desert. The synthesis—if it can be called that—is that we come out of the desert more or less intact and keep on complaining. Judaism has positioned itself as the eternal antithesis: "Whatever is," says Alexander Pope, "is right." "Whatever it is," we say, "it isn't good enough." Adam gave names to all created things; his Yiddish-speaking descendants offer critiques.

IV

Now combine this institutionalized contrariness with the fundamental absurdity of Jewish existence in the world. We are God's chosen people; it says so over and over in the Bible, His favorites. And how does He show it? Just look at Jewish history: persecution and pariahhood are both tributaries of the one big river of *goles*—exile—the fundamental fact of Jewish life for the last couple of thousand years. Indeed, scholars question whether pre-exilic Judaean society can even be called Jewish, in the sense in which we understand the term. Judaism is defined by exile, and exile without complaint is tourism, not deportation: "By the rivers of Babylon, there we sat down and wept when we remembered Zion" (Ps. 137:1). If we stop kvetching, how will we know that life isn't supposed to be like this? If we don't keep kvetching we'll forget who we really are. Kvetching lets us remember that we've got nowhere to go because we're so special. Kvetching lets us know that we're in exile, that the Jew, and hence the "Jewish," is out of place everywhere, all the time.

Yiddish, the national language of nowhere, is the spoken and written version of this displacement, and its single best-known expression—found numerous times in the Bible—is hardly a word at all. *Oy* is the involuntary expression of shock and dismay produced when a medicine ball of *tsuris*—troubles, trials, and

6

tribulations—slams into your gut without any warning. The air that's been exiled from your innards departs your body in the form of a *krekhts*, a moan or groan that begins in the *kishke* zone between navel and spine, then proceeds up your chest and throat, gathering momentum until it issues from your mouth.

This unwilled rush of breath, this *kishke*-driven release of disaffected air, is the primal phoneme, the embryonic unit of kvetch. The fact that the term *krekhts* is also used to denote the musical sob characteristic of so much klezmer music helps to underline the more significant fact that Yiddish has produced an aesthetic in which ideas of beauty and standards of artistic worth are inextricably linked to expressions of longing and pain. Rooted as it is in the long wait for a Messiah who's in no hurry to get here, Yiddish sometimes approaches fulfillment but never quite achieves it; until the Messiah comes and the Temple is rebuilt, there isn't much apart from pining and dissatisfaction. Disappointment—awareness of the difference between things as they are and things as they're supposed to be—is the basis of kvetching, and the *krekhts*, the involuntary physical reaction to the revelation of things as they are, is the dynamic force that powers it.

V

It took roughly 2,500 years, from the Exodus until about 1000 C.E., to shape the ideas upon which Yiddish is based into the forms that gave birth to the language. Without some understanding of these ideas, we can learn a lot of Yiddish, but we'll never know what we're really saying.

Like Jelly Roll Morton, Ashkenazic tradition holds that our folks "came directly from the shores of France;" they were Frenchmen who migrated to German-speaking territory in the tenth and eleventh centuries of the current era. Important as such a fact might be to the history of Yiddish, it is a matter of strictly academic interest from the traditional Jewish point of view. Countries come and countries go, and until the Messiah puts an end to our exile, a Jew's own brain is as close as he's going to come to a homeland. For centuries, the Jews' only real home was a way of thinking designed to make their exile meaningful, a way of thinking designed to arm them against the threats and attractions of the people around them and make them prefer the danger and instability of their own homelessness to being at home with anyone else.

It started with the Exodus from Egypt. Seven weeks after leaving the country, the Hebrew ex-slaves received the Torah on Mount Sinai. Most of the Torah—the Hebrew name for the first five books of the Bible—is made up of orders, orders that the ancient Israelites were so eager to receive that a well-known Talmudic tradition states that the Lord held the mountain over them like a bucket, threatening to crush them if they didn't say yes to His rules: "If you accept the Torah—good. And if not—this is where you'll be buried" (*Shabbos* 88a).

It was a Torah they couldn't refuse, and after 210 years of servitude, they must have felt that it was being given them *aftselakhis*, to make freedom as full of obligations as slavery. The orders or commandments that they received are known as *mitsves* (singular, *mitsve*), and tradition says that there are 613 of them: 248 "thou shalts" and 365 "thou shalt nots," one for every day of the year. The Jewish calendar follows the moon instead of the sun, though, and has only 354 days—a single Jewish year isn't long enough to hold all the things we're not supposed to do.

These *mitsves* are the foundations of every aspect of Jewish life; in a very real sense, they *are* Judaism. You can be as monotheistic as you like, without the *mitsves* you're still not Jewish. It's the *mitsves* that forbid pork, enjoin circumcision, and keep us out of the Knights of Columbus; they are the root of Jewish difference, of everything that makes Jews Jewish. According to Rashi, whose commentaries on the Bible and Talmud are an integral part of traditional methods of study, "The whole point of the Torah is its *mitsves.*" What the chosen people have been chosen for is the obligation of fulfilling *mitsves* that are incumbent on nobody else. The Jews have been chosen not to: *not* to have that BLT; *not* to sit on Santa's knee; *not* to catch the Saturday matinee or blend in with the people around them. The election of Israel, as the theologians call it, is like the election of the kid who has to practice the violin while the rest of the neighborhood plays ball—what's normal for everyone else is a sin for the one who's been chosen.

Mitsves are like any other rules, though; they have to be fleshed out, explained, applied. The Bible jumps from one commandment to the next without slowing down for details. It tells you what, but never how. Imagine a *mitsve* that reads, "Thou shalt not park illegally." First we need to define parking and specify the kinds of vehicles to which such a law applies: Can I leave my bicycle on the sidewalk? My motorcycle? What about my Maserati? We must define the terms *legal* and *illegal* with respect to parking: Why is parking on Main Street sinful at 8:59 A.M. but virtuous at 9:00? Why is parking on certain streets always evil, while notions of permitted and forbidden reverse themselves on certain others on the sixteenth of every month? Does this reversal of permitted and forbidden apply equally to ham sandwiches and gefilte fish, and if so, when?

Imagine between 2 and 3 million words of this, most of them in Aramaic, and you'll have some idea of what the thirty-seven tractates of the Babylonian Talmud look like. The Talmud was composed in two languages, Hebrew and Aramaic; comprises two essentially separate works, the Mishna and Gemara; took roughly

seven centuries, from before the invention of Chanukah until after the Fall of Rome, to compile; was not supposed to have been
compiled at all, and will never be considered complete. It is the
sine qua non of what we think of as Judaism.

Much of the Talmud consists of attempts to work out the rules
of day-to-day conduct from the rather bald imperatives of the
Torah. Of course, much of it also consists of jokes, anecdotes,
natural history, gossip, innuendo, and—above all—endless, almost literally endless, debate about virtually every topic raised between its covers. Of the 523 chapters of the Mishna, there is
exactly one without an argument about *halokhe* (Jewish law)—
they only disagree 99.8 percent of the time.

VI

As the real basis of Judaism as we know it, the Talmud is indispensable to the worldview and development of Yiddish, and deserves to be looked at a little more closely. The Mishna, the earlier
of its two main components, was compiled around the year 200 in
the land of Israel and is written in Hebrew. It functions primarily
as a direct investigation of the text of the Bible and is divided into
sixty-three different tractates, spread over six "orders" or major divisions. A rabbi quoted in the Mishna is known as a Tanna.

The later component, the Gemara or Talmud, was compiled in
Babylonia around the year 500 and has lent its name to the entire
collection. It is mostly in Aramaic and takes the Mishna, rather
than the Torah, as its point of departure; but to say that the
Gemara is a commentary on the Mishna is like saying that the
works of Shakespeare are a development of the blank verse pio-
neered by the earl of Surrey. It might be true, but it tells you
nothing. The Gemara is a world all to itself, something to be ex-
perienced rather than described.

The first page of the first tractate can serve as an illustration of the sort of thing that goes on in the Talmud. It opens with a discussion of the biblical commandment (Deut. 6:8) that the Shma—"Hear, O Israel," the Jewish confession of faith—be recited "when you lie down and when you arise." The text opens with a brief Mishna, which is then followed by nearly sixteen folio-sized pages of Gemara before the next Mishna appears:

> *Mishna.* From what time can the Shma be recited in the evening? From the hour when the priests go in to eat their tithes until the end of the first watch—the words of Rabbi Eliezer.
> And the Sages say: Until midnight.
> Rabban Gamliel says: Until the break of day (*Brokhos* 2a).

Directer than this it *doesn't* get. The passage doesn't really say much about the matter at hand other than that night precedes day (see Genesis 1:5,1:8, etc.) and midnight means dawn. "From the hour when the priests go in" would have been a lot more definite if there had been a fixed time at which the priests went in to eat their tithes—but there wasn't. The reference is to priests who had become impure and were forbidden from eating the food tithed to them until they had immersed themselves in a ritual bath and a new day had begun at sundown.

The Shma, which consists of three nonconsecutive paragraphs from the Bible in addition to the verse quoted above, is not defined here. Rabbis Eliezer and Gamliel flourished *after* the destruction of the Second Temple, and were hardly accustomed to being able to see priests eat their tithes. The Mishna itself was not compiled until almost a century and a half after the Temple had been destroyed, and thus defines evening in terms of a world that no longer existed, as distant from its original audience as the Civil

War is from us. It's as if someone in the year 2250 were to say that evening begins when the cleaning crews enter the World Trade Center. Why doesn't the Mishna just say "sundown," then? Because "sundown" on its own fails to make the point that such cosmic events as sunrise and sunset exist primarily for the sake of the Jews and their rituals—the rest of the world merely enjoys the fringe benefits. "Sundown" wouldn't have helped much, anyway—look what happens when the Sages say "midnight," which is always at twelve o'clock.

Note that none of the opinions offered is said to be right. This reluctance to make a definitive commitment to a particular position is one of the most striking features of the Talmud. Overtly negative statements—"Pay no attention to that man behind the prayer shawl"—are relatively rare and tend to be directed against extremist absurdities. More usually, you find an interrogative demikvetch similar to the one with which the accompanying Gemara begins:

> *Gemara.* Where is the Mishnaic sage coming from that he starts off with "from what time"? And why does he start in the evening? He should deal with the morning first.

Centuries before there was any such thing as Yiddish, the Yiddish tone of voice, the Yiddish approach to external reality, was already being elaborated:

> *Mishna.* Whenever the Sages say "until midnight," the obligation extends until the break of day. . . .
> Then why did the Sages say "until midnight"?
> In order to keep people from transgressing (*Brokhos* 2a).

When the Mishna explains, on the very first page of the Talmud, that the Sages sometimes say one thing but mean another, the ground is unwittingly being laid for a language characterized by irony, a language in which the term *Tanna,* when not directly associated with Talmudic study, generally means "male idiot." In *kuk im on, dem tone*—look at that Mishnaic sage—the Tanna in question is almost always a misbegotten hybrid of Homer Simpson and a woodchip, the kind of person also known as a *khokhem belayle,* a sage at night, when there are no witnesses around to convict him of intelligence.

Acceptance of Talmudic authority marks the real difference between Jews and the rest of the world, especially Christians, who don't even realize that when the Ten Commandments say "Thou shalt not steal," they aren't talking about money or property. Theft of money or goods is dealt with elsewhere in the Torah, so in looking at this commandment the Talmud bases its interpretation of "steal" on the word's context. The previous two commandments, both part of the same run-on sentence as "Thou shalt not steal," prohibit murder and adultery, capital sins involving the abuse of human beings. While theft of property is never punished by death, theft of people is a capital crime, just like murder and adultery. It is therefore *obvious* that the Ten Commandments forbids the theft of human beings and not of movable or even immovable property—like, who could miss it, unless they were unacquainted with folio 86a of Tractate Sanhedrin or didn't live in a society in which people who *are* acquainted with folio 86a, along with the four thousand or so other pages of the Talmud, can become bigger celebrities than Shakespeare, Confucius, and the Beatles put together.

Contrary to the usual "people of the book" shtik (the phrase, incidentally, comes from the Koran), Judaism is a Talmudic, not a biblical religion; without the interpretive guidance of the Talmud, the Hebrew Bible can lead to Jesus on the cross as easily as to me at my bar mitzvah. The Talmud is even called the Oral Torah and is considered to have been given to Moses along with the Written Torah. In the Jewish system of belief, you can't have one without the other: Judaism relates to the Bible *only* as it is refracted through the Talmud and Talmudic ways of thinking. Public-relations-minded anti-Semites who claim to dislike only "Talmudic" Jews are saying that they don't like any Jews: no Talmud, no Jews. It's like saying that they love everything about Christianity except for the skinny guy on the cross.

The Oral and Written Laws are both at considerable pains to emphasize the idea that it is the *mitsves* that make the Jews unique: "And gentiles are never exiled? Even in exile, though, they're gentiles and their exile is no exile: they will eat the bread and drink the wine of the people among whom they are exiled. But the Jews won't eat their bread and won't drink their wine—the Jews' exile is *Exile*" (*Eykho Rabbo* 1).

The *mitsves* act as hedges against this sort of assimilation, and in the medieval society in which Yiddish arose, assimilation without formal conversion to Christianity was a virtual impossibility. As such, the Jews sought as much independence from the surrounding society as was practicable for people who still needed to make a living and eat, and this independence reached a climax of sorts in precisely those regions in which Yiddish was developing. As historian I. A. Agus put it:

> . . . the reliance of German and French Jewry on Talmudic law, as the foundation of all phases of organized life, was probably far greater than that of any other Jewry in historical times. . . . In Germany and

France at this period [tenth century C.E.] all coercive powers were derived solely and exclusively from sovereign Jewish law. . . . In these countries Rabbinic law controlled all phases of life. The organization of communal agencies; the establishment of political contact with the secular authorities; the raising of funds, through taxation, to cover all expenses and financial obligations; the enforcement of individual cooperation; the regulation of business practices . . . all these were grounded, *probably for the first time in history,* exclusively on Jewish law. Rabbinic scholarship for the Jews of Northern Europe, therefore, was not a peripheral interest, not a mere luxury, but the mainspring of their being, the essence of life itself.[1]

Talmudic ways of speech and thought are not so much the forerunners of Yiddish as its matrix, the womb and long-term gestational home of a language that was waiting to happen, a language that couldn't help but be born. From a linguistic point of view, the Talmud is nothing less than Yiddish in utero. The Jews who initiated the transmutation of German into Yiddish were those Jews most deeply connected to Jewish law, people for whom the categories and mental processes of *halokhe,* of Jewish law, were practically second nature.

VII

The French and Italian Jews who began to settle in the German-speaking areas mentioned above were quick to replace the vernaculars they had brought with them with the German spoken by their new neighbors. Although certain affectively charged terms

---

1. I. A. Agus, "Rabbinic Scholarship in Northern Europe" in Cecil Roth, ed., *The World History of the Jewish People,* Second Series, Vol. 2: *The Dark Ages,* Rutgers University Press, 1966, p. 190, my italics.

from the earlier Romance languages were absorbed into the Jews' new vernacular, these did not amount to much more than islands in a sea of German. Yet, as the Romance influence continued to shrink, the Semitic elements that had crept into those Romance vernaculars not only held their own on German soil, they increased and multiplied, in accordance with the very first commandment in the Torah. Although Hebrew and Aramaic had not been spoken languages for centuries, the Jews living in Germany had the same access to classical sources as their French and Italian forebears, and were producing large amounts of religious literature of every type, culminating in a virtual golden age of German-Jewish thought in the twelfth and thirteenth centuries. German was able to efface almost any trace of the Romance languages spoken by the Jews, even as the other foreign component of Jewish speech, the far more exotic stew of Hebrew and Aramaic known as *loshn-koydesh,* the holy tongue, took root and flourished in German linguistic soil.

The German component is far and away the largest in Yiddish, and close resemblances between Yiddish and German are still to be found today. *Du bist alt,* you are old, is identical in both languages, but such one-to-one correspondence is the exception rather than the rule. There are usually differences in pronunciation or inflection, even when the words are fundamentally the same: the Yiddish *ikh shrayb a briv,* I'm writing a letter, would be understood by someone accustomed to the German *Ich schreibe einen Brief* (and vice versa). Some common Yiddish words of German origin have dropped out of German itself—*haynt* (today), for example—while modern Yiddish has no trace of others that have remained in German, such as *heute,* which is German for *haynt.* These, though, are the kinds of differences to be expected in such circumstances—Dutch, too, has diverged from

German in similar ways, just as English did sometime in the sixth or seventh century.

The most important difference between Yiddish and German goes far beyond mere accidents of linguistic history. It's the difference between Jewish—which is what the word *yidish* means in Yiddish—and non-Jewish, and the way in which that difference made itself felt in the Middle Ages, when religion was the organizing principle of Western society. It's no coincidence that *haynt,* the word for "today" that has dropped out of German, actually meant "tonight" in Middle High German; the Yiddish meaning depends on the notion of evening preceding morning, on the lunar calendar implied on the first page of Genesis and explained on the first page of the Talmud. We're talking about a society in which both Judaism and Christianity were comprehensive ways of life, not lifestyle options, a society in which Jews and gentiles could live side by side without being able to agree on what day it was. A Jew who believed in nothing but had not converted to Christianity still ate, slept, walked, talked, and went to the toilet *yidish*—like a Jew—while Christians did all the same things *goyish,* like gentiles.

We're back to what we said before about the relationship between Judaism and the Talmud. It's no surprise that *loshn-koydesh* provides Yiddish with such words as *shabbes, seyfer toyre* (Torah scroll) or *mikve* (ritual bath), which simply don't exist in non-Jewish languages; what's important is that it also supplies the words for such superficially neutral, "non-Jewish" concepts as "during," "almost," "face" and "dream." The whole point behind Yiddish, its whole raison d'être, is the need or desire to talk *yidish,* as distinct from *goyish,* Jewish instead of gentile. Rambunctious kids used to be told, "*Fir zikh vi a yid,* act like a Jew!" If the same kids answered in English instead of Yiddish, they'd be asked, "*Vos reyd-*

stu goyish, why are you talking *goyish?*" The opposition could not be more plain. Yiddish arose, at least in part, to give voice to a system of opposition and exclusion that we will be referring to throughout this book.

VIII

The opposition was made flesh in the person of Jesus. To the Jews, Jesus was, in the words of the early medieval *Toldos Yeshu* (Life of Jesus), a Jewish antigospel written in Hebrew, a *mamzer ben ha-nidoh,* the bastard son of an unclean woman. Official Jewish opinion has nothing in common with, say, the Muslim view of Jesus as a prophet. Jesus was considered so loathsome that Jewish legend views St. Peter, of all people, as a *frumer yid,* a pious and heroic Jew, who deliberately set out to effect a complete separation between "real" Jews and Judeo-Christian traitors by establishing the Catholic Church, which thus becomes *good* for the Jews because it saved us from having to pray with goyim.

Unless otherwise specified, a goy is usually assumed to be a Christian, the kind of goy with whom almost all Yiddish-speaking Jews were living. No one who ever described an argument or excuse that doesn't hold water as having *a mamoshes vi der goyisher got,* as much substance as the god of the gentiles, thought that the god might be Zeus. The only *goyisher got* who matters is Jesus, and an expression that means "It's as close to the real truth as the notion that the blood of Jesus has set us free," tells us a good deal about the oppositional nature of a language like Yiddish, and why it could not rest content with German as already spoken.

We have to start by asking why it's *mamoshes*—substance—rather than truth or power that Jesus is said to lack. *Mamoshes,* reality or substantiality, derives from the adverb *mamesh,* which means "really, truly, literally," but is used most often in a strictly figurative sense. Its Hebrew original, *mamash* (note the difference in pronunciation), developed from a verb meaning "to feel, to touch," and the basic meaning of *mamesh* is comparable to that of the English "palpable." While you can say that someone *iz mamesh alt*, really old—where *mamesh* really means "really"— you're just as likely to hear that the sweet table at a bar-mitzvah was *mamesh*, totally, groaning under the weight of the goodies.

Mamesh in the sense of substantial or tangible has even influenced English literature. There's a well-known *medresh*, a rabbinic commentary, on the plague of darkness visited upon the Egyptians that speaks of *khoyshekh mitsroyim she-yeysh boy mamesh*, the darkness of Egypt, which was palpable. Not a simple absence of light, but a substance, a positive force all on its own, darkness with a backbone that not even the noonday sun could have made any lighter. Now, anyone who's ever suffered through freshman English is probably familiar with the beginning of Milton's *Paradise Lost*, where it says "No light, but rather darkness visible." Milton, who was interested enough in such things to have gone and studied Hebrew, either got the idea from the *medresh* itself or from someone else who shared his interests.

The *mamoshes* in *a mamoshes vi der goyisher got* is merely the noun that derives from *mamesh*, and in the phrase we're looking at, the idea of substantiality is closely connected with the person whose divinity is being denied. We've seen that *goy* in Yiddish refers primarily to Christians, but this qualification can be narrowed down even further. The overwhelming majority of the Christians among whom Yiddish-speaking Jews used to live were members of either the Orthodox or Roman Catholic Churches. Despite the many differences between them, both Churches believe that when the priest takes the host and wine and says, in one language or another, "*Hoc est enim corpus meum,* this is *mamesh* my body," the bread and wine turn into the body and blood of Christ. They don't simply represent it, they don't stand in for it—they change substance and become it. This process, which is known as transubstantiation, is the basis of the Catholic Mass, and belief in its reality lies at the heart of Catholic Christianity.

Although it's unlikely that very many Eastern European Jews were experts in the minutiae of Catholic theology, the idea that Christians believed that a piece of ersatz matzoh could become Jesus's body was far from unknown among them. Whoever first described somebody else's excuse as having *a mamoshes vi der goyisher got* was intending a dig at Catholic doctrine as well, a denial of one of the fundamental tenets of the religion.

Something that has *a mamoshes vi der goyisher got* can also be said to be *nisht geshtoygn un nisht gefloygn,* it didn't climb up and it didn't fly. Any Jew who grew up in a traditional Yiddish-speaking environment will interpret the phrase in pretty much the same way: what didn't climb or fly was Jesus, who didn't climb up into heaven and who sure didn't fly there. There's a variant interpretation, according to which it's the cross onto which Jesus didn't climb, but this has no effect on the meaning—the climax of all four gospels, the point of the whole New Testament, has just been reduced to a joke, the Yiddish equivalent of "and pigs can fly."

While the denial of Jesus's divinity would be offensive enough to Christians, its use as the gold standard of unbelievability makes it dangerous for a non-Christian minority. The very existence of such a phrase tells us most of what we need to know about how and why Yiddish came into being and about why it was never really German. Each individual word of *nisht geshtoygn un nisht gefloygn* would be comprehensible to a German-speaker, but it's unlikely that the German would ever guess what it really refers to, even if he or she caught the meaning of "bullshit." And that's the point: Yiddish started out as German for blasphemers, as a German in which you could deny Christ without getting yourself killed any more often than necessary. From day one, once they started to speak "German" to one another, the Jews were speaking German *aftselakhis,* German to spite the Germans, a German that Germans wouldn't understand—the argot of the unredeemed. Don't think of Yiddish as a union or melding of German and Semitic elements; think of it as a horror movie. Think of Hebrew as an aristocrat with a funny accent, a mysterious old language no longer used in conversation, the linguistic equivalent of the Undead. It needs body and blood to return to spoken life, the body and blood of a living language that can be taken over and put to use in the service of the Jewish brain. It wants to take over German and then say, *Hoc est mamesh corpus meum,* in a parody of transubstantiation.

William Burroughs was wrong: language is not a virus, it's a dybbuk, and as far as Yiddish is concerned, German is Linda Blair. Opponents of Yiddish who saw it as a stumbling block to Jewish "normalization" were absolutely right; Yiddish embodies the successful circumcision of every German cultural assumption. If, for instance, the goyim could have Christmas, then so could the Jews, some of whom still take a holiday from Torah study on Christmas Eve, or *nitl nakht,* as it is known in Yiddish. Since studying Torah in the name of a deceased person is a common way of praying for his or her soul, Jews were afraid that studying on Jesus's birthday might somehow work to Jesus's benefit, so they abstained from study on Christmas Eve. Instead of learning Torah, they tended either to play cards—something that pious

Jews almost never did—or prepare toilet paper for the coming year. They did something insulting and they did it at home—Jews were afraid to go out on Christmas Eve.

This fondness for mocking other religions is another feature of Yiddish that goes all the way back to the Bible, where many familiar names are really nothing but schoolyard taunts. Jezebel, *I-zevel* in Hebrew, means "daughter of garbage"; her name was probably *I-baal*, Jebaal, daughter of Baal, one of the major pagan deities mentioned in the Bible. Beelzebub, *Baal Zevuv*, lord of the flies, was a takeoff of *Baal Zevul*, lord of heaven. Nabal, the first husband of King David's second wife (called Noval in Hebrew), has a name that means "vile scoundrel, godless unbeliever" and that is used as a common noun in Psalms 14 and 53: "The *noval* hath said in his heart, There is no God."

Deprecation of this sort isn't restricted to living beings. The Talmudic word for a pagan religious festival means "disaster" or "calamity." The standard Yiddish for a non-Jewish holiday, *khoge*, comes from a biblical word that means "trembling" or "terror." *Khoge* sounds just enough like the usual Hebrew word for holiday or festival, *khag*, that it began to be used as a dysphemism (that's the opposite of a euphemism) for non-Jewish religious festivals. To this day, when the Christian holiday of Pentecost is mentioned in Yiddish, it is called *di grin-khoge*, the green terror. In North American Yiddish slang, Christmas is commonly referred to as *Krats-mikh*, scratch me, and I've even heard Easter called *Yeaster* (from the English "yeast"), because "*er hot zikh a heyb geton*, he raised himself up."

The nature of this kind of dysphemism becomes clear when *nisht geshtoygn un nisht gefloygn* is compared with an English colloquialism that also means "doesn't get off the ground"—a turkey. This was originally a showbiz term, as in Irving Berlin's, "Even with a turkey that you know will fold/You may be stranded out in the cold." A show that's a turkey flaps its wings but never flies.

And there you have one of the chief differences between English and Yiddish. What doesn't get off the ground in English is ultimately a TV dinner, with peas in the cherry cobbler and weird-tasting cranberry sauce. What doesn't get off the ground in Yiddish is . . . the single most important cultural figure in the history of the Western world, founder of its largest religion and . . . your god. Only you don't know that that's what we're saying: Yiddish is the original jive, designed to keep Herr Charlie from knowing what we really think.

IX

Disharmony lies at the heart of Yiddish. Or, to put it more simply, this is a language that likes to argue with everybody about everything—and to do so all the time, even when it's pretending not to. As the voice and, indeed, the public face of the Talmudically based program to try to make *goles*, exile, work in the Jews' favor, Yiddish begins by putting itself into an adversarial relationship with the entire physical world. As long as the Messiah is still missing and the Temple remains unbuilt, the whole world is in a sort of metaphysical *goles* from which it, too, needs to be redeemed. The world might not know it, the gentiles who are lording it over us and each other might never realize it, but anybody with real knowledge already knows that whatever is, is wrong. In a world in which even the *shekhine*, a part of God, is in *goles*, finding fault with everything is not only natural, it's the only path to the truth. Compared with the way things are supposed to be, the way things used to be when the Jews had a country and a Temple, everything sucks, and there's no point mincing words about it. There is a standard against which everything is judged and found wanting. It's rarely mentioned because everybody knows what it is—the return of the Jews to their rightful place:

> For Zion's sake I will not keep silent,
> and for Jerusalem's sake I will not rest,
> until her vindication goes forth as brightness,
> and her salvation as a burning torch
> (Isa. 62:1, Revised Standard Version).

The Yiddish tendency to rain on parades and deflate the expectations of others arises from a similar impulse to see everything *sub specie aeternitatis* and wonder if it's good for the Jews.

It rarely is, and this metaphysical disharmony is reflected socially in the Jews' relationship to the society around them. The Jews are not merely out of step with Christian civilization, they hold it in utter contempt. They might borrow the occasional concept or practice—what can you expect, it's *goles*—but the general context turns them sick. They don't want the local bread, they won't touch the local wine; they want to go home, but have no home to go to.

There is no chance of reconciliation. Right cannot be reconciled with wrong, nor can the truth make peace with lies; All can never agree with Nothing. Language, culture, existence itself, all become a matter of acting *aftselakhis,* to spite the best attempts of the cosmos and the Christians to do us in. The first step was to hijack German, then came the *Drang nach Osten.*

X

The dybbuk-infested German described above remained the indigenous Yiddish of Western Europe for centuries. Western Yiddish, now nearly extinct, was spoken up to modern times in

Germany, Holland, France, and other Western European coun-tries; if it ever used such words as *blints, knish,* and *shmate,* it did so as English does, as loanwords from Eastern European Yiddish. What differentiated Western Yiddish from the Eastern Yiddish that eventually eclipsed it was the Slavic element in the latter.

Modern Germany has borders with both Poland and the Czech Republic, and German- and Slavic-speaking territories have been adjacent to each other for as long as anyone has noticed such things. Although Yiddish developed in the western part of Germany, Yiddish-speaking Jews were quick to start moving east, and much of what we think of as characteristically "Yiddish" de-rives from the language's Slavic component. Aside from the words mentioned above, there are also such well-known Yiddishisms as *nudnik, kishke, tshatshke* and *bupkes,* in addition to thousands of others that have yet to make their way into English. Much Yiddish syntax—the way in which words are put together to produce phrases and sentences—has also been taken over from Slavic. *Es kholemt zikh mir a vayser nitl,* I'm dreaming of a white Christmas, comes out literally as: It dreams itself to me a white Christmas. *Es, zikh, mir, a,* and *vayser* are all of Germanic origin; *kholemt* is a *loshn-koydesh* word, *kholem,* that is behaving like a German verb; *nitl,* the polite Yiddish word for Christmas, is a legacy of proto-Yiddish Romance. There isn't a Slavic word in the sentence, but the construction would be familiar anywhere in Poland. Ditto for such common Yiddish constructions as *gib a kuk,* which has come into English as "give a look." Outside of Yiddish, this sort of ver-bal aspect appears in no non-Slavic language in Europe.

Some Slavic influence was felt in Western Yiddish even before an independent eastern version of the language had had a chance to develop. *Nebekh,* an interjection meaning "the poor thing, it's a pity, alas," comes from the Czech *nebohy,* which means "unfortunate," and is one of the oldest Slavic words in Yiddish, one of the few to have penetrated the Yiddish of Western Europe, where the non-Jewish population did not speak Slavic languages. It is also the root of "nebbish," which is simply a Germanized pronunciation of *nebekh*, which is usually spelled *nebbich* when transliterated into German. A nebbish is called a *nebekhl* in Eastern Yiddish, a person at whom you take one look and think, "*Oy, nebekh*, the poor thing."

The fact that *nebekh* managed to travel backwards, as it were, into non-Slavic territory indicates how indispensable it is to almost any Yiddish conversation. Jews were *nebekhing* all over Europe as early as the fifteenth century, and they haven't stopped doing so here. Many Yiddish statements would be incomplete without a *nebekh:* If you're the president's press secretary and the president isn't feeling well, you say, "The president is *nebekh* sick." If you're the kind of citizen who can separate the office from the man, you'll also say *nebekh*, even if you voted for the other candidate. But if you're a journalist with pretensions to disinterest, you say, "The president is sick." Apply the same principles to your feelings for your relatives and you'll see that the presence or absence of a *nebekh* can tell a listener all that need be known about your familial relations.

Nebekhing at the right place and time is so important as to be almost reflexive among speakers of Yiddish (for years now I've dreamed of opening a pseudo-English pub called The Nebekh and Shrug, which would never have what you wanted. "Got any beer?" "*Nebekh.*"), and it's no accident that the first Slavic word to make its way into all forms of Yiddish should fit so well into a language that has turned complaining into an art form.

Some scholars of Yiddish have laid considerable stress on the down-home nature of much of the Slavic contribution, holding that "wherever there are synonyms, or closely related words, of both Germanic and Slavic origin, it is the latter that seem nearer the folk, though the Germanic words must be presumed to be older."[2] Such Slavic words are, of course, redolent of the shtetl, the small, often primarily Jewish towns in which so many of Europe's Jews lived for so long. This scent of the shtetl spread, however, through a language that was already an independent, self-regulating entity and helped to make it even more so. Let's have a look at how.

---

2. Maurice Samuel, *In Praise of Yiddish.* Chicago: Henry Regnery Company, 1971, p. 128.

Two

Six Feet Under, Baking Bagels:
Yiddish in Action

I

The most compelling evidence that Yiddish has always been more than just a dialect of German seems to lie in the fact that the German Jews who moved to Slavic-speaking countries did not follow the example of their French and Italian forebears in discarding the language that they came with. Yiddish must already have felt like the right vehicle for what these people wanted to say, and any contributions from their new Slavic-speaking neighbors had to meet the same criteria that *nebekh* had long since fulfilled: is it good for the Jews? Is this something that Yiddish could use?

Profound as the Slavic influence on Yiddish has been, we shouldn't lose sight of the fact that Slavic words and structural features changed the feel of Yiddish, but not its feelings; they came into the language to reinforce what was already there. As increasing numbers of Yiddish speakers moved from the Slavic-speaking East to Western Europe and the Americas in the late nineteenth and early twentieth centuries, they were so quick to jettison Slavic vocabulary that the most prominent Yiddish writers of the time—the founders of modern Yiddish literature, who were still living in Slavic-speaking countries—revised the printed editions of their oeuvres to eliminate obsolete and "unnecessary" Slavisms. Whatever the Slavic content of their day-to-day Yiddish, these authors weren't in the least uncomfortable with eliminating large numbers of Slavic words from writings that were already considered the defining texts of modern written Yiddish. On the other hand, syntactic features derived from the Slavic languages had become so essential to the structure of Eastern European Yiddish that they could not be discarded without destroying the very fabric of the language. These are as prominent in today's Yiddish as they were a hundred years ago, despite the fact that most Yiddish speakers no longer use Slavic languages to communicate with gentiles.

This is not to say that vast numbers of Slavic words have not been retained in contemporary Yiddish, only to point out that those that were either tend to be unique—*blintse,* for example, which gives us the English "blintz," has no real Germanic equivalent—or else have a resonance that their Germanic synonyms lack. So, for example, Yiddish has retained the Germanic *nopl* as the formal and even technical term for the navel, but unless you're speaking to a physician or reading a learned paper on the absence of the *nopl* in paintings of Adam and Eve, the word is generally felt to be a little prissy in comparison with the more popular Slavic *pupik* (often pronounced *pipik*). More belly button than navel, *pupik* is preferred for day-to-day use, where it can also refer to the gizzard of a chicken or turkey—you can still hear "Who wants the *pupik*?" at plenty of kosher Thanksgiving dinners.

Each word has its uses. If you want to curse someone in a distinctly Yiddish manner, you can say, "*Zol dir dreyen farn nopl,* you should go dizzy in the navel"—and never in the *pupik*. Imagine your navel as the hole in a vinyl LP; now imagine that LP on a turntable, your midriff and its contents spinning while the rest of you stays still; then take away the turntable and imagine feeling that way forever. This idiom probably favors the "fancier" word because certain types of Yiddish curse are best regarded as ill-tempered subdivisions of diagnostic medicine. On the other hand, *a dank dir in pupik,* thank you in your *pupik,* can never be expressed as "thank you in your *nopl*"; it means thanks for standing by and looking on, thanks for nothing. *Moyshe Pupik,* Moses Bellybutton, is never *Moyshe Nopl;* he's a nobody, a nothing, a *nebekhl* who's not even much of a nebbish. Mickey Katz's version of the American pop standard, "You Belong to Me," features the wonderful couplet: "You'll love it in the South Pacific, /Some enchanted evening with Moyshe Pipik."

But the story doesn't end in the South Pacific. *Pupik* is an eastern Slavic form. The same word comes into Yiddish all over again in its Polish form, *pempik,* to mean a squat, tubby person, someone who might be described as being built like a fireplug. *Pempik* is simply the Polish version of *pupik;* the nature of its specialized Yiddish meaning might well offer evidence of a preponderance of "outies" (as distinct from "innies") among the navels of Eastern European Yiddish speakers.

Nopl, pupik, and *pempik* can serve as examples of specialization brought on by abundance. When it came to designations for the navel, Yiddish suddenly found itself with an *embarras de richesses* and decided to take advantage of the surplus. But it was also quite happy to use the Slavic component to restructure existing idioms. One of the most popular expressions in the language, *bobe-mayse*—a cock-and-bull story, something that never took place—provides a wonderful example of the Slavic effect on Yiddish borrowings from non-Jewish cultures. We're about to see how Western Yiddish went to work on Romance material before the Slavic component of Eastern Yiddish went to work on them both.

Bobe (often pronounced *bube*) is Yiddish for grandmother; a *mayse* is a story or tale, a description of events that may or may not have happened. It's only an accident of Jewish history, though, that *bobe-mayse* appears to resemble the English "old wives' tale" so closely, and the phrase didn't become a "grandmother" until fairly late in its life. It began as a *Bove-mayse*, a Bove story, Bove being the Yiddish form of Buovo, which is the Italian form of the English and Anglo-Norman Bevys. Along with Sir Lancelot, Robin Hood, and Guy of Warwick, Sir Bevys of Hampton was one of those fictional knights whose adventures were once a staple of vernacular literature, the medieval counterparts of the action movie hero. He seems to have made his first appearance in Anglo-Norman (the French spoken in England after the Norman Conquest), then been adopted by the English, and subsequently translated into a number of other languages, including Italian. Though never as big a star as the knights of the Round Table, Bevys certainly had his fan base, and if the Middle English version of his exploits is any indication, he came by it honestly. Anyone who can ride into London, which had a population of about 5,000 at the time, and kill 32,000 citizens with no help from anyone but his twin sons and a combat-happy horse called Arondel, definitely makes it as a fourteenth-century Steven Seagal, if not a full-blown Schwarzenegger or Stallone.

Bevys's adventures were translated from Italian into Yiddish in 1507–8 and published in 1541, the first nonreligious book to be printed in the language. The translator was called Elye Bokher, i.e., Elijah the Kid, known to the non-Jewish world as Elijah Levita, the eminent Hebrew philologist and grammarian, whose *Mesorath Ha-Masoreth*, on the cantillation marks printed in Hebrew Bibles, is still regarded as a monument of biblical scholarship. Levita was a German Jew who somehow ended up in Italy, where he eventually spent thirteen years as Hebrew teacher to a cardinal and much of the rest of his time looking for work.

How I wish I could say that this Yiddish romance of chivalry featured scenes of princesses going to the *mikve* and knights winding phylacteries over chain-mailed arms, but as we've already started to see, disappointment is what makes Yiddish Yiddish. The story of Bove is basically Hamlet meets Mickey Spillane—on a horse. Bove's mother arranges to murder his father, the king of Antona, and then marries the killer. Fearing that Bove will grow up to avenge his father, mom and her new husband try to kill him, too. Bove escapes, gets sold into slavery in Flanders, saves Flanders from invasion by—who else?—the Babylonians, jumps onto a magic horse (Arondel is called Rundele in Yiddish), and goes off to free the Flemish king from captivity—another day in the life of a Yiddish-speaker, lightened only by his love for the Princess Druziana, daughter of the king of Flanders. Many more adventures ensue before it all works out in the end. Bove kills mom's boyfriend, shuts his mother up in a convent (where the nuns, unless they'd taken a vow of silence, would also have been speaking Yiddish), and lives happily ever after with Druziana and their twins.

It's unbelievable enough on the face of it. Knights and ladies speaking Yiddish isn't much of a problem—think of all the Nazis who speak English to each other in movies and TV shows—but, except for a lengthy scene in which Bove refuses to convert to Islam, even when threatened with death, the general behavior is completely non-Jewish; even the more realistic parts of the poem are outside the realm of Jewish possibility. The most credulous reader, someone who might have believed everything else in the book, could never have been convinced of the existence of a Jewish knight—*that* was as unimaginable then as Jewish Knights of Columbus are today.

Even once allowance has been made for such necessary impossibilities—*Bove* is no more implausible than most action movies—parts of the poem remain bizarre even by the standards of knightly romance. It's scarcely got under way when we stumble upon what must qualify as the single most incredible act in all of Yiddish literature.

Bove's mother, Brandonya, decides to use poison to get him out of the way. This is unusual, but not unheard of in literature. Only a Jewish poet, though, a poet with Yiddish in his soul, would depart so far from his source material as to have her try to poison him in the most underhandedly Jewish way imaginable. Bove comes home one night, tired and hungry. Mom has left him a snack, and it is only Bove's good luck—and his central place in the plot—that the servingmaid warns him that the chicken, source of the life-giving soup that also figures in the plot of this poem, has been poisoned.

The *Bove Bukh* was a raving, smash success and has remained in print almost constantly for nearly five hundred years. Towards the end of the eighteenth century, modernized adaptations began to be published under the title *Bove Mayse,* and the last popular edition, in more or less modern prose, was published in 1909–10. Although never completely forgotten, the *Bove Bukh* began to lose ground in the popular imagination once the vogue for knightly romance had passed. Bove himself had long since entered the language, and he remained there long after most of its speakers had any idea of what the *Bove* part of a *Bove mayse* was really supposed to mean.

The phrase seems to have been so well entrenched that it was felt to be indispensable, though, so the Yiddish-speaking masses subjected the word *Bove* to a process known as assimilation. Assimilation takes place in virtually all languages, and has nothing to do with dating gentiles or buying a Christmas tree; all that happened to Bove was that his name got changed. And changing the name is the essence of this kind of assimilation. A word that has otherwise dropped out of the language continues to appear in compounds or phrases where it no longer makes sense, so it's assimilated to—replaced by—a similar-sounding word, regardless of whether the replacement makes any more sense than the term that has been displaced. It's familiar, it's comfortable, and people will find a way to make it fit.

Look at the English *bridegroom*. It started out as *brydguma* in Old English and became *bridegoom* during the age of Chaucer and Bevys of Hampton. *Guma*, later *gome* or *goom*, is one of a large number of archaic words that meant "man," and a *bridegoom* was simply the male counterpart of the bride, the male principal in a wedding ceremony. *Goom* was too silly to last—"Who you callin' a goom?"—and dropped from common use after one too many tavern fights. In order to restore some sort of literal meaning to a word which the language still needed, English speakers took something that sounded like *goom* and joined it to the *bride*. The fact that the primary meaning of *groom* at the time was a boy, specifically a boy who looked after horses, doesn't seem to have bothered a soul. *Groom* was a word that they knew, and that's all that really mattered; once the usage has been established, people stop worrying about the dictionary definitions of its parts.

Once Bove receded from the general imagination, he had to be replaced. What's interesting about *bobe*, the word chosen to stand in for him, is its Slavic origin. In over 5,200 lines, there is no more than one Slavic word in the *Bove Bukh*. As it was only in Levita's lifetime that the center of European Jewish life began to shift to the east, the apparently trivial substitution of *bobe* for *Bove* contains a capsule history of Yiddish-speaking Jews and their language. To go from *Bove* to *bobe* would have taken a minimum of a century, and a century is an optimistic estimate.

The fact that *bobe-mayse* fits into the same general frame as "old wives' tale" is, as we've already said, nothing but a happy accident. Speakers of Yiddish had no trouble reinterpreting "unbelievable tale of knights and their deeds" as "unbelievable story about the good or bad ol' days such as your grandmother might tell." Bullshit is bullshit, and any bull can make it. To go from a hero on horseback to a toothless old lady, to make Errol Flynn into Granny from *The Beverly Hillbillies*, requires a trip from Venice to Vilna, and everything that such a trip implies.

II

You can dismiss a *bobe-mayse* or any other piece of flagrant bullshit by saying *a nekhtiker tog*, "nothing of the kind," literally "a yesterday's day." It's the Yiddish equivalent of "Tell it to the marines." If you tell the teacher that you were carrying your homework to school when Jesus Christ appeared out of nowhere, snatched it from your hands, and flew up into heaven, the teacher will probably look at you and say *"A nekhtiker tog!* No way!"

The source of *nekhtiker tog* is the sort of thing that helps put the Yid into Yiddish. In the fourth verse of Psalm 90, which is recited every Sabbath and festival, we read: "A thousand years in Thy sight are but as yesterday when it is past." A more literal translation of the Hebrew would say that the thousand years are "as a yesterday's day." The *taytsh*, the standard Yiddish version of the text (which used to be printed in prayer books the way English translations are today), translates the thousand years as being like unto *"a nekhtiker tog."*

Clear enough so far, but how does this come to mean BS? The point of the thousand years in this verse is that even a person who lived for all of them would be nothing but a *pisher* in the eyes of God, as substantial to Him as yesterday is to us. And if Fleetwood

Mac has taught us nothing else, it's that yesterday's gone; it doesn't climb back and it can never fly. The psalm goes on to compare human life with a dream, with grass that blooms and withers in a single day: your excuse might look green and fresh and healthy when you think it up, but it decays to nothing, turns into yesterday, as soon as it hits contemporary air.

Day-to-day Yiddish is full of phrases like *a nekhtiker tog*, idioms and expressions whose origins in the Bible or rabbinic literature are often obscured by their German or Slavic garb. Note that the sacred—a text from the Psalms—is not profaned by being made to mean "bullshit." Instead, it's been infused, so to speak, into the realm of day-to-day life. Somewhere deep in the structure of the language, beyond the conscious knowledge or recall of the speaker, lies an image of God smiling down with rueful indulgence on the vanity of human endeavor. We're dealing with a language in which yelling out "Bullshit!" can be a form of biblical exegesis.

III

There's more to it than the Bible, though; there's a way of thinking that owes something to Talmudic logic and can be applied to absolutely anything, as in the idiom *hakn a tshaynik,* to knock a teakettle. More often than not, this phrase is used in the negative: *Hak mir nisht ken tshaynik,* don't knock me a teakettle—that is, you don't have to shut up completely, but I'd really appreciate it if you'd stop rattling on about the same damned thing all the time. The English slang term "huk," as featured in so many episodes of *Law & Order,* is a direct borrowing from *hak mir nisht ken tshaynik:* "Tell the DA that he'd better stop hukking me," needs only a kettle to turn back into Yiddish.

Knocking or hitting or chopping a teapot is the kind of image that causes kids from Yiddish-speaking families to wonder about their parents' thought processes, and generations have been disappointed to realize how pedestrian the image really is. Think of a kettle with a cover or lid on the top. You pour the water into the kettle, put the lid back on top, turn the burner on, go off to make a phone call, and forget all about it. The more water boils away, the more the cover rattles. The fewer the contents, the less it has to offer, the louder and more annoying the noise. The lid is moving up and down, banging against the kettle like a jaw in full flap, clanging and banging and signifying nothing. *Hak mir nisht ken tshaynik*—don't bang away at me like the lid on an empty kettle.

The image is so striking that *hakn a tshaynik* has become one of the most popular idioms in the language, making its way into millions of Jewish and non-Jewish homes through the medium of Three Stooges shorts: Moe is on his way to a hockshop; when Larry hears where he's going, he says, "While you're there, hock me a *tshaynik*." During a manhunt for the Stooges, who are suspected of having kidnapped a baby, Larry disguises himself as a Chinese laundryman; confronted by a cop who asks, "What kinda Chinaman are you?" Larry bursts into rapid-fire Yiddish, beginning with "*Ikh bin* [I am] *a Chinaboy fun di Lower East Side*," and concluding with, "*Hak mir nisht ken tshaynik* and I don't mean *ef-sher* [maybe]."

While the Stooges were banned in many homes because of their eye gouging, nose pulling, face slapping, and occasional propensity to violence, these activities were called discipline in my own household. What bothered *my* parents was their Yiddish, which can get pretty salty, especially when Moe dresses up as Hitler. Along with Lenny Bruce and early *Mad* magazines, the Stooges are responsible for exposing millions of children born after World War II to Yiddish and its ethos; "Don't hit me a ket-tle" could have come right out of *Mad.*

Tshaynik hakking was not confined to the commercial media, ei-ther. A Yiddish copy of the New Testament left in my family's milk box by some of our thoughtful neighbors in southern Alberta—they must have dropped it off in the middle of the night, just to give us a taste of what we were missing—rendered the sounding brass of St. Paul's well-known statement in 1 Corinthians 13 ("Though I speak with the tongues of men and angels and have not charity, I am become as sounding brass or as a tinkling cym-bal") as . . . *"hak ikh nor a tshaynik."* I definitely got Paul's point, but who needs a Bible that sounds like someone's *bobe*? His message went *in der linker peye,* into my left sidelock, but didn't make it as far as my ear.

IV

From the examples we've seen in the last chapter and a half: *nisht geshtoygn un nisht gefloygn, a nekhtiker tog, hakn a tshaynik,* and *in der linker peye,* it's probably clear that the metaphors on which Yiddish idioms and expressions are based tend to be drawn from three major sources: empirically observable phenomena, the literal meaning of a particular word or words, and the sphere of religious and traditional Jewish life. Let's look at these areas in more detail.

PHENOMENA

Let's thank God that James Watt wasn't Jewish. *Hakn a tshaynik* is based on the same principle as the steam engine, but no one's ever going to write a children's book called *The Little Tshaynik That Hakked*—it wouldn't be good for the Jews. An intelligent Scots-man looked at his kettle and came up with the Union Pacific; an equally intelligent Yiddish speaker looked at a similar kettle and started to complain about someone else's complaining.

Watt abstracted a principle and expanded its application; the Yiddish speaker saw a resemblance between two otherwise disparate processes and used one to describe the other. The ability to see such resemblances is the basis of metaphorical thinking, and the less obvious the resemblance, the more striking the metaphor. So why say only that you're suffering, that death is the only way out of your problems, when you can make your kvetch more memorable by describing yourself as *lign in dr'erd un bakn beygl,* lying in the ground, baking bagels.

The phrase is both kvetch and mission statement, a perfect prologue to any future complaint. Why it has to be bagels that you're baking I don't really know, but *lign in dr'erd,* to lie in the ground, can mean to be dead. It can also mean that things are not, perhaps, going quite so well as you might have wished. So, if you run into an acquaintance on the street, and say, "Hello, Moyshe. How's business?" and Moyshe replies, "The business is *in dr'erd,*" he's telling you that you can sit shiva for the business, it's the business of blessed memory. You can even tell somebody to go *in dr'erd*—it's the Yiddish equivalent of "go to hell."

But in this phrase, in *lign in dr'erd un bakn beygl, in dr'erd* is clearly meant to describe where it is that you happen to find yourself. And it's as if being dead isn't bad enough, you've got to spend all of eternity in hellishly hot bakery conditions, baking bagels that, being dead, you have no need to eat; that, being dead, you've got no one to whom you can sell them; that, being dead, you don't even know anybody except other dead people, who also don't need to eat and who also don't have any money and who are all busy baking their own lousy bagels that they can't get rid of either.

This is the Yiddish myth of Sisyphus. But Sisyphus is a

mythological Greek. He pushes the rock, the rock rolls back. He pushes the rock, the rock rolls back—at least Sisyphus comes out with muscles. A Jew finds no peace even in death, only new opportunities for complaint.

Lign in dr'erd un bakn beygl is similar in its subtlety to a lot of the curses for which Yiddish is so justly famous. Take a look, for example, at *ale tseyn zoln dir oysfaln,* all your teeth should fall out, *nor eyner zol dir blaybn af tsonveytik,* but you should keep one to get a toothache with. Note that it is not specified that the toothache begin immediately. No, that one tooth remains as insurance; the toothache isn't going to come until the person doing the cursing is good and ready to inflict it. *A klole,* as they say, *iz nisht ken telegram;* a curse is not a telegram—*zi kumt nisht on azoy gikh,* it doesn't arrive so fast. Meanwhile, the poor cursee can sit and wait and worry and, with any luck, drop dead of a heart attack before the toothache even arrives. Again, it's the cursee who does all the work and becomes complicit in his own demise.

The dialectic apparent here, the process that renders the victim the agent of his own downfall, is one of the major contributors to the idea of Yiddish as a *goles* language, a language conditioned by exile that must be abandoned once the Jews get a land of their own. Yiddishists sometimes explain Zionist opposition to Yiddish as a product of ignorance or misunderstanding, despite the fact that most first-generation Israeli politicians were native speakers of Yiddish and felt that a language that encouraged victimization would hinder the creation of the new nonghetto Jew. The idea that Israel might take its place among the nations of the world with a coat of arms depicting heartburn rampant on a field of brisket and an inscription reading, *Zolst onkumen tsu mayn mazl,* you should have my luck, was anathema to them.

They fought and they won, but still couldn't escape their Yiddish fate: in a truly stunning variant of *lign in dr'erd un bakn beygl,* David Ben-Gurion, the first prime minister of the state of Israel, was posthumously converted to Mormonism.

Next week he gets the toothache.

LITERAL MEANINGS

Think of how "dough" is used to mean "money" in English and you've got the right idea—the metaphor depends on your ability to see what the original and the extended meanings have in common.

As a language in which almost any noun or verb can instantly be turned into an insult, Yiddish is particularly rich in this sort of thing. *Klots* has come into English as "klutz," and shouldn't need any explanation. The basic meaning of the Yiddish is a "wooden beam." A barely animate idiot, the Yiddish equivalent of a bump on a log, can be called a *glomp,* the stalk of a head of cabbage or lettuce. A *lemeshkhke,* a milksop, bears a title that means porridge.

Similar things can be found in any language, of course, but only Yiddish can produce the *klots kashe,* the wooden-beam question, a question so stupid as to put an end, at least briefly, to all discussion. A *klots,* as we have just seen, is a wooden beam. A *kashe* is more than just a question; in the Talmud, a *kashe* is a rhetorical question used to attack an opponent's assertion: "So, then, are you saying that essence precedes existence?" The word *kashe,* which has nothing to do with the identical-sounding buckwheat dish, derives from the *loshn-koydesh* for "difficult" and comes generally to mean a fairly involved question, something that cannot be answered in one or two words or by pointing to some object or other.

Most Jewish people who are even vaguely observant are familiar with the term *kashe* from the Passover seder, where the term *fir kashes,* four questions, is still used for the questions that the youngest child recites at the beginning of the seder ritual. As anybody who has ever attended a seder can tell you, it can take hours to get from the *fir kashes* to the meal, hours spent in answering these questions.

A *klots kashe* is the antithesis of this sort of question. It is like a giant log that won't let anyone go forward, and affects further discussion the way a tree in the middle of the highway affects traffic. It's a stupid question, to be sure, but a stupid question with pretensions . . . and the pretensions are always to intelligence. Imagine a group of history professors discussing the Exodus from Egypt or the Civil War when one of them asks, "But is slavery necessarily bad for the slaves?" *That* is a *klots kashe*.

RELIGIOUS AND TRADITIONAL LIFE

This is probably the most important source of Yiddish idioms. The vocabulary and images come from traditional and religious life (which were often difficult to distinguish until two or three generations ago), but their meaning lies elsewhere. A doting mother might tell her daughter, or even her son, "*Es nisht di khale far a-moytse,* don't eat the challah, the bread, before you've made the appropriate blessing." This is perfectly sound, if rather pedestrian, religious advice. The meaning of the Yiddish idiom, though, is: no wedding, no bedding. No sex before marriage. Like eating, the act of sex is forbidden until certain ritual *mitsves* have been fulfilled.

In order to make the relations between these sources stand out more clearly, let us take a look at three ways of saying that somebody is looking completely exhausted, each drawn from a different source:

1) A simile drawn from direct observation of natural phenomena: *oyszen vi a hon nokh tashmish,* to look like a rooster after the hens

have been trod. Anyone who's spent any time on a chicken farm or read Chaucer's *Nun's Priest's Tale* knows that a rooster will service any number of hens in a single night, thus giving the rooster's owners a chance to sleep late the next day. Using a word like *tashmish* makes the expression cute. *Tashmish* is the generally accepted shorthand for *tashmish ha-mite*, use of the bed, which is the standard rabbinic euphemism for sexual intercourse. Commentaries and legal codes from Talmudic times to today discuss *tashmish ha-mite*, which is usually translated as "conjugal duty" or "nuptial rights." A man is obliged to "pay" these to his wife on her return from the *mikve* at the close of her menstrual period. Of course, it's absurd to discuss conjugal duties or use vocabulary of this type when you're talking about poultry; it's like saying "to look like a rooster *post copulam carnalem*" in English. The difference is that any Yiddish speaker knows the rabbinic term *tashmish; copula carnalis*, the scholastic term for the same thing, used frequently by St. Thomas Aquinas, is known only to priests and medievalists. But the visibly fatigued rooster can be found in any barnyard in the world; Yiddish simply takes the image and combines it with the idea of punctilious performance of a religious duty— the sort of thing that once kept many Jews from a full night's sleep. The rooster is turned into a Jew, and a Jew—for the sake of this expression—is always losing sleep because he has so many *mitsves* to fulfill.

2) The simple, literal phrase *oysgemutshet un oysgematert*, rundown and weary, exhausted and exhausted. That's what the words happen to mean. Note that both of them have the German prefixes *oys-*, which here means "all the way, completely," and *ge*, which indicates the past participle. *Mutshet* comes from the Slavic component, *matert* from the German. There is no real

distinction made between them, and they are certainly indistinguishable with respect to the kinds of prefixes and suffixes that can be attached to them. This is a fixed phrase, and neither word would have quite the same effect on its own. This sort of repetition is not uncommon in Yiddish and is generally attributed to the influence of parallelisms in the Bible. Even in this very literal and fairly pedestrian idiom, we find Germanic and Slavic material used promiscuously to fulfill the demands of a Hebrew-based rhetoric.

3) A specifically Jewish simile: *oyszen vi an opgeshlogene heshayne*, to look like a beat-out willow twig. The image comes from the festival of Sukkes or Tabernacles, when different plants are used as part of the holiday ritual. The fifth day of Sukkes is known as Hoshana Rabba, the great Hoshana, when worshippers recite a large number of supplicatory prayers called Hoshanas (whence the English word Hosanna). When all the Hoshanas have been concluded, each worshipper takes a bundle of five willow twigs (which have come to be called *heshaynes* by association with the prayers) and strikes it against the ground five times. By the end of the fifth stroke, these dainty little twigs look even worse than the randy rooster. The idiom has a sense of someone buffeted by the winds of fate, bloodied and far from unbowed. It's a typical piece of Yiddish irony that the prayer that accompanies the beating of the willow twigs should concern the resurrection of the dead.

Note that even the most literal of these three idioms has an aspect that has been determined by traditional Jewish culture. Regardless of where they come from, German and Slavic words end up as the products of Jewish, rather than Germanic or Slavic, sources, because they have been transplanted from gentile to Jewish intellectual soil. We're going to look more deeply into that intellectual soil very shortly, but before we do so we need to glance briefly at the different types of Yiddish that were spoken on the physical soil of Eastern Europe.

THREE

Something Else to Kvetch About:
YIDDISH DIALECTS

I

Imagine a situation in which one-half of the U.S.A. pronounced "poodle" to rhyme with "toodle," the other half pronounced it "piddle," and each resented the other for doing so. If you change the Americans to Jews and forget about English, you'll have a fairly accurate portrait of conversational Yiddish—a language in which you can't open your mouth without finding out that, no matter what you're saying, you're saying it wrong.

There were three main groupings of Eastern European Yiddish speakers: *polyakn, litvakes,* and *galitsiyaner*—Poles, Lithuanians, and Galicians. *Polyakn* and *galitsiyaner* would have said "piddle"; *litvakes* preferred the "poodle." The significant Yiddish-speaking populations of what are now Romania and Hungary shared a basic southeastern dialect with their fellow Austrians (or ex-Austrians) in Galicia, a province of Austro-Hungary that included large areas of present-day Poland (e.g., Cracow) and Ukraine (L'viv, for instance). The idea of *galitsiyaner* as a distinct society is a late development that depends on the existence (or, after World War I, the memory) of an Austrian administrative department with well-defined borders. The Yiddish spoken there—southeastern, as already noted—inclines more to the *poylish* side of the great Yiddish divide between Polish (*poylish*) and Lithuanian (*litvish*) Yiddish.

With respect to Yiddish, the ideas of *poylish* and *litvish* are a little more involved than the names might lead one to believe. As far as Yiddish is concerned, residents of such places as Minsk and Kiev, which have as much to do with Lithuania as Tulsa does with Trenton, are *litvakes*, even though nobody thinks that Kiev is full of Lithuanians. Yiddish got a map of Eastern Europe 450 years ago and never bothered to replace it with a new one. Until World War II turned virtually all Yiddish dialects into matters of ancestry rather than birthplace, the basic dialect boundaries of Eastern European Yiddish corresponded to the political boundaries in place at the time of the Union of Lublin, the 1569 treaty in which Poland and Lithuania united into a single entity to defend themselves against Russian aggression. The Lithuania of 1569 was considerably larger than it is today, and Poland included large areas of Ukraine within its borders. When people speak of *poylish* or *litvish* with respect to Yiddish, the borders implied have been obsolete for nearly five hundred years. In light of what we've already learned about Talmudic ways of thought, this makes perfect Yiddish sense. One of the pioneering works of modern Yiddish literature, *Dos Poylishe Yingl (The Boy from Poland)*, is about a boy from the southern Ukraine; it's as if Twain's *Life on the Mississippi* were actually set on the Colorado—and nobody really cared. The more academic names for the dialects—Central and Eastern Yiddish—are fine for linguists, but are usually explained to nonspecialists by reference to the more popular folk classifications of *poylish* and *litvish*. A language with no permanently defined territory of its own defines itself in terms of territorial designations that have been either hopes or memories for most of the term of their use. Independent political entities known as Poland and Lithuania have existed only sporadically since 1569, and never with permanent borders. The names used to shed light on the language of a people with no country of its own are those of countries that flicker in and out of existence.

Regrettably, the issue of dialect is becoming ever more academic. Aside from children born into the various Hasidic communities, most Yiddish speakers under forty have learned the language in universities—often from teachers who learned it in university themselves—and speak no dialect ever used in synagogues or marketplaces, in bedrooms or bathrooms, in heaven or on earth. This is *klal-shprakh*, the standard language first developed in the 1920s and '30s by scholars associated with YIVO (Yidisher Visnshaftlikher Institut, the Jewish Scientific Institute, founded in Vilna and now based in New York). Their ideal—a sort of unlocalized "broadcast Yiddish" for use in mass media, public addresses, educational institutions, and so on—answered a deeply felt need at a time when Yiddish seemed to have a long-term need for such a thing, if only to keep *litvishe* academics from stomping out of lectures on Boolean algebra that might have been delivered in *poylish*.

Klal-shprakh was a tool, a way of trying to establish consistent standards of spelling, pronunciation, and usage in areas where a lack of agreed-upon standards was hindering development. Broadly speaking, it uses the *litvishe* pronunciation of vowels and diphthongs and *poylishe* ideas of gender and case. It wasn't supposed to wipe out regional variations. You weren't supposed to dandle your children or mourn your dead in it. The whole point was that it was nobody's *mame-loshn:* it was the Yiddish of the owner's manual in your car's glove compartment, not of your mother kissing a boo-boo. To speak *klal-shprakh* at home would have been like talking to your kids as if you were all on *Meet the Press*.

While plenty of intelligent people made use of *klal-shprakh* and contributed to its development, it also attracted a number of strident nudniks for whom *klal-shprakh* (or their particular circle's version of it) became the only acceptable Yiddish. These people actually *did* talk to their kids as if they were all speaking Yiddish on *Meet the Press*. Fortunately for everyone, these proofreaders of the human spirit had no influence outside their own circles, which seem to have been structured, in North America at least, along the lines of Bossidy's Boston, where "The Lowells talk to the Cabots/And the Cabots talk only to God."

Just change the names and leave out God. The stiff-necked character of the Jews, first noted by God Himself, combined with the general population's indifference to the left-wing politics and perceived linguistic censoriousness of many amateur Yiddishists to give *klal-shprakh* very little currency outside of *klal-shprakh* circles. Poles and Galicians didn't want a bunch of Litvaks telling them how to talk, and the Litvaks resented having their dialect cleaned up for purposes of standardization.

Klal-shprakh satisfied no one. Someone once characterized it as "the Yiddish of people who only talk about Yiddish." While *klal-shprakh* certainly influenced written Yiddish, its effect on the language spoken by *amkho*, the Yiddish-speaking masses, was not great. The decision to base so much of it on the Eastern European dialect felt to be closest to German rather than the one with the greatest number of speakers turned out to be fatal to its widespread acceptance in pre-World War II Europe. Even today, Hasidim in Brooklyn—for whom Yiddish has remained an intimate part of religious life—look at *klal-shprakh* as a curiosity, a Yiddish spoken by people who have no reason to speak it now that it's no longer the basic language of every segment of the Jewish community. The Yiddish of these Hasidim—usually a Hungarian dialect modified by six decades on American soil—must sound like a Folkways record of mountain music to many *klal-shprakhnikes*, but it serves as the primary means of communication for every level of a virtually self-standing society. *Klal-shprakh* has adherents; Hasidim have babies.

II

Klal-shprakh, which is based on idealized Lithuanian pronunciations, sounds almost nothing like the Yiddish once spoken in Warsaw, and students learning Yiddish in university often have considerable difficulty understanding Polish (and Galician/Hungarian) Yiddish. Compare two versions of the same sentence. First, the *klal-shprakh:*

Mayn man voynt in a guter shtot mit a sheyner froy.

It means: "My husband lives in a good city with a beautiful woman." Here is the same sentence in the Polish Yiddish that I grew up with. Words that have changed in any way are in bold:

Maan *man* **vo:nt** *in a* **giter shtut** *mit a* **shayner fro:.**

One noun stays the same, and there isn't very much that can happen with *in, mit* and *a;* otherwise, every adjective, every pronoun has undergone some sort of change:

KLAL-SHPRAKH	POYLISH
1. *mayn*—*ay* (as in English "mine")	*maan*—*aa* (superlong *a*)
2. *voynt, froy*—*oy*	*vo:nt, fro:*—*o:* (as in English "oh")
3. *guter, fun*—*oo* (as in English "boot")	*giter, fin*—*i* (as in English "pit")

4. *shtot*—*o* (between "aw" and long "o")   *shtut*—*u* (as in English "puss")

5. *sheyner*—*ey* (as in English "hey")   *shayner*—*ay* (as in English "mine")

The most important of these differences is the third, which produces such well-known and frequently argued-over doublets as *meshuge/meshige,* "crazy," and *kugl/kigl,* "noodle or potato pudding." While English uses only *kugl,* both forms of *meshuge* have managed to cross over, together with their inflecting forms *meshugener/meshigener,* which mean the same thing but must be accompanied by an article or a noun. You say, "He's *meshuge*" or "He's a *meshugener*"; "She came in with a *meshigene* plan because she's *meshige*"; "What are you, *meshuge*?" Just remember the old Louis Prima song: "I'm *meshuge* for my sugar/And my sugar's *meshuge* for me," and compare it with Slim Gaillard's "*Meshugene* Mambo." And if you can't remember that, don't forget the dual versions of one of the best personal descriptions in the language: *frish, gezunt, un meshuge* and—with better assonance—*frish, gezint, in meshige:* "hale, hearty, and unhinged."

The *meshuge/meshige* split reflects a Babylonian development in Hebrew that happened well before the birth of Yiddish. The *u* sound in *meshuge* is a Hebrew vowel called a *kubuts,* which is represented by three dots in a descending slant: ֻ . The system of Hebrew vowels used today was first elaborated in Tiberias, in the land of Israel. It was not the only system going, however; a competing Babylonian system assigned the *kubuts* the sound of a double *e* ("ee," as in "feet") instead of "oo." A Hebrew word that would have been pronounced *kubuts* in Israel was pronounced *kibuts* in Babylonia, and even today Hebrew dictionaries give *kibuts* as an alternative name for *kubuts.*

Yiddish took this Babylonian preference and extended it to another Hebrew vowel, the *shureq,* which sounds the same as a *kubuts.* Many non-Lithuanian Yiddish speakers—Poles, Hungarians, Romanians, western Ukrainians—retained this preference in their treatment of the Hebrew and Aramaic words that came into Yiddish, words like *meshige* and *side* (instead of *sude,* "formal meal, banquet"). The holidays of *shvues* and *purim* became *shvies* and *pirim,* and, to move to the Hebrew of the liturgy, the well-known prayer *Ovinu Malkeynu,* "Our Father, our King," morphed into *Uvini Malkayni,* while *ve'al kulom,* "and for all these things," a phrase near the end of the *shminesre,* the central prayer of every Jewish service, turned into the legendary *ve-i'll kill 'im.*

This "oo" to "ee" shift in Hebrew anticipates Dave Seville's "Witch Doctor" by about fifteen hundred years and predates the development of Yiddish. A similar development in German helps get us from *kugl* to *kigl,* but before we look at it, please be warned: if you've never wondered about the difference between *kugl* and *kigl* or *meshuge* and *meshige,* the remainder of this chapter could prove a little heavy going. You might want to go on to Chapter Four and return to this section after reading the rest of the book. If, however, you're tired of people telling you that your Yiddish is "wrong," that you don't know to talk, that nothing that even pretended to be human would speak the way your parents or grandparents did, the following few pages should give you all the ammunition you need.

The word *Kugel* still exists in German, where it means "ball, sphere, bullet"; a *Kugel Eis* is a scoop of ice cream in a cone. Like today's German vowel, the *u* in the Yiddish was originally long because it comes at the end of a syllable: *ku-gel* is pronounced *koo-gel,* with the accent on the *koo.* This kind of syllable, one that ends in a vowel, is called an open syllable; a syllable ending in a consonant is closed. The vowel at the end of an open syllable is lengthened: the *u* goes from the vowel in "put" to the vowel in "poot."

So *ku-gel*, a German word, has two syllables and a long initial vowel that sounds like the English "oo." In Central German dialects *u* was often "fronted" to *i* (i.e., the vowel was moved closer to the front of the mouth; *u* is a back vowel, *i* a front vowel), leading to a situation in which Yiddish has two official forms of the same word: *nutsn*, which originated in High German, means "to use," as does *nitsn*, which is based on a Central German form. Each was taken into Yiddish independently, which is why you can sometimes hear *nitsn* from people who eat *kugl* rather than *kigl*—the *i* was there when they got it. The same lengthening process operates independently of the German dialects, too, and turns *kugl*, with its long vowel, into *kigl*, whether Central German does so or not.

So we see the same thing happening at different times in Hebrew and German; a sound that was originally rendered as "oo" gets pushed up to the front of the mouth (sent into exile, as it were) and emerges as "ee." In the Babylonian tradition of Hebrew, though, this change takes place right across the board: all "oo" vowels are transformed into "ee." In German, the long vowel undergoes these changes only in an open syllable. As far as the shift from "oo" to "ee" goes, some dialects of Yiddish follow the Babylonians with respect to words of Hebrew and Aramaic origin and make the change regardless of the vowel's position in a word, at the same time as they apply the originally German distinction between open and closed syllables to words of *goyishe*—and not only German—provenance: along with the Hebrew *shvies* and the German *kigl*, there is also *pipik*, the fronted version of the East Slavic *pupik*.

Some of these words were fronted at very early stages. The

German *Jude,* "Jew" (from Hebrew by way of Latin) comes very close to rhyming with "Bermuda" and consists of two syllables, *Ju* and *de*. The "oo" moved to "ee" in some forms of Central German and in all varieties of Yiddish; *yid,* with the fronted vowel and without the *e,* is the only form in the language.

If, however, the German *Ju-de* ends up as *yid* because of the *u* in an open syllable, how do you explain the German *gut,* "good," coming out as *git* when the syllable seems to be closed? The truth is that Yiddish discriminates against gentile words. A word from *loshn-koydesh* needs only one consonant after a vowel in order to close a syllable; a non-Jewish word, be it Slavic, Germanic, or anything else, pays double: it has to have two consonants after the vowel if the syllable is going to be closed.

This lengthening underlies many of the differences between the dialects: *voynt/vo:nt* and *froy/fro:* are based on pre-*oy* German vowels—the modern German *Frau* was *frou* and, in some positions, *frô* in Middle High German—but the lengthening is then extended to words from other sources. Residents of Warsaw used to talk about a *go:* instead of a *goy*. Lengthening also explains the distinctively Ashkenazic—i.e., Yiddish-based—treatment of many Hebrew words. Moses in Hebrew is *Moshe;* in Yiddish, though, it's *Moyshe*. As far as Yiddish is concerned, *Moshe* consists of two syllables, *Mo* and *she*. The long version of the short *o* (which has no precise English equivalent) is the diphthong *oy*. In a closed syllable, it remains a short *o:* the Yom in Yom Kippur is *yom* in Yiddish, too.

The "oo" to "ee" process is paralleled in the treatment of the Hebrew *segol,* ֶ and non-Hebrew short *e* (as in English "pet"). In such Hebrew words as *derekh,* "way," and *melekh,* "king," the syllables break up as *de-rekh* and *me-lekh*. Following the Germanic rule that applies here, the short *e* is lengthened to the diphthong *ey* (as in English "hey") and you end up with *deyrekh, meylekh,* or *peysakh,* Passover, instead of the Israeli-influenced *pesakh.* The same lengthening takes place in such common non-Hebraic words as *redn,* "to speak," which turns into *reydn,* and *betn,* "to ask," which comes out as *beytn.*

This lengthening never takes place in real Lithuanian Yiddish, which has no long vowels at all. Such forms as *redn* and *gut* are the only ones possible in that dialect, and were the preferred forms of the Vilna-based framers of standard Yiddish.

III

The one important *litvish* deviation from the *klal-shprakh* of our sample sentence occurs in the word *voynt,* "lives," which comes out as *veynt* (rhyming with the English "paint") in the language once spoken on the *litvishe* street. The standard-language verb *veynen* means "to cry"; Lithuanian Jews make no distinction between crying and living. This unrounding of *oy* to *ey* is typical of real *litvish* Yiddish, and produces such well-known phenomena as the name Yale, the *litvish* version of *Yoyel,* which is Yiddish for Joel; a Yiddish-speaking actor friend once described eating at a McDonald's in New Haven as "going to the Scottish restaurant by the Litvak college."

The rounding or unrounding of vowels is more than just another Yiddish dialect marker; it proves that Rod Serling, creator of the *Twilight Zone* and *Night Gallery,* was a Litvak. In his play, *Requiem for a Heavyweight,* the heavyweight's manager, played by Jackie Gleason in the movie, is named Meysh. Meysh is short for Meyshe, Meyshe is *litvish* for Moyshe, and Ralph Kramden weeps in Brooklyn.

We've already seen how the Hebrew "o" is lengthened to "oy" in Moyshe. Watch the position of your lips when you say "oy" and note how round they get. Now try to make the same sound without rounding your lips. Hold them tight and see what comes out. Next, try to say "Moyshe" without the rounding and listen to how it sounds. *Litvakes* simply unround or refuse to round something that is rounded by other Yiddish speakers. They keep their lips tight in the face of any temptation to relax. The folklore image of the *litvak* as stiff, severe, and carrying a pole up his ass is based in part, at least, on habits of pronunciation.

Polish Yiddish extends the rounding process to other sounds, other diphthongs that are not always rounded in the standard language. Hence the contrast between the *klal-shprakh* "ey" and the *poylish* "ay" in *sheyner* and *shayner*. The substitution of "ay" for "ey" is considered a defining feature of Polish and Galician Yiddish.

A similar rounding is apparent in the "o"/"oo" contrast in such pairs as *shtot* and *shtut* or *foter* and *futer* (father). The long "a" in the German *Vater* (note the open syllable), is labialized: the lips are pursed, the tongue's lifted and drawn back, and the sound comes out as the English "o." *Poylish* speakers then round this "o" to "oo." This particular shift is crucial to Anglo-Yiddish, as it is responsible for turning the *klal-shprakh tsores, bobkes, shtopn,* and *tokhes*—troubles, goat dung, screw, and ass—into *tsuris, bupkes, shtupn,* and *tukhes*.

And now that *tukhes* has brought us back to fundamentals, it's time to move on to religion.

Four

Pigs, Poultry, and Pampers:
THE RELIGIOUS ROOTS OF YIDDISH

I

If terms originating in religious and traditional practices referred only to religious and traditional practices, Yiddish would be as whimsical as auto insurance, as exciting as alphabetical order. Sure, you could ask for Chanukah gelt and get yourself a quarter—as long as you asked on Chanukah—but you'd miss what Richard Wagner would have called the "Jewification" of otherwise nonsectarian things and activities. Good Talmudic language that it is, Yiddish takes terms based in religious and traditional practices and applies them to just about everything. For instance, people unfamiliar with traditional Judaism are often surprised to learn that observant Jews recite a blessing called *asher yotser* ("He Who has created") after going to the toilet, but there isn't a Yiddish speaker alive who can make do without the phrase *asher yotser papir*, the paper of "He Who has created," the usual Yiddish term for toilet paper. You can deny the existence of God from now until *meshiekh*—the Messiah—comes, but your atheist ass is going to grumble and kvetch until it gets the paper that confirms God's plan for humanity:

Blessed art Thou, O Lord our God, King of the Universe, Who has created man with wisdom and made him with orifices upon orifices, hollows upon hollows. It is known and revealed before Your Throne of Glory that if one of these were to rupture or another to be stopped, it would be impossible to remain alive and stand before You for even a single hour. Blessed art Thou, O Lord, Who heals all flesh and does wonders.

Although terms like *tualet-papir* (toilet paper) and *klozet-papir* (water closet paper) do exist in Yiddish, they are rarely found in the mouths of its speakers, for whom every successful trip to the john is memorialized as a triumph over death. They don't need to recite the blessing or even believe in God—the mere name of the paper lets them know that they've cheated the reaper yet again. Stalin's suspicions were correct: a Yiddish-speaking Communist had less in common with a non-Jewish commissar than with a Yiddish-speaking rabbi, even if neither of them cared to admit it. Stalin—or his advisers from the Yevsektsiye, the "Jewish Section"—grasped the all-important notion that people who are fluent in Yiddish are also fluent in Jewish culture: cultural knowledge, cultural literacy, is essential because Yiddish is the language of a self-defined culture group, and not of a geographic location. To be ignorant of *yidishkayt*—traditional Jewish culture in the broadest sense—is to have no reason to speak Yiddish, no way to understand it properly. Which is why Stalin tried to exterminate secular Yiddish culture along with Jewish religious practice: the Yiddish idea of toilet paper contradicts the basic principles of dialectical materialism.

When normal digestion is portrayed as cosmic drama, a term like "toilet paper"—which stresses appliance over apocalypse—has got to look pretty plain. As Comrade Stalin realized, Yiddish speakers who avoid the term *asher yotser papir* or do not understand its gastrointestinal and theological underpinnings won't be speaking Yiddish for very much longer. Somewhere along the way, they have failed to make the crucial distinction (and remember that crucial means "pertaining to a cross") between thinking like a *yid* and thinking like a goy.

II

Such distinctions are the lifeblood of Yiddish. Deciding what is in and what is out, assigning everything to a place on one side or another of a religiously-based dividing line, is a fundamental Jewish activity. On Saturday nights, observant Jews recite a blessing to mark the end of the Sabbath: "Blessed art Thou, O Lord our God, King of the Universe, who separates sacred from profane, light from dark, Israel from the nations, the seventh day from the six days of creation."

Judaism is obsessed with separation, with boundaries. The Mishna enjoins us to "make a fence for the Torah," and generations of sages have erected walls around that fence to keep it safe: If the Torah forbids us from cooking a kid in its mother's milk (see Exod. 23:19), then not eating meat and dairy together is a "fence" that keeps any slaughtered kid out of any kind of milk. Keeping separate sets of dishes for meat and dairy foods is a further fence that prevents any contact at all between the kid and its mother's milk by making it impossible to cook the kid in any kind of milk. Each successive fence takes on the character of a full-fledged legal ordinance and spawns its own system of hedges and subfences until the starting point—the kid in its mother's milk—is forgotten amid a welter of rules concerning a dairy knife accidentally used to cut a roast beef: was the roast beef hot or cold? What happens to the knife, the roast beef, the plate? Can the beef be eaten, the knife be used again? Anyone who keeps a kosher home deals with similar questions every day.

Milk and meat are only one small example, though. Similar

fences are so taken for granted that *porets,* the Yiddish word for nobleman, is a shortened version of *porets geder,* fence breaker, a term that first occurs in the Book of Ecclesiastes: "Whoever breaks through a fence will be bitten by a snake" (Eccles. 10:8).

"To break through a fence" means to transgress, to put no boundaries to one's own behavior, and two millennia of Mishnaic influence have left many Jews with a near-innate inclination for erecting barriers and devising prohibitions. The standard *secular* Jewish living room of my youth was an unwitting example of Mishnaic thinking in action: painstakingly arranged chairs and sofas, shrouded in plastic and arrayed in a room that no one but cleaning help and the lady of the house was ever allowed to enter. "Make a fence for pricey upholstery" and pretty soon the whole room is off limits. Those permitted to enter did so with vacuum in hand.

The covers and restricted access are only secularized echoes of the Mishna's fence around the Torah and are psychologically similar to the *mekhitse,* the divider that separates men from women in an orthodox synagogue and often *is* an indoor fence. The Saturday night ceremony that helps to fence the Sabbath off from Sunday is called *havdole,* division or differentiation, as if the sanctity and exaltation of the Sabbath must be kept away from the profane neutrality of Sunday or Tuesday. If the Sabbath is a living room, Sunday is a kid with muddy shoes, and *havdole* is a plastic cover for the Jewish soul.

Less formalized, nonritual *havdoles*—verbal fences, if you will—are an integral part of Yiddish. *Lehavdl,* from the same Hebrew root as *havdole,* means "to divide, separate, or differentiate," and is used to point up the contrast between two people or things that are mentioned in the same breath but should not really be associated with each other: "Gandhi and, *lehavdl,* Hitler were twentieth-century political figures"; "the cow and, *lehavdl*, the pig . . . ." Forced or prissy as "pardon the expression" would seem in equivalent sentences in English, *lehavdl* is so vital to the idiomatic structure of Yiddish that its absence would be marked immediately. In fact, Gandhi is so different from Hitler that a single *lehavdl* might not be enough: you might want to say *lehavdl be-elef havdoles* or even *be-elef alfey havdoles,* to separate with a thousand or even a million divisions.

The numbers aren't as important as the fact of separation. Whether you're keeping away from gentiles or using different sets of dishes at meat and dairy meals, you are taking an active part in the system of exclusions produced by the *mitsves.* You can never stop deciding what's in and what's out, who's this and who's that: every sentence passes sentence. A person who puts a *lehavdl* between the Beatles and Frank Sinatra will have nothing in common with one who doesn't. To put an "excuse me" between Gandhi and Hitler is a matter of choice in English; to leave out the *lehavdl* in a similar Yiddish sentence is to speak the language like a goy—like someone who knows Yiddish words but does not understand the principles that bind them together—and to place yourself on the wrong side of the biggest fence of all: "Blessed art Thou, O Lord our God, King of the Universe, for not having made me a goy."

This blessing, recited every morning, is generally interpreted as an expression of thanks for all the *mitsves* that we are obliged to perform. Since fulfillment of these *mitsves* is the *takhles*—the real purpose—of all human life, the *yid,* the adult Jewish male, is the most privileged member of the human species: Jewish women have fewer *mitsves* than men, gentiles have none at all. If a diminished connection to the Torah and its *mitsves* is felt to diminish one's human potential (and if it did not, there would be no difference between *yid* and goy), there is no reason not to use *yid* as a synonym for *mentsh,* "member of my species, generic human being."

Yid equals man plus *mitsves.* A stranger coming into a synagogue—where his religious affiliation is unlikely to be in doubt—will be asked, *Fun vanet kumt a yid?* "Whence comes a Jew?" To ask someone how he is, you say *Vos makht a yid? Yid* means "you" as often as "Jew," and is the only polite way of refer- ring to a Jewish stranger (as long as he's a man). *Reb Yid,* Mr. Jew, is a term of considerable respect, the equivalent of "sir." If you were to ask a stranger, especially one your age or older, for direc- tions, you would say, "*Zayt moykhl,* Excuse me, *Reb Yid,* is this the way to Carnegie Hall?" The only thing more polite is to refer to him in the third person and call him *der yid,* the Jew: *Tsi ken der yid mir zogn?* . . . "Could the Jew tell me? . . ." A literal English translation not only misses the point, it inverts it: "I was standing on the corner when a *yid* came up to me. . . ." All it means is "somebody," but not everybody is somebody.

The protean character of the word *yid* extends only as far as the sign of Abraham's covenant with God. The verb *yidishn,* to make someone into a *yid,* means "to circumcise," and every *yid* is by defi- nition circumcised. Yiddish has long since lost any proper female equivalent of *yid,* any single defining word with which to address or denote a Jew with no penis to trim. *Yidene,* the feminine form of *yid,* lost its neutrality long ago and has come to mean "a petty, sen- timental, talkative Jewess" (Uriel Weinreich, *Modern English- Yiddish Yiddish-English Dictionary*) or an "elderly" or "old-fashioned Jewish woman" (Alexander Harkavy, *Yiddish-English-Hebrew Dic- tionary,* fourth edition, 1928). You can't address a Jewish woman as *yidene;* the overtones of small-mindedness, stupidity, and emo- tional instability would probably get you slapped.

If there was real Yiddish hip-hop, though, *yidene* would be in there where English has "bitch." If there were real Yiddish football coaches, they'd call a losing team a bunch of *yidenes*. The generally accepted form of address for a Jewish woman with whom you're not acquainted is "Mrs.," as in, "*Zayt moykhl*, Mrs." In Israel you'd use *geveret*, in South America, *señora*.

Aside from a couple of idioms like *brokn ligns vi a yidene lokshn* (to make up lies the way a *yidene* makes noodles; see Chapter Nine for more on this idiom) and *tseveynen zikh vi a yidene* (to burst out crying like a woman), *yidene* is now used primarily by Yiddish Ralph Kramdens to refer to their wives: "The *yidene* won't let me go bowling tonight." It's the equivalent of "the missus," "the ol' lady," "the li'l woman," and is of a piece with *di ployneste*, also "the missus," but more literally "the what's-her-name." *Ployneste* is a feminine form of *ployne*, "name unspecified." Such jocular usage acknowledges the existence of a problem—and refuses to do anything about it.

Thank heaven, then, for attributive adjectives. Since you can't call a Jewish woman a *yid* and it isn't nice to call her a *yidene*, you call her either *a yidish kind*, a Jewish child, or *a yidishe tokhter*, a Jewish daughter, regardless of the woman's actual age. These terms are usually used of adult, married women, and imply, if not absolute fidelity to every single Jewish tradition, at least a modicum of traditional feeling and behavior. Think of *yidishe tokhter* as "daughter of her people," and you'll get the general idea.

In Yiddish, the Jewish male *is;* the Jewish woman is described. But at least she's described as Jewish. Exclusion, even when involuntary, is equated with apostasy. Someone who has been passed over for an honor or promotion or been unjustly and unexpectedly excluded from a social event will ask the rhetorical question, "***Ikh hob zikh geshmat?*** *I* converted to Christianity? I don't count any more than a Christian when Jews are being sought for a minyen?" This is the real Yiddish original of "What am I, chopped liver?" and the answer is likewise, no.

No apostate Yiddish speaker would use this phrase, any more than the term *goyisher kop,* gentile head, would ever be applied to a real non-Jew. *Goyisher kop* means "idiot," "simpleton," as in the old joke about the Jewish convert to Christianity who gets up on the morning after his baptism, puts on *tallis* and *tefillin* and starts to daven. "Moyshe," says his wife, "*Host zikh nekhtn opgeshmat,* You converted to Christianity yesterday." Moyshe stops praying, gives himself a slap in the forehead, and cries out, "*Goyisher kop!*"

I'm not sure if it's funny, but it gets the idea across. *Goyisher kop* is closely related to the synonymous but less common *poyersher kop,* peasant head, which developed from the German *Bauern-schädel,* peasant—i.e., thick—skull. Aside from their initial letters, *poyersher* and *goyisher* sound quite similar in spoken Yiddish, while *Bauer,* the German for farmer or peasant, already encompasses all the basic meanings of *goy,* including the implication of Christianity. And the *poyer,* the peasant, the *Bauer* of *Bauernschädel,* was the type of goy with whom Jews had much of their contact. The widespread Yiddish idea of goyim as stupid seems to owe as much to German ideas about Germans as to Jewish ones, and the *goyisher kop* probably developed under the influence of the *poyersher.*

Not every goy was a *poyer,* but every *poyer* was a goy, and to the Yiddish speaker they were all Jed Clampett. On the great chain of Yiddish being, gentiles fall somewhere between Francis the Talking Mule and Bigfoot, and *goy* is almost always as much as to say uneducated, uncouth, uncircumcised—not necessarily good, not necessarily bad, but never anything like one of us. To the Jews, whose behavior was hedged in at every turn, goyim seemed creatures of pure instinct, masses of appetite intent on gratification.

There was no Torah to stand between them and their desires, no system of fences to hinder or defer their satisfaction. As the folk song has it:

Shikker iz er,	He is drunk,
Trinken miz er,	Has no choice but to drink,
Vayl er iz a goy.	Because he is a goy.

Men, women, and children: they drink, they fight, and they screw. Once in a while they beat up a Jew. And since drinking is drinking and screwing is screwing, goyim are goyim: the politics at play between *yid* and *yidene* scarcely exist between the male *goy* and the female *goye.* The only real difference is that licentiousness takes a greater toll on women, and the word *goye* carries with it a whiff of desiccation, a sense of having seen better days. Clark Gable could have been described as a *sheyner goy,* a handsome non-Jew, but to call Ingrid Bergman—or anybody else—a *sheyne goye* would make no more sense than saying that she was a good-looking hag. Ingrid Bergman, Marilyn Monroe—a gentile woman of any age in whom the sap is still running is a *shikse,* not a *goye.*

III

It is not youth that the *goye* has lost so much as allure. Jane Fonda was a *shikse* at sixty; Elizabeth Taylor, despite her conversion, a *goye.* Like Ingrid Bergman, Cyd Charisse, or the characters on such television shows as *Sex and the City,* Fonda is an exception to the general rule that *shikse* is the female counterpart of *sheygets,* a gentile youth, a goy still green in years.

Sheygets started out with no connection to gentiles or youth. It began as the Hebrew *shekets,* a reptile or amphibian, an abominable

or detestable creature, cold-blooded *treyf*. Most of the eleventh
chapter of Leviticus is devoted to enumerating the *shkotsim* (that's
the plural of *shekets*) that are not to be eaten by Jews, who became
impure if they so much as touched the carcass of a *shekets*. This
touch-me-not aspect of the *shekets* is expanded from food to family in the Talmud, where the word is used in a well-known passage
about the types of family to avoid in marriage:

> Let him not marry the daughter of an unlearned and unobservant
> man, for they are an abomination [*shekets*] and their wives a creeping
> thing, and of their daughters it is said: Cursed be he who lieth with
> any manner of beast [Deut. 27:21] . . . Rabbi Meir used to say, "Any-
> one who marries his daughter to an unlearned and unobservant man
> can be said to have tied her up and set her down in front of a lion. For
> just as a lion treads upon its prey, then eats it and has no shame, so
> does an unlearned and unobservant man hit his wife, then lie with her
> and feel no shame" (*Pesokhim* 49b).

If an ignorant Jew of suspect religious observance can be called
a *shekets*, then how much the more so a gentile, whose ignorance
and utter nonobservance can be taken for granted. But that doesn't
mean that the gentile's bestial daughters are lacking in animal
magnetism. In 1 Thessalonians, St. Paul, who shares the Talmudic
opinion of shikses, advises a group of Jewish Christians to "take a
wife . . . in holiness and honor, not in the passion of lust like the
heathen who do not know God" (1 Thess. 4:4–5). Find a nice
Jewish girl, says the Apostle to the Gentiles, and don't live it up
with the shikses.

Sheygets and *shikse* were meant as barriers, fences between Jewish youth and the easy sexuality of "the heathen who do not know

God," vital bits of propaganda in the never-ending war against mixed dating: if it's too loathsome to touch, it's too loathsome to sleep with.

Sheygets lost most of its sexual charge a long time ago, and tends to call forth an image of testosterone-fueled loutishness—loud, boozy, and violent, what the British refer to as "laddish." It is seldom specifically sexual. Indeed, Jewish boys are often called *shkotsim* if they're misbehaving, mouthing off, running around, or playing sports. A command like "Enough with the baseball, *sheygets*. Be a *mentsh* and do your biochemistry homework," can be directed to Mendel but never to Chris. When *sheygets* is used of a Jewish boy (compare "rascal" in English), it is often pronounced *shkots*—a form developed by working backwards from the plural—so that everyone will know that the *sheygets* in question is a Jew. To call a Jewish boy a *sheygets* or a *shkots* is a matter of Jewish behavior, not gentile ethnicity. *Zayn a shkots,* to be a *shkots,* means to enjoy whoopee cushions and attitude; GIs named Brooklyn in movies about World War II are usually textbook *shkotsim.*

There is also a pastry called a *sheygets,* an oblong strip of honey-glazed dough stuffed with poppy seeds, named for its resemblance to a gentile boy's uncircumcised member. The usage is perfectly polite, and there was a time not so long ago when a *yidene* could come beaming from the kitchen with a tray full of treats for dad and the kids: "C'mon everybody. Who wants Christian boys with poppy seeds?"

Note that the pastry is a *sheygets,* not a goy. While ideas of desire, sexuality, and penile appearance do come into play, they do so against a backdrop of seventeen hundred years of ritual-murder libels, accusations of slaughtering Christian children and using their blood for baking. A slightly vulgar joke about pastry and prepuces conceals exactly the sort of irony that Yiddish arose to convey: "*Shkotsim*, sure, we eat 'em all the time. But it isn't their blood that we're after." The English wiener or weenie—where the metaphor travels in the opposite direction—never gets past the skin tube and the smirk; the Yiddish goes where Twinkies fear to tread. And *shkotsim*, incidentally, cannot be eaten on Passover.

There is a baked shikse, too—an unraveled, flattened-out version of the *sheygets*—but it's hardly as popular or well-known: the poppy seeds don't stay put and the word *shikse* lacks the affective range of *sheygets*. "Domestic servant" and "backstreet mistress" are about as complimentary as *shikse* ever gets—"Talk louder, the shikse's vacuuming"; "Soon as the business took off, he went and got himself a shikse"—and it's no accident that shikse has entered other languages with the meaning of "slut" or "floozy," retaining so little of its original sense that well-educated Germans and Poles are often surprised to discover that the word isn't native to their own languages, let alone that it has anything to do with Judaism.

The shikse is freedom from the yoke of the *mitsves* expressed in terms of nocturnal emission. Since a shikse has no *mitsves,* a shikse has no morals. She is the Other in a garter belt, Ellie Mae Clampett after the censors go home. But Ellie Mae soon turns into Granny; a woman passes from *shikse* to *goye* once she loses the ability to tempt a Jewish male. *A yunge shikse*—my mother recited it, my mother's friends and my friends' mothers, they all recited it, it was a secular hymn to endogamy—*a yunge shikse vert an alte goye,* a young *shikse* turns into an old *goye.* This is the Yiddish gloss on the Wife of Bath's, "Age, allas, that al wole envenyme," and the Wife of Bath is a perfect illustration of the shikse at sunset: "I have had my world as in my tyme." I had my fun? No good Jew could ever say such a thing.

IV

Calling a desirable woman a *shikse* or an attractive man a *sheygets* is not much different from calling a fat person Tiny. Referring to nubile non-Jews as abominations is an obvious form of irony, but Yiddish irony can get much more elaborate than simply calling the beautiful ugly. There is a children's finger-counting game similar to This Little Piggy in which the baby finger is called the *yid* and the thumb is called the *goy*. In some versions of this game, the middle finger, halfway between *yid* and *goy*, is known as the *galekh*, the priest, but for reasons that no priest could ever guess.

Six mornings a week, a *yid* gets out of bed and puts on *tefillin*. He winds a leather strap around his arm, places a leather chaplet on his head, then winds the arm strap around his middle finger, and says: "And I [God] will *betroth* you to me forever; I will *betroth* you to me in righteousness and justice and kindness and mercy. And I will *betroth* you to me in faithfulness and you shall know the Lord" (Hos. 2:21–2 in the Hebrew).

It's the betrothal that gives the finger its name; the one person a Jew was likely to encounter for whom engagement and marriage were impossible was the *galekh*, the Roman Catholic priest. While calling the finger a *galekh* is yet another way of mocking Catholic beliefs, it isn't the irony itself that is so remarkable as its presence in a game aimed at people who are still learning how to count. Whatever they're doing, they know that they're doing it *aftse-lakhis*, to get at, the priest and his beliefs. T. S. Eliot, a prominent anti-Semite, claimed that great poetry moves us before we understand what it's saying; Yiddish makes us ironic before we even know what "opposite" means.

The irony even extends to euphemisms, many of which have become more taboo than the words that they were designed to conceal. A real SOB, for example, is said to be a *dover akher,* "something else," "another thing," something that you don't want to mention. It's a *loshn-koydesh* phrase. *Dover* means "thing"; *akher* means "other"; the two together were used as a means of getting from one interpretation to the next in rabbinic literature (as, for instance, in the Passover *hagode,* where *dover akher* has the basic meaning of "there is a different or alternative explanation of Deuteronomy 26:8"). Rabbinic Hebrew used *akher* on its own to mean "that person or thing that I prefer not to mention" or "Mr. X, whose identity we all know." Rather than mention the name of Elisha Ben Avuya, a prominent second-century scholar who turned his back on Judaism and became a pagan, the Talmud prefers to call him *akher,* which it also uses to mean "non-Jew." Fundamentally, it's calling Elisha a *sheygets.*

When the source of the indelicacy or repugnance is not human, *dover* is joined to *akher* to produce a you-know-what, an I-don't-have-to-spell-it-out-for-you. The Talmud uses *dover akher* to refer to things as diverse as sodomy, coitus, idolatry, and leprosy. Most often, though, *dover akher* means "pig," and it is this meaning that has been carried over into Yiddish. Unlike the ostrich, the camel, or the pussy cat, which are equally unkosher, the pig is loathsome in a metaphysical as well as a culinary way. Rather than call it by its name, the Talmud treats it just as it treats the metaphysically repugnant Elisha and uses *dover akher,* best rendered in this context as "you-know-what": "It would have been better for that righteous man [King Solomon] to be the valet of a *dover akher* than that it be written of him that 'he did evil in the sight of the Lord'" (*Shabbos* 56b). There is a wonderful collision of *dover akhers* later in the same tractate: "If a man who has just been bled encounters a *dover akher,* he could become a *dover akher*" (*Shabbos* 129b). That is, if he bumps into a pig, he could become a leper—swine were thought to carry the disease—but at first reading it still looks like he bumps into a you-know-what and becomes a whaddya-call-it. It all depends on how you say it.

A Yiddish *dover akher* is always human, and likely to be harmful to your health. A *khazer*—the basic Yiddish word for pig—can be a greedy, slovenly person or a barnyard animal with a curly tail. A *dover akher* will lie, cheat, and steal; he'll stab you in the back and say that you left him no choice. A human *khazer* can be a very nice person with an eating disorder and no sense of personal hygiene just as easily as he can be a grasping, avaricious miser, but *dover akher* is always a moral judgment. Porky Pig is cute and a *khazer;* Orwell's Napoleon is a *dover akher.* A *khazer* is any kind of pig, a *dover akher* a human swine.

The development of *dover akher* illustrates how a bland, almost meaningless euphemism can end up needing a euphemism of its own: call a man a *khazer* and he might argue, call him a *dover akher* and he'll sue.

Now, a certain type of *dover akher* will try to trip up his victims by means of a process known as *aroysshteln a kosher khazer-fisl,* sticking out a kosher little pig's foot (and note that it has to be a *khazer-fisl;* there's no such thing as a *dover akher-fisl*). The pig's foot here is the legitimate-seeming come-on to something that isn't quite what it seems and might even be illegitimate or unkosher, as when a concern with social justice is used to turn people into terrorists or questions about the importance of family lead to an attempt to change your religion. The phrase can also mean to show only the good parts: when your blind date is described as having "a real personality," that's the *kosher khazer-fisl.* The image goes back to Leviticus 11:7: "And the pig, because it parts the hoof and is cloven-footed, but does not chew the cud, is unclean to you." Because it fulfills the most visible prerequisite of *kashres,* a pig can look kosher from certain angles. A popular *medresh* (*Bereyshis Rabbo* 68) describes how that *dover akher* of a pig lies on its back, waving its cloven hooves in the air, and cries, "Eat me, I'm kosher." If you take the feet at face value, you'd think that it was.

Someone caught sticking out a *kosher khazer-fisl* usually receives a good *oyssheygetsn,* a good bawling out. The *sheygets,* whether you think of him as an actual gentile or an ill-mannered Jew, is knocked out of him. He is de-sheygetsed and reproved for his *yandes. Yandes* is best defined as circumcised chutzpah. If chutzpah can be characterized as murdering your mother and father, then throwing yourself on the mercy of the court because you're an orphan (a "definition" borrowed from the American humorist Artemus Ward, who died in 1867 without knowing of his influence on American Jewish folklore), *yandes* would consist of asking for a Jewish jury so that you could say Kaddish in the courtroom.

While chutzpah derives from a Hebrew root meaning "to be insolent or impudent"—chutzpah is as chutzpah does, so to speak; it's extremely negative in Yiddish—*yandes* represents the other side of the rhetorical coin and has come to mean the opposite of its original dictionary definition. *Yandes* derives from *yahadus,* Hebrew for "Judaism," and came to mean "conscience" in Yiddish, which used it so often of people who had none that serious use of the word became impossible. "Mighty Christian of you" is a compliment that one Christian pays to another, but when a Jewish-speaking Jew commends the Jewish conscience of another Jew, it means that the second Jew is . . . mighty Christian.

Whether he has a *sheygets* inside of him or not, every *yid* has a *ruf-nomen,* a call name, which contains his metaphysical essence and by which he is called to the Torah in the synagogue. It is generally given at his *bris,* the circumcision ceremony, and consists of one or more Hebrew given names joined to his father's Hebrew given name (or names) by the word *ben*, "son of." A *ruf-nomen* is a man's official Jewish name, the one he uses when signing or witnessing a contract or participating in most religious rituals. Hence the expression *avekleygn dem tatn*, to lay your daddy down, the Yiddish equivalent of "put down your John Hancock." Even today, Orthodox businesspeople will sign contracts with other Orthodox businesspeople as "Avrohom ben Khayim-Yankl, *ha-mekhune*, also known as, Goldstein."

The a.k.a. is merely a courtesy; once the *ruf-nomen* appears on the page, the contract is valid. It is a contract *vi in posek shteyt*, as prescribed by the biblical verse concerning contracts. A *posek* is a verse in the Bible, and any yeshiva boy worth his shiny black jacket should be able to tell you that the Torah consists of 5,845 *psukim*, the numerical equivalent of the words "the sun" in gematria. Gematria is an interpretive technique based on assigning numerical values to letters of the alphabet. Before the development of purely numeric notation—1, 2, 3, and so on—the letters of certain alphabets also served as numbers. Remember Roman numerals? The Romans used relatively few letters, but Hebrew assigned a numerical value to every letter of the alphabet, and even today religiously oriented texts (not to mention Jewish calendars) continue to favor Hebrew letters over Arabic numbers, which run in the "wrong" direction. If you wanted to write that 450 people attended a meeting, you'd write: "There were ת"ן people at the meeting," with only the quotation marks to show that ת"ן is a number and not the imperative form of the verb "to give."

The possibility of being able to see a group of letters as either a word or a numeral makes the use of gematria in biblical exegesis almost inevitable. Any word can be replaced by any other word with the same numerical value in order to make a point. On Purim, for example, we are commanded to get so drunk that we can't tell the difference between "blessed be Mordechai," mastermind of the Jewish triumph, and "cursed be Haman," who wanted to exterminate the Jews. Most people take this as a straightforward injunction to get as wrecked as possible, but more than one wet blanket—the kind of vinegar puss called a *yoyz,* a Jesus on the cross, in Yiddish kids' slang—has noticed that the letters of *borukh Mordekhay* and *orur Homan* both add up to 502: "Put the bottle down and return to your studies. There is no reason to enjoy yourself."

Although gematria has the capacity to be both ingenious and enlightening, it can also serve as the last refuge of a speaker with nothing to say: anyone who knows the drill can come up with some kind of gematria about almost any word or phrase in the Bible. It's an impressive-looking trick, and nowhere near as difficult as it seems. As the Mishna puts it, gematria is a side dish, a diversion that is not to be confused with real learning.

The best-known manifestation of gematria in day-to-day Jewish life is the habit of giving charitable donations and gifts of money in multiples of eighteen, the gematria of *khay* (as in the chunky gold medallions), which means alive or living. The best-known Yiddish idiom to employ it is *redn fun akhtsn un draytsn,* to talk about eighteen and thirteen. Depending on where you come from, this can mean either to stop pussyfooting around an uncomfortable subject or else to talk about money:

> "Mr. Wex, we'd like you to come in and lecture about Yiddish next week."
>
> "I'd be delighted, but *lomir redn fun akhtsn un draytsn,* tell me what you're going to pay."

The secret here is the gematria of the Hebrew *loy,* which means "no," and comes out to thirty-one, the sum of eighteen and thirteen: let's talk about that no-no, that issue that we'd prefer to avoid.

As mentioned above, a biblical verse to which such techniques are applied is a *posek,* and *vi in posek shteyt,* "as it is written in the biblical verse," "as the good book says," means with all the requisite details, with bells on, par excellence. If I *am* the blues, you can say that I am a blues singer *vi in posek shteyt*—I satisfy every one of the Torah's rules for blues singing. The fact that the Torah says nothing about singing the blues is the point here: the idiom depends entirely on the thing in question *not* being mentioned in the Bible. You don't say that somebody is a Jew *vi in posek shteyt;* the Bible has so many rules for being a Jew that not even Moses was able to get them all right. *Vi in posek shteyt* means that even though the Bible never deals with the matter at hand, whether it's holding a luau or singing the blues, if it *did* have a verse detailing the requirements for this sort of thing, this singer or luau would have them all, right down to the pineapple-ring yarmulke on the roast suckling pig.

v

The tension between the will to do things as the Torah commands and the will to do them the way that you want to, between the desire to live for the Torah and the will to live for yourself, has been given concrete form in Yiddish, which absorbed the idea of the *yeyster tov,* the good inclination, and the *yeytser hore,* its fun-loving evil twin, directly from the classical sources. The good inclination is mentioned so infrequently that it is always referred to by its full name; the evil is so familiar that it is often called simply the *yeytser,* the inclination: "Who is a man of might?" asks the Mishna. "He who conquers his *yeytser*" (*Avos* 4:1).

Yeytser can refer to any kind of passion for any kind of thing.

According to the *medresh*, "Were it not for the *yeytser hore*, no one would build a house, get married, have children, or do any business" (*Bereyshis Rabbo* 9:7). It drives people to satisfy their urges and gratify their egos; William Blake called it Energy. *Der yeytser hot zi ongenumen*, the *yeytser* seized her, means that she fell into a passionate desire—for a dress, a new house, or finding the cure for cancer—anything that could be desired or even lusted for. And just as the word *lust* without any specified object implies sexual desire in English, so *yeytser* by itself denotes the same thing in Yiddish. It's Inclination with a capital *I*, immune to cold showers or thoughts of Santa. There's only one way to resist: "Shlep [the *yeytser*] into the *bes-medresh* [study house]. If he's made of rock, he'll be crushed; of iron, he'll be smashed to pieces" (*Sukko* 52b).

Rock, iron—the only thing that's supposed to get hard in a *bes-medresh* is the book you're trying to read, and Yiddish idioms in which the *yeytser* pops up have nothing to do with study. There is the fabulous *yeytser-hore-bleterl*, a small blotch of the evil inclination, standard Yiddish for a hickey. *Zi hot gekrogn baym Teanecker drive-in aza yeytser-hore-bleterl az zi iz gegan' a gantse vokh in turtlenecks*, She got such a hickey at the Teaneck drive-in that she went around all week in a turtleneck. In the same way as *asher-yotser papir* is paper pertaining to the blessing *asher yotser*, so this *bleterl* belongs to the *yeytser hore*, who takes the fall for what you or your lover have done.

The *yeytser's* demonic qualities move further to the fore in *kuperner yeytser hore*, a *yeytser hore* made of brass, a brazen *yeytser hore*: a fetish, that is, an abnormal or "unnatural" sexual desire that won't be kept down. The brass comes in by analogy with *kuperner shtern*, a brass forehead, an impudent and shameless person: "I know that you are obstinate, and your neck is an iron sinew, and your forehead brass" (Isa. 48:4). The *taytsh* renders the concluding phrase as *"dayn shtern iz kuper,"* and the expression *kuperner shtern* for someone full of chutzpah is extremely common.

Some of these *kuperne yetsorim* (the plural of *kuperner yeytser*) are simply distasteful, others are illegal. Possession of material pertaining to the wrong kind of fetish can land you in *khad gadye:* stir, the clink, the hoosegow. The Yiddish version of Jimmie Rodgers's "He's in the Jailhouse Now" would be *Er zitst in khad gadye itst.* As anyone who has ever lasted to the end of a Passover seder knows, *khad gadye* means "one kid"—that's kid as in baby goat—and is the title of the song that ends the seder. Said to be the earliest known instance of the House-that-Jack-Built motif in Western literature, *Khad Gadye* is an allegorical rendering of the history of the Jews and includes events that have still not come to pass.

The one thing never mentioned in *Khad Gadye'*s catalogue of retribution and deliverance is prison or confinement; the title's new meaning has more to do with Poland than with prayer, and provides a clearer-than-usual illustration of the way in which aspects of non-Jewish culture are translated into Jewish religious terms for the sake of a laugh. Goat in Polish is *koze,* and *koze* is also slang for jail. In a humorous reversal of *fartaytshn,* the translation and explication of the Bible that formed the basic technique of traditional education, a piece of Polish slang is "translated" into a well-known piece of *loshn-koydesh,* which then takes on the meaning of the Polish slang term—and the more incongruously, the better.

As *khad gadye* nearly makes clear, Yiddish can have as much impact on Jewish rituals as the rituals do on Yiddish. The Ashkenazi custom of eating carrots on Rosh Hashana as a means of asking the Lord that our "merits might increase" derives from the fact that the Yiddish verb for "increase" is *mern,* which is identical in sound and spelling with the plural form of the noun *mer,* which means "carrot." Most Yiddish speakers are aware of this folksy bit of sympathetic magic, in which the food becomes the image of its blessing, but far fewer realize that the play on *mern* is already a precocious instance of dumbing-down, that *mern* and *mern* are only stand-ins for an earlier, more esoteric pun. The supplication recited over the carrots is in Hebrew, not Yiddish. The pun on *mer* is reserved for explanations; what people actually say is, "*she-yirbu zekhuyoyseynu,* that our merits might increase." Among the foods that the Talmud (*Kereisos* 6a) prescribes for consumption on Rosh Hashana is fenugreek, a legume which is called *rubyo* in Aramaic (in contemporary Hebrew, the same word means black-eyed peas). Originally, one ate fenugreek—*rubyo*—and said *she-yirbu,* "may they (our merits) increase." But fenugreek must have been hard to find in Ashkenaz, or perhaps carrots were simply easier. In any event, the Aramaic *rubyo* sounds a lot like *Rübe,* a German word that still means carrot in some dialects (in standard Modern German, it most often means turnip). As fewer and fewer Yiddish speakers could understand the connection between fenugreek and increase, they began to replace *rubyo* with *Rübe.* As fewer and fewer Yiddish speakers were able to understand *Rübe,* it was trans-lated to the more common *mer* (compare the standard German *Mohrrübe,* carrot), which necessitated the translation of the He-brew *yirbu,* increase—which was no longer the scene of the pun—to the Yiddish *mern,* the only known instance of re-*fartaytshn* for the sake of a carrot.

VI

The best example of how far Yiddish can go with a single religious activity is found in a pre–Yom Kippur ritual in which a live chicken is waved in the air while the following incantation is recited: "This is my stand-in, this is my substitute, this is my atonement. May this hen/rooster go to its death while I go off and continue on a good, long, and peaceful life."

Christians embrace Jesus, Jews buy poultry. The ceremony, currently undergoing a bit of a revival after a century of contempt and neglect, is known as *shlogn kapores,* and even the people who practice it know that it looks a little weird. In its heyday, *shlogn kapores* was so widespread as to arouse sporadic opposition from rabbis, so unlike anything else that the translator of the *Epistolae Obscurorum Virorum,* the *Letters of Obscure Men,* a sixteenth-century monument of European satire, uses it to defend the Children of Israel from their detractors. The *Epistolae* are concerned with the controversy that sprang up around Johannes Reuchlin, a Christian scholar, and his defense of Talmudic study (Talmudic study for Christians, that is). The bad guys, against whom the *Epistolae* were directed, were fronted by a *meshumad,* an apostate Jew, called Pfefferkorn. The translator, a non-Jewish scholar named Francis Griffin Stokes who wrote in 1909, has no patience with Pfefferkorn's Jew-baiting, and mocks him for saying that Jews invert their pockets beside a river on their New Year and wave live chickens around their heads on the eve of their Day of Atonement.

And there you have the tragedy of Jewish life in exile, the ground from which Yiddish had no choice but to grow: accurate descriptions of your religious activities are taken as racist slander. Inverting the pockets on Rosh Hashana is called *tashlikh,* from a verse in Micah (7:19): "*Tashlikh,* You will cast all their sins into the depths of the sea." It is still widely practiced, but hasn't produced any idioms in Yiddish. *Shlogn kapores,* on the other hand, extends far beyond Yom Kippur.

The word itself, *kapores,* is the plural of the *loshn–koydesh* term *kapore,* which comes from the same root as the Kippur in Yom Kippur and means "forgiveness, atonement, absolution." *Shlogn kapores,* literally to beat or strike *kapores* (where *kapore* is used to represent the chicken), is the only term for performing the ritual. The bird is lifted up by the feet and waved around your head in a circle. After the third revolution, it is taken off to be slaughtered. The birds used to be given to the poor, who were understandably upset at a largesse which would leave them to consume the sins of their more prosperous brethren; these days, the financial value of the fowl is donated to charity.

Why chickens? Because cows are too heavy. Asking "Why the chickens?" is like asking "Why the Jews?" The chicken is snatched, terrorized, and executed—because it is cheap and easy to lift, and because the Hebrew word for cock, *gever,* is the same as the Hebrew word for man. An eye for an eye, a tooth for a tooth, a *mer* for a *rubye,* and a *gever* for a *gever:* half the religion is based on puns, and people wonder why Jews are so funny.

The bird is grabbed out of the blue, raised aloft, and waved in the air. The bird is scared. It doesn't know what's happening. And what do birds do when they're afraid? . . . My own mother had a lifelong aversion to chickens and anything to do with them as the result of a *kapore* mishap in her childhood, and she was obviously not alone: religious newspapers now carry ads for "live *kapores* with Pampers," and I'm sure that somewhere or other religious communities are being torn apart by controversies over whether the *kapores* should be wrapped in Pampers or Huggies. Responsibility for continuing and even expanding the *kapore* tradition rests squarely on the shoulders—or the heads—of the Hasidic population, which continued to *shlog* long after most of the religious world had replaced chickens with charity, a fact that probably explains the mystery of their wide-brimmed hats.

Someone encountering this ritual for the first time would probably be said to *kukn vi a hon in bney-odem,* to gaze the way a rooster looks at the *kapores* prayer called *Bney Odom,* Children of Adam: in clueless incomprehension, too shocked to make any sense of what is taking place. How would *you* look if you were diapered, turned upside down, held up in front of a prayer book (from which the penitent recites Bney Odom) and then waved in the air? The idiom, once a favorite of *kheyder* teachers describing a pupil's efforts to construe a text—usually in front of the pupil himself—is never used of anything truly dismaying. It usually suggests that the viewer is too stupid to make sense of whatever fairly obvious phenomenon is being beheld. "I'm pushing the doorbell and she's standing there on the other side of the screen door and *kukt vi a hon in bney-odem*"—she can't make the connection between the music in the wall and the speaker's desire to come in.

The fowl to be sacrificed is known as a *kapore-hon* (rooster) or a *kapore-hun* (hen). The *kapore hindl,* the little *kapore* hen is, however, strictly metaphorical. A *kapore hindl* is a fall guy, an innocent victim who suffers for the sins of others; it is often translated as "scapegoat." What's interesting here is that even though the notion of a scapegoat comes from the Bible, the Jews do not seem to have felt any need for the concept until well after *kapores* and Yiddish had both taken root: neither the biblical *se'ir l'azazel* nor the Talmudic *se'ir ha-mishtaleyakh* found its way into Yiddish, a fact that looks much stranger when one considers that the French for scapegoat, *bouc émissaire,* is a direct translation of the Talmudic phrase. Using a person as the *se'ir l'azazel* is a fundamentally Christian idea (Jesus becomes the *kapore-hindl* for mankind and all its sins). Yiddish speakers appear to have picked it up from their neighbors, but replaced both Jesus and the biblical goat with a ritual that they were already practicing in which an innocent being died for the sins of a guilty one.

Yiddish took a Christian reading of a sacrifice described in the Hebrew Bible and recast it as something neither Christian nor biblical—a chicken who dies for an individual rather than a goat who dies for a people or a savior who dies for humanity—not because Yiddish wanted to mock the Christians in this instance but because it was unable to escape their influence. We're dealing with a longing for the feelings of security and assurance that rituals of sacrifice seem to engender. Recitation of the biblical sacrifices is an integral part of traditional Jewish prayer, but the sacrifices themselves cannot be offered until the advent of the Messiah and the rebuilding of the Temple. The Christians, *lehavdl,* seem to derive emotional strength and even some measure of temporal power from the sacrifice associated with Jesus. All that the Jews were looking for in adapting the scapegoat idea was a way to go on with their suffering, their exile, their status of "testimony to the truth of Christianity," without having to feel as if it were all their fault. The *kapores* ritual simply helped to provide them with a model.

Vicarious atonement is, however, only one of the Yiddish chicken's functions. There is a close, if oblique, relationship between the *kapore-hindl* and the idiom *vern di kapore,* which is involved with sex and death. If you tell someone simply to *ver di kapore* or *ver mir di kapore*—become my *kapore*—you'd be telling them to drop dead. They should be waved around your head three times and then slaughtered—preferably for something *you* did. If, however, you were to tell someone that they should *ver di kapore far* you—*far* means "for"—you'd be commanding them, however absurdly, to get a crush on you. *Vern di kapore far* a person implies that you're so besotted that you'd let them wave you around their head and then distribute bits of you to the poor. Ira Gershwin's well-known "I've got a crush on you, sweetie-pie" comes out in Yiddish as *Ikh ver di kapore far dir, ketsenyu,* I'm turning into a penitential chicken for you, pussycat.

Should you then pass from becoming to being, if you progress from *vern di kapore far* to *zayn di kapore far,* to be the *kapore* for somebody, what you're saying is that you've been snatched, waved, and slaughtered already. You've gone beyond infatuation all the way to mad, all-consuming, self-negating love, the kind that has weathered every obstacle, whether from without or from within. Only in Yiddish could the plot of *Wuthering Heights* be expressed in terms of poultry.

Shlogn kapores mit, to *shlog kapores* with a person, can mean either to abuse or revile them, or else to kick them out of someplace. The line between the ceremony and the meaning of the idiom is pretty straight, as it is in the very common *toygn af kapores,* to be good for *kapores,* i.e., good for nothing. Good to wave around your head three times and then throw away. *Toygn af kapores* is often used in association with *helfn vi a toytn bankes,* to help like cupping a corpse. The idea, of course, is that the remedy has come too late, the patient has already died.

The other side of the coin from *toygn af kapores* is *darfn af kapores,* to need something for *kapores,* to have no earthly use for it. This is virtually synonymous with *darfn vi a lokh in kop,* which has entered English as "I need it like a hole in the head." More emphatically, you might need something *af tish-un-nayntsik kapores,* for ninety-nine *kapores* (as garage rockers ? and the Mysterians would have sung, had they but sung in Yiddish). The Yiddish for ninety-nine is *nayn-un-nayntsik;* the *tish* here represents the Hebrew *tishe,* which also means nine, but otherwise appears in Yiddish only in *tishe b'ov,* the ninth of Av, the date when both

Temples were destroyed, the saddest day of the Jewish year. *Tish* lends the phrase a sense of dignified absurdity, as if ? and the Mysterians had sung of six and ninety rather than "Ninety-Six Tears."

Closely related to the drop-dead meaning of *vern di kapore* is the wonderfully ill-bred and extremely common *a sheyne, reyne kapore*, a beautiful, pure *kapore*. This is an interjection that means "good riddance (to bad rubbish)," "the hell with her," "I'm better off without him." The death of the other party isn't necessary, but it'd sure be nice. People who speak a traditional Yiddish will always say *borekh dayan emes*, blessed be the righteous judge, on hearing of the death of any decent, respectable person. *A sheyne, reyne kapore* is its opposite and is also equally popular among less traditionally oriented speakers who hear of the death of a personal enemy, a public figure they can't stand, or any anti-Semite. "Benedict Arnold's dead? *A sheyne, reyne kapore*."

Divested of the *sheyne* and *reyne*, a lone *kapore* preceding a noun means "the hell with, who cares about, don't gimme none of that." "*Gelt?* You speak to me of *gelt? A kapore gelt*, it's art that's important."

Kaporenitse was once thieves' slang for a chicken, and *kaporenik*, the masculine form of the same word, was general Jewish slang for a gentile, the sort of word that would be used when there was a gentile present who knew the meaning of *goy*. It's about as nice as the black English "ofay," and motivated by a similar idea of needing him for *kapores*.

Kaporenik is a fine example of a once widespread conversational strategy known as *ivre be-loy*, "Hebrew, so no [understand]," that is, "The gentile who can hear us understands Yiddish. Use Hebrew words that haven't entered standard Yiddish so he won't know what we're saying." Although comparatively few Jews had much more than a *kheyder*-level education, almost all knew enough to be able to turn "the rain in Spain" into "the *geshem* in *Sfarad*" without having to pause too long to think. Versions of *ivre be-loy* were, not surprisingly, quite common in the argot of Jewish criminals, and a surprising amount of this underworld Hebrew found its way into non-Jewish criminal speech, some of which then penetrated into general usage. We have only to recall that the gun in "gun moll" comes from the Yiddish *gonef*, a thief, to see how the process could work.

But for every gun, there were plenty of terms that never crossed over. The preferred substitute for goy is *orel*, which means "be-foreskinned one, an uncircumcised male." The foreskin is taken as a simple statement of fact, and the term has none of the overtones of stupidity or viciousness that so often accompany the word *goy*. You can call a stupid or irreligious Jew a goy; you could never call him an *orel*. There was a classified ad that ran for years in *Der Yid*, the weekly newspaper of the Satmarer Hasidim, that began, "*Farleslekher orel*, reliable male with prepuce seeks work as a handyman."

Certain *areylim* (the plural of *orel*) are mocked by being transformed into Hebrew texts. Virtually any Jew of South African origin will tell you that Afrikaaners, the Boers who make up so large a part of the white population, are known as *khateysim* (singular, *khatas*). *Khatas* derives from the Hebrew *khet*, a sin, and means sin-offering, a sort of official *kapore* sacrifice. *Khatas* retains this meaning in Yiddish, where it acquires the additional, and more common, sense of sinner or rogue. There is a well-known line in the Mishnaic tractate *Avos*, which every Orthodox male studies every Saturday between Passover and Rosh Hashana: "*Eyn bor yerey khet*, a *bor* [uncouth ignoramus] is not afraid of sin." The coincidence of sound was too much to ignore, and since someone not afraid to sin must therefore be a sinner, South Africans of Dutch descent—Boers, that is—became known as *khateysim,* as if Boer (which is related to the Yiddish *poyer* and the German *Bauer*) were not only Hebrew, but a Hebrew word as defined in an authoritative Hebrew text. The Boers end up at the same transgressive destination as the nobleman, the *porets geder,* whom we saw at the beginning of this chapter, but by a very different exegetical path.

VII

As a final example of the areas into which religious imagery can extend, we can look at the phrase *sheyne moyshe ve-arendlekh,* beautiful little Moses-and-Aaronses. Inevitably preceded by the words *zi hot,* she has, the idiom means "stacked." Moses and Aaron sneak in by way of the Song of Songs, which is recited every Friday in much of the Yiddish-speaking world and every Passover throughout the whole of the Jewish world, and was thus familiar to large numbers of people who were not especially scholarly. One of its verses reads: "Your two breasts are like two fawns, twins of a gazelle, that feed among the lilies" (Song 4:5).

Since the time of Rabbi Akiva, every traditional commentary on the Song of Songs has been at pains to prove that it has nothing to do with erotic poetry or physical love. It is generally taken as an allegory, usually of God's love for the Jews. The popular Artscroll prayer book, which is rapidly becoming standard issue in all sorts of synagogues and temples, provides an easily accessible illustration of this sort of interpretation. In their introduction to the Song of Songs, the editors state quite openly that "a literal translation would be misleading—even false—because it would not convey the meaning intended by King Solomon." In this spirit, the second verse—"Let him kiss me with the kisses of his mouth, for thy love is better than wine"—comes out as "Communicate Your innermost wisdom to me again in loving closeness, for Your friendship is dearer than all earthly delights." The misleading version of Chapter 1, verse 12—"While the king sat at his table, my spikenard sent forth its fragrance"—is corrected to: "While the King was yet at Sinai my malodorous deed gave forth its scent as my Golden Calf defiled the covenant," which sounds a lot dirtier to me.

To be fair to the editors, they aren't making this stuff up. They are following Rashi's commentary fairly closely, and it's important to stress that Rashi's commentary has been indispensable to traditional study for nearly a thousand years: Jewish learning without Rashi is like pop music without the Beatles.

In his comments on the first verse quoted, Rashi refers to the *medresh* on the Song of Songs: *"Your two breasts, which give you suck. That is, Moses and Aaron."* The two things that sustain the Children of Israel are the law, as given by Moses, and the sacrifices performed by Aaron the High Priest and his descendants. Of course, there is no mention of any of this in the text, and generations of schoolboys have noticed the disjunction between what the words are saying and what grown-ups insist that they mean. Over and over again, kids—boys in this case—took the commentary on its own terms, then extended those terms beyond the sacred page: now that we know what "breasts" really means, it "would be misleading—even false" to call any breasts "breasts." Where the Boers were read into a text, Moses and Aaron are being read out of one. The commentary has been applied to the things described, not to the literary description of those things, but it has also kept its character as a commentary on a specific verse of the Bible. If the breasts of the woman in the Song of Songs are Moses and Aaron, then *all* women's breasts are Moses and Aaron, and all the really good ones are beautiful Moses and Aarons—and now we know what Hooters will be called if the company ever goes kosher.

FIVE

Discouraging Words:

YIDDISH AND THE FORCES OF DARKNESS

I

Anyone who has spent much time with European-born Yiddish speakers is likely to have noticed that, agreeable as many of them might otherwise be, they never seem to get too enthusiastic about the things that they don't dislike. Indeed, they never really seem to *like* anything.

> YOU: How was the movie?
> THEM: Eh [rhymes with the other possible answer, *feh*].

> YOU: How are you?
> THEM: Old.

> YOU: How's your brother?
> THEM: Dead.

> YOU: What's doing?
> THEM: Nothing.
> YOU: Nothing?
> THEM: Nothing.
> YOU: Nothing?
> THEM: Thank God, nothing.

YOU: Good news! Your son has been nominated for the Nobel Prize.

THEM: And who do you think bought him the ticket?

They can be chilly, these people, but that doesn't mean they don't care. If anything, they care too much. In their view of the world, though, liking is only the first step to losing: if "they" know that you love it, "they'll" try to take it. Generations of Jews with parents were told that the only thing "they" can't take away from you is an education. So, if you've got to like something, like it quietly, so no one can see; but you're better off to develop a code, a way of letting those in the know know what you feel without alerting "them" to the fact that you're attached. Express approbation by saying nothing—only disapproval can come out in the open; if something nice should slip out, be sure to spit; if you can't resist a compliment, turn it into a curse: "*Iz zi sheyn?* Is she beautiful? *Mayne sonim zoln zayn azoy miyes,* My enemies should be as ugly [as she is beautiful]."

Yiddish isn't social work; it would rather vent its feelings than share them. But don't go blaming the Jews; they are at the mercy of forces beyond their control. As if endless exile and ravening goyim were not enough, let us not forget that *klal yisroel,* the Jewish people as a whole, is besieged twenty-four hours a day by *sheydim, rukhes, klipes, leytsim, mazikim,* and *dibukim*—demons, spirits, gremlins, sprites, goblins, and devils, whose only reason for living is to wreck your hopes and rain on your parade. They hate human happiness and can't stand prosperity. And there's no getting out from under them: "Abba Binyomin says: If the eye were granted the ability to see demons, no creature would be able to bear the terror. Abbaye says: They are more numerous than we are, and rest on us like piles of dirt beside a ditch. Rav Huna says:

Every one of us has a thousand of them to his left and ten thousand to his right" (*Brokhos* 6a). And they're all waiting for someone to say, "You have such beautiful children" without adding a *keynehore*—"no evil eye"—or spitting three times at the end of the sentence. Although few living Yiddish speakers would admit to believing in demons or the evil eye, such formulas and practices are so deeply rooted in the language that things just don't sound right without them; there aren't too many Yiddish-speaking materialists willing to omit a *keynehore* when bragging about their children (as long as those children are not within earshot).

Compared with contemporary English, Yiddish is a regular haunted house where demons frolic and sinister forces rage nearly unchecked. These *sheydim* (singular, *shed*) are generally thought of as being Jewish—they believe in the Torah, observe all the *mitsves* incumbent on Jewish demons, base their lives on being unable to stand prosperity, and exist, with God's blessing and active co-operation, *aftselakhis*—just to spite—the rest of the world. They're us, but invisible; like us, they prefer to prey upon their human coreligionists.

Made famous through the work of Isaac Bashevis Singer, these Jewish demons are grouped under such collective rubrics as *di yenike* (them, those others), *di nisht gute* (the ungood), *di gute layt* (the good folk), and *di rekhte layt* (the real things, the you-know-who's). They are *khitsoynim*, "outsiders" or "outcasts," spirits of impurity. Together they make up the *sitre akhre*, "the other side," every member of which is also a *klipe*, a husk or shell that has grown up around a spark of holiness, masking its light and imprisoning its sanctity.

Klipe is used colloquially to mean "shrew" or "bothersome child," creatures who resemble their namesakes "over yonder" by

93

seeming to have blocked out any warmth or serenity. An adult *klipe* is what used to be called a "common scold," Elvira Gulch crossed with Joan Rivers, such a nonstop, ill-tempered, screaming nag that it is impossible to imagine how anyone can live with her. A child *klipe* is clingy and demanding, a precocious little kvetch who always feels neglected and for whom no amount of attention is ever enough. The two different types were considered mutually exclusive until Courtney Love came along.

The supernatural *klipe* comes in many forms. Though the different categories tend to be used interchangeably when referring to actual demons, there are important colloquial distinctions between them. The most frequently invoked Yiddish demons are the *mazik*, the *lets*, and the *ruekh*.

The *mazik*, whose name comes from a Hebrew root that means "harm" or "damage," is part poltergeist, part the sort of elf who comes by at night to destroy the shoes that you'd been making all day. *Mazik* also means a clever kid who's full of mischief—a circumcised Bart Simpson—or a swashbuckling adult daredevil, Errol Flynn or Douglas Fairbanks, Sr. If someone is a *mazik af epes*, a *mazik* when it comes to doing something, he has a real knack for it. *Er iz a mazik af zingen* means that he is a devil of a singer, one hell of a vocalist. A *mazik* can also be a beloved rascal, Bart as an adult, Victor McLaglen as a cavalry sergeant. If you were to give him a friendly, half-admiring punch in the shoulder and say, "You big lug" in English, your Yiddish translator would render it as "*mazik vos du bist, mazik* that you are."

A *lets* is a scoffer or mocker, a smart-aleck (the same root also produces the Hebrew word for clown), and a particular kind of poltergeist. Where the *mazik* is interested in destruction for its own sake, the *lets* likes to stick around and yuk it up at all the trouble he has caused. He's a mischievous imp, a Mr. Mxyzptlk who can never be tricked into saying his name backwards. A person described as a *lets* is a wag, a dab hand with a quip, someone who sits at the back of the room and cracks wise.

There is also the *ruekh,* a disembodied spirit that can take up residence in a human being—*a ruekh in dayn tatn,* "a disembodied spirit in your father," is Yiddish for "your mama." A spirit that has left one body or being in order to settle in another is called a *dybbuk.* The best-known of all Jewish demons, thanks to S. Anski's play of the same title, the *dybbuk* is the spirit of a demon or recently deceased person or animal that moves into someone else's living body to wreak metaphysical havoc or right a metaphysical wrong.

II

Piety and clean living are no proof against such forces. We need to arm ourselves with apotropaic formulas and practices, protective sayings and actions that can stop a *ruekh* dead in its tracks. "Apotropaic" comes from the Greek for a factor or steward, someone whose job consists in looking out for the welfare of another; apotropaic speech or behavior is designed to take care of bad metaphysical forces bent on doing you harm.

Traditional Judaism is rife with apotropaic practices that have been given newer, more rational explanations in an effort to try to disguise their essentially superstitious nature. The best known is probably the practice of breaking a glass at the end of a wedding, "to symbolize," in the words of the Artscroll prayer book, "that until the Temple is rebuilt our joy cannot be complete." It is interesting—and symptomatic of something—that Artscroll's ultra-Orthodox editors should prefer this nationalist-rationalist explanation to the original rationale as given in the Talmud itself: "Mar, the son of Ravina, made a wedding party for his son.

Noticing that the assembled sages were merrier than was meet, he fetched a precious goblet worth four hundred *zuzim* and smashed it in front of them. They grew sad" (*Brokhos* 30b–31a).

Similia similibus curantur, like cures like, and sadness is being used in the service of safety. Mar was engaging in a kind of metaphysical homeopathy that was meant to keep something worse from happening. According to the Toysfes, the so-called "Supplements" to Rashi's commentary compiled between the twelfth and fourteenth centuries, "It is from here that the custom of breaking a glass at a wedding originates." When the usually gnarly and complex Toysfes are this easy to understand, you know that there's no room to argue. The glass is broken to fool the *sitre akhre,* to give it its share in the celebration. It wets its beak, gets its props, and is then free to go on its way and ruin someone else's wedding.

Sometimes, though, a slight change in the practice will provoke a new explanation that leads to the protective function being completely forgotten. One of the high points of the Passover seder is the recitation of the ten plagues visited upon the Egyptians: as each plague is named, participants dip their index fingers into their wineglasses and shake the wine back onto their saucers—and woe to the wayward child who licks a finger afterward.

This custom is usually held up as an example of Jewish moral largesse. We are so tenderhearted, so unvindictive with respect to our enemies, that we deprive ourselves of half a teaspoon of Manischewitz, thus decreasing our pleasure and leading us to compassion for the sufferings of the Egyptians. This is the ethical equivalent of a Ramones record: an ingenious, indeed a brilliantly successful, attempt to make the primitive look progressive. The basic idea has been traced back to Isaac Abarbanel, a prominent fifteenth-century exegete, but it took roughly four hundred years to catch on: the standard traditional view of the seder was that we reduce the amount of our wine in the same way as God reduced the number of Egyptians, an interpretation that can't be accused of trying too hard. Abarbanel's idea was picked up and popularized by Samson Raphael Hirsch (died 1888), the founder and guiding spirit of Frankfurt neo-Orthodoxy, a German-Jewish movement that sought to reconcile punctilious religious observance with advanced secular education and a good command of German. A sworn enemy of Reform Judaism, Hirsch was still quick to recognize the difference between the immutable and the expendable, and was happy to explain it all in German—a language that even gentiles could read—rather than Hebrew or Yiddish.

If Hirsch was hoping to make us look rational, the Germans don't seem to have been paying attention; but the Jews embraced the idea so wholeheartedly that most people no longer realize that there is any other explanation for the custom. Originally, though—a very long time ago, well before the development of Yiddish—people named each plague and then, instead of dipping their fingers in the wine, spat three times, as if they were ptoo-ptoo-ptooing after mentioning a calamity or disaster in casual conversation.

They did so at long tables, with lots of people sitting opposite each other. Lots of relatives, many of them nursing grudges or looking for a fight, sitting across from each other and spitting. There are ten plagues: three little spits per plague equals thirty spits per person, not to mention eighteen other little spits, nine before the plagues proper and nine after, for a total of forty-eight expectorations per seder guest. Multiply by the number of participants, get a raincoat, and run for cover.

Rhyming off this list of plagues without doing *something* apotropaic never seems to have been an option. The problem was how to do so while avoiding bad manners, poor hygiene, and domestic strife—they needed the spittle, but didn't want to spit. The process by which they arrived at dipping a finger in the wine-glass is possible only in a culture that bans the use of umbrellas on Saturday because the Torah won't let us pitch a tent then.

Jews and non-Jews alike spit to ward off bad luck; everybody seems to know of the demon-repelling powers of human saliva. Spitting can be defined as the deliberate projection of saliva into the area around you. Neither standing saliva inside the mouth nor involuntary drool outside it is believed to protect against anything but dating—it's the propulsion or transfer, rather than the mere presence of saliva that does the trick. Granted that the saliva must be in motion in order to be effective, "Where," asked these Jews of yore, "*shteyt geshribn*, is it written, that the motion of saliva has to originate in the mouth? Why don't we just find some that's al-ready part of our surroundings and transfer it to another part of those surroundings in such a way as to give it the same deterrent effect as actual expectoration? But where are we going to find traces of our own saliva and how will we propel them? They're only traces, after all."

God, as they say in Yiddish, *shikt di refue far der make*, He sends the remedy in advance of the plague. *Halokhe* obliges us to drink four glasses of wine over the course of the seder and everybody, children included, has a glass which is filled (and drained) at spec-ified points in the proceedings. The first of these compulsory liba-tions takes place well before we get to the plagues, which means that everybody's glass contains enough saliva for apotropaic pur-poses and enough wine to get that saliva moving. The finger does duty for a human tongue.

And so the Passover wine-dip was born. The logic was a little too subtle, however, and the lack of actual spitting caused the origins of the custom to be forgotten; most people who did it did so because . . . that's what you do. Hirsch's reinterpretation of the motives underlying this act managed the brilliant feat of translating something that was intended to cover our own asses into a show of concern for the asses of others.

III

As this need to protect ourselves when naming plagues that took place thousands of years ago might suggest, Judaism—as a civilization and a system of thought—has a deep-seated belief in the power of words and the significance of names. It could never countenance the logic of Shakespeare's Juliet:

> What's in a name? that which we call a rose
> By any other name would smell as sweet;
> So Romeo would, were he not Romeo call'd,
> Retain that dear perfection which he owes
> Without that title. Romeo, doff thy name,
> And for that name which is no part of thee
> Take all myself
> (*Romeo and Juliet*, II:2:43–49).

Juliet is taking the *goyishe* side in a debate that has bedeviled Western philosophy since the days of the Greeks: is the name of a person or thing just a label that derives its meaning from convention or is it an integral part of the being to which it refers? Can the name be doffed without affecting the thing, or is the essence of the thing contained in its name? Juliet takes the former position, which is known as nominalism; the other, more Jewish one is called realism, and so far as the Jews are concerned, a rose by any other name would have a very different smell. What happened with *sheygets* and *shikse* was just an early application of realist theory. Call a rose a pile of crap and the flower turns into something else.

The same process is put to different use in Jewish name-changing practices. A Jew is thought to have one real name and one real name only, the *ruf-nomen*, which stays with a person even in the other world—proof, as if any were needed, that the name is somehow a part of the soul. It can be changed only to confuse the demons who cause illness and death, i.e., to change the being and destiny of someone who is seriously ill. Sick children are given new names such as *Alter*, Old One, in hopes that the demons will leave a dotard alone (because he's going to die soon, anyway); a boy or man has his name changed to *Khayim*, Life, or else has *Khayim* added to the names he already has, in order to take a stand against the demons and get around the Angel of Death.

This is all as it should be in a culture that has been radically realist from its very beginnings, when God created the world by means of speech. As the Mishna tells us, "The world was created with ten utterances" (*Avos* 5:1); God said, "Let there be light," and there was light. Utterances such as this, words that produce physical effects in the world, are the serious theological underpinnings of such half-serious expressions as *me zol nor dermonen meshiekhn*, "we should have mentioned the Messiah"—the Yiddish equivalent of "speak of the devil" that is used when Mendel turns up only seconds after his name has been mentioned. This is a joke, of course—no one has ever tried to second-guess God and hasten the advent of the Messiah by going "Mendel, Mendel, Mendel"—but just try to get any Yiddish-speaking Jew to say "cancer" (*rak* in Yiddish) or, if you want to go back a couple of generations, "epilepsy" (*nikhpe*). Even in published obituaries, the former is usually referred to as *a gevise makhle*, a certain sickness, or *a bitere makhle,* a bitter sickness, while the word *nikhpe* was used in curses more often than in descriptions. Epilepsy was known as *di gute zakh* and *di shlekhte zakh,* "the good thing" and "the bad thing," *di shvere krenk,* "the severe illness," and *der rekhter inyen,* "the real thing, the real McCoy." It was sometimes even called *di kindershe zakh,* "the children's thing"; using its real name could cause it to appear as quickly as Mendel.

The reluctance to separate a being or thing from its name is fundamental to the Jewish idea of God, whose real name, the so-called Tetragrammaton—usually transliterated as YHVH, as if the Lord were my health club—is spoken so rarely that its proper pronunciation has been lost for two thousand years. God Himself is quite clear about the significance of this name: "I am YHVH. I appeared to Abraham, Isaac, and Jacob as El Shaddai, but my name is YHVH: I did not make myself known to them" (Exod. 6:2–3).

The English versions of the last clause are usually similar to the Revised Standard Version: "By my name the LORD I did not make myself known to them." The Hebrew grammar, though, is closer to the translation above: by not revealing His real name, God did not reveal His real self. Indeed, the *real* name is so closely identified with the divine being that the standard way of referring to God outside of prayer and Torah reading (where YHVH is read as Adonay, the holiest name currently available for utterance) is Ha-Shem, "the Name." "The Name will avenge us; he died to sanctify the Name; thank the Name for the nighttime"—substitute Ha-Shem for "the Name" and every one of these phrases is perfectly idiomatic orthodox English.

Again, we don't praise God Himself; it's His name that gets the laurels. *Yisgadal ve-yiskadash*—even non-Jews are familiar with the opening of the Kaddish: "Magnified and sanctified, *shmey rabbo,* be the Great Name, in the world which It [the Name] has created according to Its will. . . ." It's another case of "as his name, so is he," because He and His Name are One: omnipotent and awful, beyond the scope of human comprehension. The high priest was allowed to pronounce the Name on Yom Kippur—and it is understood that his staying alive after doing so was an instance of heavenly grace. Just as the Greeks thought that looking upon a god in his full glory would prove fatal to any mortal (as in the story of Zeus and Semele), so did the Jews believe that the sound of their invisible God's name would have a similar effect.

On a more mundane level, the identification of name and ontological essence underlies the Ashkenazic prohibition against naming children for people who are still alive. *Zol zayn nomen aheymkumen*, "may his name come home [with somebody else attached to it]," is another way of saying, "He should drop dead."

Just as the *ruf-nomen* is the only name of metaphysical record, so it is that only Hebrew nouns are really identified with the things that they name. The ten utterances with which God created the world were in Hebrew. The Bible goes on to tell us that just about the first thing that Adam does in the Garden of Eden is give names to other life forms: ". . . the Lord God formed every beast of the field and every bird of the air, and brought them to the man to see what he would call them; and whatever the man called every living creature, that was its name" (Gen. 2:19).

And the Torah lets us know that he was speaking Hebrew: "She shall be called Woman [*isho*] because she was taken out of Man [*ish*]" (Gen. 2:23). According to Rashi, who cites a *medresh*, "The play on words [*ish/isho*] indicates that the world was created by means of the Holy Tongue." The *Sifsey Khakhomim, The Lips of the Wise*, a medieval commentary on Rashi's commentary, goes on to claim that "only in the Holy Tongue is the word for woman derived from the word for man." It doesn't matter that this is incorrect; what is important is the belief that the Hebrew word for a thing, and the Hebrew word alone, actually *is* the thing. Realism begins and ends in the Hebrew with which God created the world and Adam gave things their names: once we start talking *goyish,* we're free to turn into Juliet.

Since Yiddish, like other Jewish languages, is written in the Hebrew alphabet, it can still be construed as part of the Hebrew reality of authentic existence. If combinations of Hebrew letters actually *are* the things that they serve to denote, it stands to reason that unpleasant, dangerous, or frightening things may not be mentioned—not even in the Bible itself, where certain unspeakable ideas are expressed only in terms of their opposites. The passage at the beginning of the Book of Job, which every English translation renders as "Curse God and die" (Job 2:9), reads "Bless God and die" in the original. The notion of cursing God is so horrific, so literally unspeakable, as to remain taboo even in direct quotation. Likewise, when the evil queen Jezebel decides to frame Naboth in order to steal his vineyard, she instructs her suborned witnesses to accuse him of having "blessed God and the king" (1 Kings 21:10). The standard English translations all say "cursed."

Strictly speaking, this kind of benign doublethink is called antiphrasis, not euphemism, and is known in Yiddish as *loshn sgey-nehoyr,* a *loshn-koydesh* phrase that means "the language of 'rich in light.'" It is a Talmudic and Midrashic designation for a blind person (the Aramaic *sagi nehor*), and serves as an archetype of how to say the opposite of what you really mean and still get your message across. As a rhetorical device, *loshn sgey-nehoyr* manages to block the taboo word or subject in such a way as to make sure that those who really do have "lots of light"—Jews who are hip to the jive—are able to appreciate the irony and understand what is really meant.

Anyone with a reasonable Jewish education knows that the Talmudic tractates Greater and Lesser Mourning are never referred to as anything but *Semakhos*—Happy Times—and that funeral services are listed in prayer books under the rubric *inyoney semakhos*, "matters pertaining to happy occasions, a guide to good times." This penchant for antiphrasis is yet another Talmudic factor that helps pave the way for Yiddish, a language in which irony tends to be used for simple communication as well as comic effect, and it isn't hard to find in the German component of Yiddish, either. Anything "bad" or "black" becomes "good": the *beyz oyg*—the evil eye—is often called a *gut oyg*, a good eye. A *shvarts-yor*, which looks like it should mean "black year" but actually means "the devil," is often called a *gut yor*, "good year," with no reference to blimps or tires. A cemetery can be called *dos gute ort*, "the good place," when it isn't simply called *beys khayim*, "house of life."

In a world in which virtually any statement or action is likely to attract the attention of the powers of evil, little white lies, tiny feats of artifice and deception, are needed just to get through the day. Unambiguous communication carries grave risks. Want to know how many of your fellow Jews are hanging around the synagogue, waiting to say Kaddish and praise the Great Name? Don't even think about counting them. "When you take the census of the people of Israel, each shall give a ransom for himself to the Lord when you number them, that there be no plague among them when you number them" (Exod. 30:12).

"Counting," says Rashi, "is subject to the evil eye." The ransom, half a shekel a head, was more than just a fund-raising device; it allowed the census officials to count coins instead of people, and so evade the threat of a plague. Numbering Jews is dangerous on two counts: the apparent blasphemy involved in appearing to doubt or contradict God's promise to Abraham—"Look up to the sky and number the stars . . . so will your descendants be" (Gen. 15:5)—and the virtual invitation to demonic forces to come and do something to reduce that number. Although the Bible never mentions the evil eye, it seems to make allowance for both sources of danger in its descriptions of the census ordered by King David, which didn't go as well as the one in the desert. The story is told twice, first in the Book of Samuel and again in the twenty-first chapter of First Chronicles (written about half a millennium after the account in Samuel). According to Samuel, "Yet again God was angry with Israel, and He stirred David up against them, saying: 'Go, count Israel and Judah' " (2 Sam. 24:1). In the Chronicles version, though, it isn't God who gives the orders: "Satan stood up against Israel and incited David to count Israel" (1 Chron. 21:1). David's commander in chief goes so far as to ask why David seems to want to "bring sin upon Israel," but to no avail: both accounts state that seventy thousand people died in the ensuing plague.

Better not to count Jews at all, best not to speak of numbers. When specific numbers cannot be avoided—"We have 380 students in our school"—the sentence usually ends with *keyn yirbu*, "so may they increase," though the all-purpose *keynehore* is sometimes heard as well.

Counting or not counting becomes an issue in Jewish life because of the minyen, the quorum of ten necessary for public prayer. How do you know how many people you've got if you're not allowed to count? What's a Jew supposed to do? The most common solution is "not-counting": instead of pointing at each person and saying, *"Eyns, tsvey, dray,"* until you see how close you come to *tsen,* you point and "don't-say" *eyns, tsvey, dray* by saying, *"Nisht eyns, nisht tsvey, nisht dray*—not-one, not-two, not-three." Depending on your point of view, this will either deceive or placate whichever supernatural force you're trying to get around—you get all the thrill of the forbidden, free from any of the risks. Not-counting is only one way of having your metaphysical *treyf* and eating it, too. In some synagogues, feet are counted. In others, well-known ten-word sayings are used. With each word, you point to a different person. The *moytse*, the blessing over bread, is the most common of these formulae, followed closely by the ninth verse of the Twenty-eighth Psalm, "*Hoyshiyo es amekho*, Save your nation and bless your inheritance; be their shepherd and lift them up forever," which has only ten words in the Hebrew. Shakespeare can also be used in place of these more traditional phrases: "To daven or not to daven, that is the question."

Regardless of which method of noncounting is used, the non-sum is always the same: *Undz felt nokh X*, "We need X more people." You can only number the nonexistent. To specify the number of people already there would be to invite the sudden and possibly permanent departure of one or more of them.

There are times, however, as with the plagues at the seder, when you simply can't avoid mentioning things that would be better left unsaid. You can't describe the sinking of the Titanic by antiphrasis: "And the next thing you know, it didn't hit an iceberg." But if misfortune is to be discussed without being incurred, the forces of evil have to be turned away before they can turn up and wreak havoc. One of the most common ways of doing so is to add the phrase *nisht far aykh gedakht*—idiomatically, "heaven preserve you"—to the offending sentence, as in *er layt, nebekh, fun der biterer makhle, nisht far aykh gedakht*, "The poor man is suffering from cancer, heaven preserve you." *Dakhtn*, the infinitive from which *gedakht* comes, doesn't actually mean "preserve" or "defend"; it means "to mention," and the literal meaning of *nisht far aykh gedakht* is "may it not be mentioned for [i.e., with regard to] you." What is being said is, "Although I am unable to continue the conversation without mentioning this unpleasant and highly undesirable matter, I'm doing everything I can to make sure that the forces capable of bringing it about won't be bringing it to you." Among other things, such a formula helps to allay any suspicion that might fall on you if the evil in question ever does befall your listener. Coverage can be extended to people who are absent or out of earshot by saying *nisht do gedakht*, it shouldn't happen here, and can even go global with *nisht far ken yidn gedakht*, it shouldn't be mentioned with regard to any Jew. If this idea of mentioning seems forced or farfetched, consider its less ambiguous opposite, something you might say when you hear that Mendel has just won the lottery: "*Af ale yidishe kinder gezogt*, May it be said on [i.e., decreed for] all the Children of Israel."

The unspeakable can also be averted by using the less specific *loy aleykhem*, "may it not befall you," and *loy oleynu*, "may it not happen to us." Literally, these mean "not for you" and "not for us," and are similar in construction to the Yiddish word for corpse, *barmenen* (accent on the *bar*), literally "outside of us, not us, anybody but us." When it comes to death, we all sound like Ralph Kramden: "The undertaker prepared the not-this-kid for burial."

The truly all-purpose *rakhmone litslan*, "may the Merciful One save us," is even less specific than *loy oleynu* and *loy aleykhem*. The real advantage of *rakhmone litslan*, a phrase that seems to get prissier with every year that passes, is that it can also express disapproval and moral superiority (*your* moral superiority); it can mean "out, demons, out" and it can also mean "tsk-tsk." "There was a terrible crash on the highway, *rakhmone litslan*," is meant to keep such crashes away from everyone present. "There he was, nibbling the foot of a live pig on Yom Kippur, *rakhmone litslan*," is meant to dispel the mental image of such loathsome and non-Jewish behavior. Both usages are perfectly idiomatic, with the latter being particularly favored in Jew-on-Jew religious debate: "They call themselves Jews? They eat nonkosher lettuce, *rakhmone litslan*."

Rakhmone litslan, loy oleynu, and *nisht far aykh gedakht* appeal directly to supernatural forces. God is asked to intervene, devils are commanded to go away—similar forms exist in every language. Yiddish, however, also makes use of what might be called the Demon Double Whammy, in which the demons are commanded *not* to do what you think you want them to do—because you know that you don't really want them to do it. "You kicked your sister?" asks the outraged mother. "*Zol dir nisht tsebrokhn vern a fus,* may you not break your leg! *Zolst mir nisht geharget vern,* don't drop dead!" At the same time as the mother is telling the kid that he should break the leg that he used to kick his sister and then drop dead, she's also telling the demons that she isn't really serious and their services are not required. When my mother found me hanging over the railing of our apartment balcony she said, "*Gay, heng, 'est zakh dem karek* nisht *brakhn,* Go ahead, hang there—you *won't* break your neck." A child not weaned on antiphrasis might not have known enough to come down.

IV

You can't take living for granted. If you mention someone's age, especially your own or that of the person to whom you're speaking, you usually throw in *biz hundert un tsvantsik,* "until a hundred and twenty," lest the demons decide that, since you seem to like your present age so much, they'll do their best to make it permanent. "How old are you, Mr. Goldberg?" "*Dray un zibetsik, biz hundert un tsvantsik,* seventy-three [I should keep on living] until a hundred and twenty." A polite way of asking Mr. Goldberg how old he is (and there are scores of old jokes for which this is the punch line) is, *"Vi alt zayt ir, biz hundert un tsvantsik,* How old are you, until a hundred and twenty?" thus freeing Mr. Goldberg to respond with a simple *"Dray un zibetsik."*

Why 120? The usual answer—that's how long Moses lived—fails to explain why Moses lived to 120, rather than 110 or 130. The reason goes back to the time of Noah, when God decided to reduce the human life span from the 900-plus years that people had been living up until then: "My spirit shall not remain in man forever, because he is flesh; his days shall be one hundred and twenty years" (Gen. 6:3). It takes a few generations for this limit to become effective. Abraham lives to 175, Isaac to 180, Jacob to 147; poor Joseph is only 110 when he dies, the first major figure in biblical history not to have been grandfathered into a longer life span. The rabbis tell us that God imposed His new limit gradually, in order to give people time to retool their expectations. Where Joseph, who is not considered one of the patriarchs, is subject to the new limits, Moses, who was as close to perfect as a person can be, is graced with a complete human life span, without temporal demerits for sin or misdeed. The only other person said to have lived for the whole 120 years is Rabbi Akiva, who is as much the hero of the Talmud as Moses is of the Torah.

Biz hundert un tsvantsik can only be used in conjunction with another number. If you mention a person only by name—and again, "person" here tends to imply a relative or close friend—you say *zol lebn,* may he or she live, which is generally taken as an abbreviated form of *zol lebn un gezunt zayn,* may he or she live and be well. This keeps the demons from messing up your relationships with the people you really care about. *Zol lebn* doesn't take any chances with their health, either; trust the Jews to bring it to the foreground. There's even a blessing that goes *a gezunt af dir,* "health to you," which means, "well done, way to go, attaboy/girl." I'm pretty sure that Spock's "Live long and prosper" on *Star Trek* owes as much of a debt to *zolst lebn un gezunt zayn* as the Vulcan salute does to the hand motions of the priestly blessing administered in the synagogue.

Zol lebn itself owes a good deal to the Hebrew, where the acronym *shlita* is usually appended to the name of a living rabbi. The letters stand for *she-yikhye le'oyrekh yomim toyvim, amen,* may he live long and well, amen (the feminine form, *tlita,* reserved for the rabbi's wife, is seen primarily in invitations and social announcements). Hasidim will often refer to their leader as *der rebbe, shlita,* the rebbe, long may he live and prosper, or *der rebbe, zol lebn.*

It is easier to keep the demons away from living loved ones than it is to keep them from reuniting you with any of the dear departed whom you might mention. After a dead person's name, you can say *opgesheyt zol er/zi zayn,* "may he/she be separated from us"; this is a version of the Hebrew *le-havdil beyn ha-khayim ve-ha-meysim,* "to separate the living from the dead," which is the conversational *havdole* used to separate us from the deceased: let them stay dead and let us stay alive. Indeed, you can avoid any unnecessary (and hence dangerous) direct reference to death by saying *aykh tsu lengere yor,* more years to you ("you" being the person to whom you're speaking), after the name of the deceased has been mentioned. "Why, Mendel, you sing like a second Elvis, *aykh tsu lengere yor.*"

Like "rest in peace," even the nicer sayings about the dead are intended, if only in part, to keep them happy and at peace so that they won't come back to haunt us like bad decisions. The most common of these, *olevhasholem,* "peace be on him" (feminine, *olehasholem*), is primarily honorific and is virtually never considered to have even the slightest apotropaic function. The phrase is found in the Talmud and Midrash, where it is used only in association with people who figure in the Bible: Abraham, Isaac, Jacob, Moses, King David, et al. As such, it shows considerable respect for the deceased, who are placated by being placed in such august company, and is always used when the speaker's late parents are mentioned—"My father, *olevhasholem*"—though it isn't necessarily confined to family members and is often used in the same sense as the English "sorely missed." Note that an actual name need not be used; you can say "my father, my mother, my friend," and so on.

Olevhasholem gives rise to a couple of mocking versions— *olevhashnobel* and *olehasholekhts,* "a beak on him" and "a peel on her"—that depend entirely on similarity of sound. It's also open to jocular usage. A person who's recently been fired can speak of "My job, *olevhasholem.*" "My relationship, *olevhasholem,*" means that you two have finally broken up, and so on.

Heaven, where the dead people go, is technically known as *ganeydn,* "the Garden of Eden, paradise," but people tend to speak more of *yene velt,* "that world, the other world," the one where we're really not so anxious to go, which is why we aren't calling it paradise: the spirits might get the wrong idea.

V

The general reluctance to offer a foothold to evil eyes and evil spirits lies at the root of the previously mentioned niggardliness with compliments and pleasant remarks. Good wishes or unqualified praise can turn into frightening and incomprehensible minefields of *keynehores, zol lebns, biz hundert un tsvantsiks,* where every wish must be protected, fenced in, and finally nailed into its protective coffin with three good spits if it isn't to turn into its opposite. It is often easier (and always less dangerous) to rely on the fact that other Yiddish speakers will know exactly what you mean when you shrug your shoulders and wave dismissively or nod curtly in someone's general direction while saying something that sounds like "u-whu-e." Unhappiness is never shy about speaking up, but approval is expressed as indifference, satisfaction as lack of enthusiasm.

Rashi's comment on Numbers 12:1 gives us a comprehensive illustration of how compliments work in the Yiddish-speaking world. The Bible tells us: "Miriam and Aaron spoke against Moses because of the Cushite woman whom he had married, for he had married a Cushite woman."

A Cushite is an Ethiopian or a black person. Yet the Targum, a second-century Aramaic translation of the Bible, still printed, like Rashi's commentary, alongside the original in every Hebrew Bible, translates "Cushite" as *shapirto*, which means "beautiful." If only this could be ascribed to precocious Jewish recognition of the idea that black is beautiful; but, as Rashi makes clear, we're unfortunately dealing with the opposite prejudice:

> *The Cushite woman:* This tells us that her beauty was acknowledged by all, just as all acknowledge the blackness of the Cushite. *Cushite:* In gematria, *yefas mare,* beautiful in appearance [each has a numerical value of 736]. *The Cushite woman:* She is called a Cushite because of her beauty, in the same way that a man will call his handsome son "Cushite" in order to protect him from the evil eye [i.e., there is no actual Cushite involved; the term is being used to describe the beauty of Moses's wife, Zipporah, without calling forth an evil eye].

There is a direct line from the Christian to the Cushite, from the antiphrasis of *shikse* to the antiphrasis of Cushite. Both women are beautiful and desirable. The shikse's beauty is dangerous to us, the Jewish people as a whole; a woman beautiful enough to marry Moses is a danger to herself—other people and evil spirits could get jealous and bring an evil eye upon her. To call the forbidden-but-desirable Christian girl a shikse, a repulsive thing, is to call down a curse on her; the demons are such *aftselakhisnikes* that praising the Christian girl would lead to an *increase* in her devilish beauty. Moses's wife and a man's handsome son are called ugly in order to protect their beauty; complimenting either of them would call forth a destructive evil eye. Rather than risk harming someone whom you like with open praise, it is safer to say nothing that isn't negative—negative and noncommittal—because there's no second-guessing the demons.

It's an equal-opportunity negativism that also applies to one-self. Just go up to a random group of Jews and ask, "*Vos makht ir?* How are you?" and listen to what happens. Like everybody else, Jews can be divided into two categories: those who take the "are" in "How are you?" to mean "right now" and those who take it to mean "How have you been?" In the Yiddish world, at least, the former are the slaves of every two-bit demon that comes down the pike and will try to change the topic immediately by answering you with another, not entirely serious question:

> *Vos makh ikh? Vos zol ikh makhn?* How am I? How should I be?
> *Ikh makh a lebn,* I make a living.
> *Ikh makh nisht ken lebn,* I don't make a living.

And from the real rakes:

> *Ikh makh kinder,* I make children (to which the proper response is *Gots vinder,* "God's miracles," which is short for *Gots vinder, a puts makht kinder,* "God's miracles, a *puts* makes children").

These and scores of similar "jokes" are also serious ways of begging a question that the speakers might not wish to answer. They are less serious versions of the once widespread *borekh ha-shem*, "Blessed be God" (or, more idiomatically, *tenks Got*), that is still nearly universal in the religious world. It is a fine all-purpose response and tells the questioner nothing more than that you're still alive enough to be able to utter it. The phrase manages to be both uninformative and a little sanctimonious, and is sometimes countered, even in the most religious circles, with *borekh ha-shem gut tsi borekh ha-shem shlekht*, "*borekh ha-shem* good or *borekh ha-shem* bad?" In other words, "Get the mush out of your mouth and answer my question already." Whatever it isn't telling you, though, *borekh ha-shem* is also saying that things could always be worse.

Almost as uninformative, but much closer to English usage, is *nishkoshe*, which is usually repeated twice in answer to *vos makht ir* and is best translated as "tol'able, tol'able." Well, of course it's "tol'able"—if you couldn't tolerate it, you'd be dead. You'll sometimes hear *gants nishkoshe*, "I have no trouble putting up with it," if things are really going well. This can be compared with the textbook-approved response of *gants gut*, which I have never heard in my life. "Real good"? As a response to a Yiddish question, it marks you as someone who knows some Yiddish words but doesn't really understand the language. *Gants gut*—if you're not afraid to say it, you have no business speaking Yiddish.

Eh, which rhymes with *feh*, can be used in response to a variety of questions. "How was the concert?" "How was the food?" And, of course, "How are you?" It is usually accompanied by a gentle swaying of the right hand, which is held perpendicular to the chest and then rocked gently, first to the left, then to the right. It means "Okay, all right, nothing to get excited about but nothing to complain about, either: three to three and a half out of a possible five stars."

These are the responses of people for whom the present really means now—not yesterday, not five minutes ago, but *now*. Yiddish speakers who take a longer view are likely to answer with *nisht far aykh gedakht*, or even a simple *oy*. Like *freg nisht*, "don't ask," and *af mayne sonim gezogt*, "it should happen to my enemies," these are the introductions to a comprehensive catalogue of petty annoyances and major disappointments that are usually of interest to the speaker and nobody else. And they're often expressed in terms of a curse.

Six

You Should Grow Like an Onion:
THE YIDDISH CURSE

I

"You should own a thousand houses
   with a thousand rooms in each house
      and a thousand beds in every room.
         And you should sleep each night in a different bed
in a different room
   in a different house
      and get up every morning
         and go down a different staircase
            and get into a different car,
               driven by a different chauffeur,
                  who should drive you to a different doctor—and *he*
               shouldn't know what's wrong with you, either."

Think of it as a kvetch with a mission, a bellyache that knows
where it's going; it's a classic example of the *klole,* the Yiddish curse.
It might be formulaic—you have to wonder if it's subtlety or an
oversight that every room in every house seems to be a bedroom—
but it shows how much you care. This kind of elaborate curse—
delivered in a Talmudic singsong—isn't an imprecation; it's a
pastime, a form of recreation that lets standard Yiddish thought
and speech run wild.

   As we have already seen, kvetching is essentially passive.

A simple kvetch is a descriptive activity that conveys disapproval, but does nothing to alter or eliminate the cause of that disapproval. A kvetch might make things easier to bear, but it doesn't actually try to change the things it's kvetching about; it's a way of dealing with circumstances and situations that we feel powerless to change. A curse, though, is directed at a person, and as such is a step in the direction of control; it's the kvetch armed, the kvetch-militant, the kvetch that sets out to silence itself. It is prescriptive, but still doesn't do much. Half kvetch, half action, the *klole* gives the curser a feeling of satisfaction while doing the cursee no real harm—and then the curser becomes the cursee and everybody's happy, or as happy as they're likely to be.

Where the kvetch is still uncomfortable with the idea of name-as-thing, the *klole* depends on it. Rather than shrink from the terrifying power of words, the curse tries to harness these powers for its own ends, only to discover that they only seem to work when you *don't* want them to, as when you forget a *keynehore*. The kvetch is often couched in the form of a simple declarative statement and makes use of verbs like "is" and "are"; the *klole* is always subjunctive, always a matter of "would" and "should." The Yiddish verb *zoln,* which we'll be seeing especially in the forms *zolst* and *zol,* means "should" or even "let," as in *zol er kumen,* "let him come." The *klole* is to the kvetch what the Messiah is to the mundane. The kvetch is the living nightmare; the curse, the dream deferred.

The path from kvetch to *klole* can be traced in a phrase that we saw at the beginning of the last chapter. "My enemies should be as ugly as she is beautiful," is a compliment, a complaint, and a curse all at once. This comment about a woman's beauty is structured as a complaint that the speaker's enemies are too good-looking, but in the ultimate analysis, it's a curse that seeks to make them a whole lot uglier. The verb in the principal clause has to do with the enemies, not the beauty—she simply "is"; whatever needs to happen, needs to happen to the enemies. Otherwise, the speaker could have said, "She is extremely beautiful, *keynehore*," and let it go at that. But that wouldn't have filled the emotional need.

If we take the kvetch as the basic form of Yiddish communication, we can trace the process of thought quite clearly. Someone asks the speaker what a certain woman looks like. He immediately falls back on Yiddish default mode and seeks to express himself by means of a kvetch, but his chances don't look good. There is nothing about the woman's character that is kvetch-worthy, at least not at the moment, and there's certainly no kvetch potential in her looks. The speaker, however, has any number of ill-wishers and enemies, all of whom are always good for a few minutes' kvetching, even to an audience that doesn't know who they are. If there's a need for an impromptu kvetch, this is the place to start.

The speaker is toiling under a double burden. There's the responsibility of answering the question about the woman's looks, as well as the basic conversational imperative to come out with a kvetch. To complicate things further, the speaker genuinely admires the appearance of the woman about whom he has been asked, and wants the questioner to know this. He has to figure out how to link his dislike of his enemies to the woman's beauty, and in such a way as to make the woman's beauty a source of suffering to his enemies. A few microseconds after the question was first asked, behold—God's verbal plenty.

Imagine what happens, then, when two people who think in this way confront each other as adversaries. The Yiddish equivalents of "drop," "get," and "screw" will be nowhere in evidence. A curse like "You should own a thousand houses" has nothing in common with "Drop dead," "Get stuffed," or "Screw you." "Screw you" leads to "Screw you, too," or else to a fight. "You should own a thousand houses" is an invitation to dialogue. It fairly screams at the victim: "Notice how it builds! Look how clever I am! Say something back and I'll answer that, too." In a culture defined by dissatisfaction and debate, even vengeance turns into an argument, an escalating series of "Oh, yeahs?" in which either party threatens the other with things over which neither has any control:

> BERL: *A beyzer gzar zol af dir* **kumen**—May an evil decree come upon you.
> SHMERL: **Kumen** *zolstu tsu dayn eybiker* **ru**—May you come to your eternal rest.
> BERL: **Ruen** *zolstu nisht afile in* **keyver**—May you find no rest even in the grave.
> SHMERL: *Zol dir lign in* **keyver** *der eyver, in di kishkes a lokh mit a sheyver*—May your penis lie in a grave, [may] a hole and a hernia [lie] in your guts.

By the time the second pair of curses begins, they have become impossible to take seriously. "Screw you" is an insult, and so is "Screw you, too." By the time we get to "Screw me, too? Then screw you three," we're dealing with a game, a performance to which the proper response is either laughter, applause, or an even more outrageous comeback. This sort of competitive cursing is one of the rarest forms of spoken communication, one in which each participant really listens to what the other is saying. Reciprocal cursing demands reciprocated attention—your response has to build on and demolish whatever has just been wished on you, or you're going to be out of the game.

The game isn't played very much anymore, at least not in Yiddish. Most of the more elaborate curses that you hear these days—either in Yiddish or in English translation—are quoted from books or old recordings, or have been passed along as jokes. The elaborate curses quoted above are pretty much a thing of the past, and even then tended to be identified with certain strata of society.

The terms for cursing—as distinct from simple use of "bad" words—are quite similar to those found in English: *sheltn vi a mark-yidene*, "to curse like a market woman"; *sheltn zikh vi afn fish-mark*, "to curse like in a fishmarket." We're dealing with the Yiddish equivalent of Billingsgate, the London fish market that lent its name to all kinds of bad language, a Jewish version of the dozens, the African-American insult game, but far less sexually oriented and far more likely to be identified as a female rather than a male activity. As in all such games, victory was strictly verbal; if all the ill wishes came true, there'd be no one left to play with.

II

If any of these fancy curses was really meant to be taken seriously, the victim would probably have walked away long before the curser got to the punch line. If you really wanted someone to drop dead, you wouldn't waste this kind of time on them. You'd tell them to drop dead and leave it at that. When Hitler comes up in conversation, he gets a simple *yemakh shmoy*, "may his name be blotted out," rather than any filigreed malediction.

Yemakh shmoy is as deadly serious as Yiddish gets, and it is not a phrase to be thrown around lightly. It isn't cute or funny or terribly memorable in translation; it isn't an insult or an expression of distaste or impatience. It's a real curse, and seeks to put an end to its object. Your boss might be a jerk, but unless he's at least as big a jerk as Lionel Barrymore in *It's a Wonderful Life*, you can't justify saying *yemakh shmoy* after mentioning his name. It's a *klole mit beyner,* this one, a curse with bones, and takes us right back to the realism at the heart of so much Jewish religious thought; blotting out a person's name is the same as blotting out that person's existence. To forget a name is one thing; to efface it completely is to efface its bearer from the Book of Life as well as the Book of Those Who Have Lived. *Yemakh shmoy ve-zikhroy,* a fuller version of the same thing, "may his name and his memory be blotted out," makes this abundantly clear: there should be no memory of this person's existence—no children, no grandchildren, nothing.

A couple of other Yiddish curses play on the same idea, but without the heartfelt seriousness of *yemakh shmoy. A kleyn kind zol nokh im heysn,* "a small child should bear his name," and *zayn nomen zol aheymkumen,* "his name should come home," at least leave the victim his existence and, in the Ashkenazic naming system, virtually assure him of grandchildren. He'll be remembered; he'll be mourned. But the person whose name has been blotted out is a person whose existence cannot be forgotten because it never took place; he and his life have been negated.

The curse begins as a *mitsve: "Timkhe es zeykher Amolek,* Blot out the memory of Amalek from under the heavens" (Deut. 25:19). The Amalekites attacked the Israelites from behind, killing women, children, and old people, and the enmity didn't pale with time. The Book of Esther says that Haman was a descendant of Agag, the Amalekite king spared by a foolishly merciful Saul. More modern tradition has sought to link Hitler to the same bloodline, even though popular Yiddish ethnography holds Armenians to be the modern descendants of Amalek. An Armenian would once have been known colloquially as a *timkhe* or a *mokh* (Ex. 17:14: "*Ki-mokho emkhe es zeykher Amolek,* I will most certainly **blot** out the memory of Amalek"), even though there seems to have been no unusual enmity between Jews and Armenians. A few names that have nothing to do with Amalek are also blotted in the Bible, but the association of *yemakh shmoy* with Amalek remains strong: the traditional way of testing a new pen is to write "Amalek" (in Hebrew letters, of course) and then scribble over it until it is "blotted out."

This seems to be the only way of fulfilling the commandment. Since Amalek is mentioned in the Torah, which is eternal and unchangeable, the commandment can never be fulfilled: there will always be a Torah with the name Amalek in it. Had Moses been allowed to act, rather than simply transcribe what the Lord dictated, the commandment would undoubtedly have read, "Blot out the memory of what's-their-name from under the heavens." Later generations would have had no knowledge of Amalekite depredations and no idea of what the commandment was about.

Yemakh shmoy is so serious that the noun that derives from it is never used about anyone about whom you'd actually say *yemakh shmoy*. A *yemakh-shmoynik* (feminine, *yemakh-shmoynitse*) is "a scoundrel, an evildoer," but not evil enough to warrant an actual *yemakh shmoy*. War criminals and terrorists deserve a *yemakh shmoy; yemakh-shmoynik* is closer to "scum-bag" or "SOB."

III

More serious cursing, the stuff with no underlying spirit of fun (which includes *yemakh shmoy*) is known as *leynen di toykhekhe,* "reading the reproof," or *oyslozn di gantse toykhekhe (af),* "to wreak the whole *toykhekhe* on someone." The *toykhekhe,* or more properly *toykhekhes,* are two separate chapters in the Bible, Leviticus 26 and

Deuteronomy 28, in which the Lord sets forth the consequences of failure to obey His voice and walk in His statutes:

> Cursed shall you be in the city, and cursed shall you be in the field. Cursed shall be your basket and your kneading-trough. Cursed shall be the fruit of your body, and the fruit of your ground, the increase of your cattle and the young of your flock. Cursed shall you be when you come in, and cursed shall you be when you go out. . . . The Lord will smite you with madness and blindness and confusion of mind; and you shall grope at noonday, as the blind grope in darkness, and you shall not prosper in your ways; and you shall be only oppressed and robbed continually, and there shall be no one to help you (Deut. 26:16–19, 28–29).

This continues for another couple of pages, in tones so frightening that it is traditional not to call any member of the congregation to the Torah when these sections are due to be read. Instead, the *shammes*—the sexton—or some other synagogue employee is called. Being called for the *toykhekhe* is understood to be part of the job; neither God nor man is supposed to take it as any reflection on the character or morals of the person standing up there. The passages themselves are read quickly and in an undertone, so as not to frighten or upset the congregation.

Transferring the name of these sections of the Torah to lava-like streams of profanity and abuse does no real injustice to the Bible and is not really intended ironically. *Oyslozn di toykhekhe* is like saying "to put everything you've got into cursing someone, to pile curse after curse on top of them."

Appropriately enough, the most versatile of these *toyte kloles* or "dead curses," vehement curses with plenty of feeling behind them, is *gey in dr'erd,* "go in the ground, drop dead, go to hell." It's simple, straightforward and makes up in applicability whatever it might lack in inventiveness. The "go to hell" aspect allows *in dr'erd* to be used in cases where "drop dead" would make no sense: "She wants to throw a passenger out of the car to make room for her suitcases? *In dr'erd mit ire tshemodanes,* the hell with her suitcases." This is the same *in dr'erd* that we saw as part of *lign in dr'erd un bakn beygl,* to lie in the ground baking bagels. Tone of voice has a great deal to do with the proper translation of these *in dr'erd* idioms. Depending on how you say it, you can communicate anything from "the hell with her suitcases" to "shit on her suitcases" to "fuck her *and* her goddamned suitcases."

The general background of *geyn in dr'erd* produces the really wonderful *ikh vel im bagrobn in dr'erd vi an oytser,* "I'll bury him in the ground like a treasure," which not only leaves the death itself in someone else's hands, but also bespeaks so exquisite a hatred that you want to make sure that he goes into the ground gently and deeply, without anyone but you knowing where he's been buried. I once heard a speaker who had just been introduced as *undzer natsyonaler oytser,* "our national treasure," get up and begin his speech with, *"Ah, a dank aykh, reb forzitser, vos ir hot mikh ongerufen 'oytser.'* Thank you, Mr. Chairman, for having called me a 'treasure.' *Itst farshtey ikh far vos ikh bin shoyn azoy fil yorn in dr'erd,* now I know why I've been *in dr'erd* all these years."

Less wide-rangingly, you can tell somebody to *ver geharget,* "get killed," or even specify the way in which you'd like to see them die: *ver dershtikt, ver dershokhtn, ver dervorgn, ver tsezest,* "get strangled, get stabbed, get choked, explode." You could go on endlessly, and there are equivalents in every language. With *farkhapt zolstu vern,* "you should die suddenly,"—i.e., right now—things start to move in a more interesting direction. *A viste pgire af dir,* "a dismal animal death on you," is careful to ensure that you don't miss the point. A *pgire* is bad enough, the wretched death of a nonhuman creature; but a *viste pgire,* a dismal or desolate death of this type, means "to croak wretchedly"—as in, you should spend the rest of your tiny life in a Colorado feedlot, then be herded off to some nonunion slaughterhouse to be turned, *painfully,* into fast-food burgers for one of the less prominent chains.

Less scurrilous but possibly more painful, *a vist bagegenish zol dir trefn,* "may a dismal event befall you," or, more idiomatically, "something really bad should happen to you," gives the cursee credit for having enough intelligence to come up with something suitably horrible on his or her own. Curses like this are a purely psychological version of Room 101 in Orwell's *1984:* the object of the curse furnishes the *vist bagegenish* that will upset her the most and moves it into her head all by herself.

The victim's complicity in his own demise leaves plenty of room for nonspecific curses whose inexactitude virtually forces the victim to furnish the really terrifying details. Hence the prominence of the *umglik.* An *umglik* is a misfortune, a calamity. Road accidents, mine disasters, stock market crashes, folk music festivals—they are all *umglikn.* Lou Gehrig was a great ball player and a wonderful guy, but *an umglik, take a vist bagegenish, hot im getrofn,* "a calamity, a really dismal event, befell him." Mothers scream at their children to desist from dangerous physical stunts because *vest zikh umgliklekh makhn,* "you'll make yourself unfortunate," that is, you'll end up crippled, damaged for life.

Based on this type of usage, *umglik* gives us the all-purpose *an umglik af dir,* "may a disaster befall you." This might be *too* nonspecific; the lack of an adjective to guide the less inventive or phobia-ridden cursee is a real weakness here. So many *umglikn* involve vast numbers of people that they might be a bit too easy to write off; if it's a matter of earthquakes or tidal waves, chances are that the person doing the cursing is going to suffer just as much as you do. The localized *umglik,* generally localized without any regard for what would normally be thought of as "rational discourse" or "the course of nature," is therefore far more effective. *An umglik dir in di zaytn,* "a calamity in your flanks," helps guide the cursee to a locus of pain, while leaving the nature and intensity of that pain up to him. Similarly with *an umglik dir in di kishkes,* "a calamity in your guts," in which things start with churning, corkscrewlike pain and then begin to build. *An umglik iz far dir veynik,* "a disaster isn't enough for you, a disaster is too good for you," is a little weak and—unless the person has just suffered an actual *umglik* which you're doing your level best to make even worse—doesn't really lead where you'd like it to go: your displeasure will certainly be noted, but don't count on the recipient's racking her brains to try to figure out what *isn't* too good for her. You're better off with the slightly longer but rather more pointed *zol es dir onkumen vos ikh vintsh dir khotsh a helft/khotsh a tsent kheylek,* "may only a half/a tenth of what I wish you [actually] befall you." This puts the onus back onto the cursee, who now knows how much you hate her, while leaving you free to add as many other curses and calamities as you feel the occasion warrants: they're all just a part of the same percentage that your victim is working out in her head.

A *beyze mehume* might be even better than an *umglik,* just because nobody's quite sure what it really is. As we've seen with *beyz-oyg,* the evil eye, *beyz* can mean "evil." It also means "angry, malicious, bad." A *mehume* is "turmoil, tumult, riot," as in, "Certain British soccer fans like to start *mehumes,*" or as the Bible has it, "Every man's sword was against his fellow and there was a very great *mehume*" (1 Sam. 14:20). A *beyze mehume,* "an evil riot, a particularly nasty instance of mass violence," is a soccer riot with an unusually high rate of injury or death, or one directed at members of a particular ethnic or racial group (regardless of which team they support). *Kristallnacht*, the 1968 Democratic National Convention, the L.A. riots in the 1990s were all *beyze mehumes*. *A beyze mehume af dir*, "an evil riot on you," implies that you'd like the victim to end up as a casualty of such a riot. Where, why, how—these are for him to figure out. *A beyze mehume af dir* is really an oblique way of saying *nem ayn a mise-meshune*, "have yourself a violent death," but it also helps to put a face, human or otherwise, on the *umglik* being wished. And speaking of faces, there's also *a sibe dir in ponim*, "may an accident befall your face," which is pretty much the same thing as *an umglik dir in ponim*.

A beyze sho, "an evil hour," is no less vicious for being so nebulous. A *mehume*, a *mise meshune*, an *umglik*—all these take place *in a beyzer sho*, as does anything else that might be harmful to you. *A beyze sho af dir* derives its real sting from the fact that *in a guter (un a mazldiker) sho*, "in a good (and auspicious) hour," is a standard Yiddish congratulatory formula. Someone gets married, has a baby, makes a *bris*, gets a new job—you say *mazl tov* and then wish that it take place in a good hour. As a result, *beyze sho* means more than it actually says; along with the visitation of an evil hour, the curse has an underlying sense of wishing that none of your dreams should ever come true. It's like congratulating someone whose life's work has come to nothing.

Geshedikt zolstu vern, "may you be hurt, damaged," derives such force as it has from a play on the word *shed*, "demon," so that it also carries the idea of "may you be beset by evil spirits." And when? *In a beyzer sho*, of course.

The *viste pgire* that we met a little while ago can also be elaborated in ways that are more, rather than less, specific, as in such well-known idioms as *brenen un brotn*, "to burn and to roast," which figures as *me zol im afile brenen un brotn,* "even if he was burned and roasted," that is, no matter what you do, he's not going to change his mind. *Brenen* and *brotn* were once used as means of trying to get Jews to change their minds about religion, and very few of them were convinced, either. *Brenen* appears in the well-known short curse, *brenen zol er,* "may he burn"—in hell, that is. There is also the more emphatic, if slightly redundant, *brenen zol-stu afn fayer,* "may you burn in (hell-) fire." If burning him doesn't work, it might be an idea to try the Yiddish version of puffed wheat: *geshosn zol er vern fun a biks,* "he should be shot from a gun." Had three-time Oscar winner Walter Brennan only been Jewish, his friends would surely have called him *Zol er.*

Considerably nastier than any of these and somewhat more oblique, *opkoyfn zol men im baym tatn zayne malbushim,* "may his wardrobe be purchased from his father," is so vicious that it could easily backfire and make the curser look bad: when you wish a person dead, you're not supposed to calculate the consequences.

These are all good, solid curses that could get you cursed back, punched out, and never spoken to again, but they'll never make anyone stop to admire your wit while you're sending them to hell with a sugar-free cereal. Neither, of course, will anything else you're likely to find in a book, but there are techniques that can be learned to help spice up your invective. Take, for instance, the well-known *zolst vaksn vi a tsibele, mitn kop in dr'erd,* "you should grow like an onion—with your head in the ground." In order to understand the curse properly, we need to consider the vegetable. The onion occupies a prominent place in the hierarchy of Jewish vegetables. Remember the kvetch about the manna in Chapter One? The Israelites lament, "the fish we ate in Egypt for nothing, the cucumber, the melons, the leeks, the onions, and the garlic." Now, the merest *kheyder* boy knows that the manna about which they were complaining could assume any taste that the eater wanted it to have, so why should they be complaining about missing particular foods? Just will the manna to taste like cucumbers and so on, and forget about it. Rashi explains it, with the help of a *medresh:* "Rabbi Simeon said: Why could the manna change its taste to that of anything but these five things? Because they are not good for nursing mothers, who are told, 'Do not eat garlic and onions because they are not good for the child.'"

Why the cucumbers, melons, and leeks seem to have been ignored by subsequent generations is a question that I cannot answer, but the onion and the garlic—two Eastern European Jewish foods par excellence—have been repaid for having been slighted in the manna's pantheon of taste. They are supposed to be eaten every *shabbes* as a means of completing the Sabbath pleasure; since these flavors were excluded from the manna, which could taste like anything else, they came to stand for every sort of exotic delicacy. Since onions were also very cheap, it was easy to get them for *shabbes;* the almost worthless onion thus became the vegetable world's counterpart of the Jew, whose status was likewise exalted on the Sabbath. Less midrashically, Jews also share the common association of onions with fertility and fruitfulness.

The need for a vegetable with strong positive associations in a curse like *zolst vaksn vi a tsibele* is underlined in a variant that is sometimes encountered: *zolst vaksn vi a mer,* "you should grow like a carrot." We've seen how highly esteemed the carrot is in Ashkenazic folklore, not least because of the wordplay made possible by its name. The point is that either version starts out looking exactly like what it is not: a blessing. *Zolst vaksn vi a tsibele* and *zolst vaksn vi a mer* would each have sounded like the beginning of a blessing in the days when this curse was young. Someone using this curse is setting up an expectation that is suddenly reversed. As with "You should own a thousand houses," everything looks just ducky until you get to the end, to the point where the whole thing turns around and smacks you in the face.

This inversion of expectation is a major strategy in Yiddish cursing and might be called the *zolst krenken in nakhes* motif, "you should suffer in the midst of pleasure," get everything you always wanted and suffer all the more for it. "Your daughter should marry the richest, best-looking boy in the country the day after he's become president of the United States, and you should have a front row pew in the church." The victim must be exalted, raised to the very pinnacle of his or her aspirations, and only then, lulled into a false sense of security, be brought crashing back to earth. It's a good wish without a *keynehore*, a contract with the devil on an episode of *The Twilight Zone*. "*Got zol dir helfn,* May God help you, *zolst shtendik zayn gezunt un shtark,* you should always be healthy and strong, *un shtendik fregn vos far a veter es iz in droysn,* and always be asking what the weather's like outside." What are you being condemned to: madness, an idée fixe, a lifetime in a padded cell, or solitary confinement? Probably the latter, but you never know—it could be the Yid in the Iron Mask.

Note the lack of specificity in these examples. Has the daughter in the previous paragraph simply married a gentile? Did she convert on her own before marrying the boy? If so, why hasn't the parent sat shiva? Is there some external compulsion that won't allow him or her to miss the wedding? Every good insult is a soap opera, and good wishes are the *kosher khazer-fisl,* the kosher little pig's foot, of the Yiddish curse: *Dayn mazl zol dir laykhtn . . . vi di levone in sof khoydesh,* "your luck should shine . . . like the moon at the end of the [lunar] month," like the moon on a moonless night.

The inversion *klole* has had a tremendous influence on what we think of as Jewish or Jewish-style humor. It is a psychic mirror of *goles,* of the conditions of exile: no matter how much you seem to have, there's always one little thing that, because it's either missing or horribly askew, sucks the value out of everything else: "*A groys gesheft zolstu hobn mit skhoyre,* you should have a large and well-stocked business—*vos du host zol men bay dir nisht fregn,* what you've got, no one should ask for, *un vos me fregt zolstu nisht hobn,* and what they ask for, you shouldn't have." You should be as out of step with your customers as the Jews are with the larger society.

The complement of *krenken in nakhes* is the *krenken in gehakte tsuris* motif, "suffering in cut-up troubles," troubles that are bleeding from their wounds. An example drawn from the classics will make it plain. *A kazarme zol af dir aynfaln,* "a barracks should collapse on you." Having a building of any kind collapse on top of you is never pleasant, but if that building is a barracks, then you're probably in the army—the last place any Eastern European Jew wanted to find himself. There's a whole history of bad luck built into the collapse of the barracks: first you get a conscription notice; then you can't hide, buy, or cheat your way out of serving; you endure the million and one horrors and humiliations of army life, along with the additional horrors and humiliations reserved exclusively for minorities; and then—as if all this weren't already punishment enough—the scene of all these crimes has to fall down and crush you—all because you hadn't succeeded in evading the draft, that is, because you had failed as a criminal.

That's what is meant by *krenken in gehakte tsuris.* Whatever is described in the curse is only the visible tip of the iceberg of *tsuris;* the remaining 90 percent plays silent havoc with the victim's mind. *Brenen zolstu on strakhovke,* "you should burn and be uninsured," is a world away from the curses with *brenen* mentioned a little while ago. Does it mean that you yourself should combust spontaneously and leave your family with no means of support, or that your home and business should burn and you should live a nice long life, blaming yourself for not having taken out the policy? Or does the curse refer to the once notorious Jewish penchant for arson, which was even known as "Jewish lightning"? Did you torch your own store without bothering to insure it first? Had the insurance lapsed without your knowing? Are you going to prison or merely the poorhouse?

Compare *doktoyrim zoln dikh darfn,* "doctors should have need of you." Probably to assure themselves of a livelihood, but who can say for sure? It could be for research purposes, as a negative example to their other patients, for the sake of finding a disease to which the doctor's name can be attached—the list is almost endless. You could even go baroque: all your children should be doctors, and still need you to support them. Because they're not working? Because your illnesses take up their entire practice?

There is something very Talmudic about all of this, not least the fact that it's the dialectic, the logical examination of its premises, that gives the curse its kick. In a culture in which every cursee is his or her own Rashi, it is axiomatic that *purim iz nisht ken yontef,* "Purim is not a real holiday," *un kush in tukhes iz nisht ken klole,* "and 'kiss my ass' is not a curse." It isn't a matter of yelling out bad words; the trick is to put good ones together in the most damaging possible way.

IV

The most prominent of these words tend to be drawn from certain key areas of human life and concern. From the realm of metaphysics, the aspiring curser has to be able to invoke and describe the visible and invisible workings of God, demons, angels, and spirits. *Got zol in dir fargesn,* "May God forget about you," is balanced by *Got zol in dir nisht fargesn,* "May God not forget about you." The former will leave the victim abandoned, with no help from heaven. Prayer will not avail because God—who is otherwise incapable of forgetting—will have made an exception in this one case. *Zayn af Gots barot,* "to be in God's care," usually means to be abandoned, forsaken, left willy-nilly to one's own devices; it's an idiom of last resort. If God has forgotten about you, though, you can't even end up in His *barot.* You've got Nothing, and no matter where you go, you're still nowhere.

Got zol in dir nisht fargesn goes to the other extreme and has Him refusing to leave you alone for a minute. One problem will lead directly to another, even before the first one has been solved, and the second will turn into a third before you've realized that the second has been visited upon you. It's the idea at the root of the joke in which God is asked to do the Chosen People a favor and choose someone else for a change.

The devil, whoever he might be in Yiddish, appears as the *shvarts-yor* in the frequently used *a shvarts-yor af dir,* "devil take you," which overuse has weakened to the point where it's a little worse than "the heck with you" but not quite as bad as "the hell with you."

He comes up under a variety of pseudonyms in the series *khapt dikh der baytl-makher, khapt dikh der vatl-makher,* and *khapt dikh der vatn-makher,* "may the purse-maker/cotton-batting-maker take you." These two needle-trade-oriented professions are examples of apotropaic language at its highest pitch. One of the Yiddish words for "devil" is the Germanic *tayvl,* which in older Yiddish spelling would have looked like this:

טײבל

In the same spelling system, *baytl* would have looked like

בײטל

and *vatl* would come out as

באטל

The fact that two of these would now be spelled very differently doesn't matter—the apotropaic shifts are obviously pretty old. *Tayvl* gets rearranged to *baytl,* which has the same letters in a different order; *baytl* then gets changed to *vatl,* which would sound very much like *baytl* in the dialects in which *baytl* is actually pronounced *baatl. Vatl* was then replaced by *vatn,* the more modern Yiddish term for cotton batting, without any loss of meaning. *Baytl* was apparently a common substitution for *tayvl* at one time—"Go to the purse," "It's a wallet of a rainy day outside." It must have been so widely used as a euphemism that it started to take on many of the connotations of the word for which it was supposed to be subbing. *Baytl-makher* on its own doesn't seem to have taken the phrase far enough away from its origins for some speakers, hence the further substitutions of *vatl* and *vatn.*

Human anatomy receives considerably more attention than the world of the spirit, and Yiddish curses cover the whole body, just like leprosy. To give a sampling, from the ground up:

fardreyen zolstu mit di fis—may your feet be twisted

a veytik/shnaydenish dir in boykh—a pain/colic in your belly

shrayen zolstu afn boykh—may your belly make you scream

krikhn zolstu afn boykh—may you crawl on your belly

a klog dir in boykh—may there be a lament in your belly

a baysenish dir in layb—may you itch all over your body

a kramp dir in layb/boykh/di kishkes—a cramp in your body/your
belly/your guts

zol dir shnaydn di kishkes—a stabbing pain in your guts

a fayer dir in leber—a fire in your liver

zol dir platsn di gal—may your gallbladder burst

zol dir dreyen farn nopl—may you be turned around by the navel (suffer
constant dizziness and nausea)

a shtekhenish dir in di krizhes—a stitch, a terrible pain in the small of
your back

zol dir shtekhn in di zaytn—you should have stabbing pain in your sides

a duner dir in di zaytn—a thunderbolt in your sides

shteyner dir afn hartsn—stones on your heart

es zol dir drikn in hartsn—you should have angina

oysdarn zol bay dir der moyekh (der kop)—your brain (your head) should
dry up

brekhn zolstu dem kop—you should break your head

*a geshvir dir in kop/in zayt/in der leber/in haldz/af der noz/af der shpits-
noz*—an abscess on your head/side/liver/neck/nose/tip of your nose

feffer dir in noz—pepper in your nose

zalts dir in di oygn—salt in your eyes

finster zolstu vern in di oygn—it should go black in your eyes

aroyskrikhn zoln dir di oygn fun kop—may your eyes crawl out of your head

Any part of the body that can be moved—hands, feet, tongue,
fingers, toes, eyelids, elbows, knees, ankles—can also be paralyzed:

es zol dir opnemen di hent, di fis, di tsung, di finger, di fus-finger, di ledelekh, di elnbogens, di kni, di knekhelekh, not to mention *der kleyner* and *der eyver,* two slang terms for the male member.

V

It is fitting that people who regard medical school as the most important non-Jewish invention of all time should put a particular emphasis on illness in their cursing. There are certain favored diseases, most of which appear below, as well as less specific but equally appalling syndromes and conditions: *geshvoln un gedroln zolstu vern,* "you should swell up and suffer from varicose veins." *Pishn zolstu mit verem* or *mit grine verem,* "you should piss worms/green worms," resembles no disease I've ever heard of, but points up the fact that many of the disease-based curses, revolting as they might be, lack the resonance, the assumed backstory found so often in other fields of cursing. There's more emphasis here on the body than on the brain. From the simple *krenken zolstu,* "you should sicken," which is somewhat stronger in Yiddish than might appear from a literal translation, to the more whimsical *arayntrogn zol men dikh a krankn,* "you should be carried in sick," on a stretcher, that is, these illnesses just seem to appear. In the reduplicating *zolstu zokhn un krenken,* "may you sicken and be ill," we see *zokhn,* "to be sick," which is used only to show contempt for a person, their illness, or both. Some of the curses refer to collections of symptoms rather than recognized diseases:

> *redn zolstu fun hits*—you should speak in a fever, fall into a delirium
> *fargelt un fargrint zolstu vern*—you should turn yellow and green
> *a meshugenem zol men oysshraybn un dikh araynshraybn*—a maniac should be crossed off the register of madmen and you should be inscribed in his place

zolst kakn mit blut un mit ayter—you should shit blood and pus
es zol dir farshporn fun fornt un fun hintn—you should be blocked up
 from in front and from behind
es zol dir dunern in boykh un blitsn in di hoyzn—you should thunder in
 your belly and lightning in your pants

Epidemic diseases are miraculously confined to a single person, and any disease can be localized to certain parts of that person's body:

a mageyfe zol af im kumen—a plague should come upon him (and no one
 else)
a mageyfe im in di zaytn—he should get the plague in his sides
a kholyere dir in di beyner—cholera in your bones
a nikhpe zol dikh khapn—you should have an epileptic seizure
remates in di pyates—rheumatism in the soles of your feet (this seems to
 be determined solely by the rhyme)
a kadokhes in dir—a recurrent fever
a kadokhes dir in di beyner—a recurrent fever in your bones

Note that cancer, tuberculosis, leukemia, and even the common heart attack are all conspicuously absent from this list. It's okay to curse, but you don't want to get heavy with anybody's health. When things look serious, realism rushes back in.

Pharmacy gives us *di kleyne fleshlekh*, "the little bottles, vials of medicine," as in *zolst trinken nor fun di kleyne fleshlekh*, "you should drink only from medicine bottles," and the equally pleasant *shraybn zol men dir retseptn*, "they should write prescriptions for you." Note the plural here: because you have so many different diseases or because nothing seems to work? In any event, it's a good way to ensure that someone's money is *farkrenkt*, spent only on their ailments.

VI

Physical illness and death are as nothing, however, before what must surely be the final frontier of human cursing, the ultimate reversal of your victim's expectations: *Zolst onkumen tsu mayn mazl,* "you should have my luck." In other words, "The worst thing I can wish on you is . . . that you should be me." *Ale tsuris vos ikh hob zoln oysgeyn tsu dayn kop,* "all my troubles should be redirected to you." It doesn't say much for my own life, but at least no one can call me conceited; we've come full circle to the language of internalized exile. Your most secret thoughts are best inflicted on somebody else: *Vos s'hot zikh mir gekholemt di nakht un yene nakht un a gants yor zol oysgeyn tsu dayn kop,* "what I dreamed tonight and last night and every night for a whole year should happen to you." And finally, one that leaves the curser safely within the bounds of Hillel's famous dictum, "Do not do that which is hateful to you to your fellow": *Vos s'iz mir bashert tsu zayn in mindstn fingerl zol dir zayn in dayn gants layb un lebn,* "may what is destined to happen to my baby finger happen to your whole body and life": What did *I* do that *you* should deserve this?

"Don't ask," is the only answer.

SEVEN

If It Wasn't for Bad Luck:
MAZL, MISERY, AND MONEY

I

As a language of *goles,* of the exile that has defined every aspect of Jewish life since the destruction of the Second Temple, Yiddish has developed an unusually extensive vocabulary of poverty, want, and stymied desire—the indispensable prerequisites for a really good kvetch. The whole point of being in exile is that you aren't where you want to be—at home; you don't have the one thing you want the most—a home; you shlep yourself from one day to the next, lurching from crisis to crisis, painfully aware that any episodes of prosperity are likely to be all too brief. *Yidishe ashires iz vi shney in marts,* Jewish wealth is like snow in March: you get it once in a while, and it vanishes overnight. Up until the Nazis, poverty, not anti-Semitism, was considered the most serious problem facing the Jews, and much, if not most, modern Yiddish culture developed in an environment of almost incomprehensible deprivation.

Gentiles also live in poverty, they also have to worry about demons and evil spirits, but the world around them is the one that they're meant to be in. *Oylem haze,* "this world," is their world. Religious Christians might see themselves as pilgrims on earth, sojourners waiting to die and go live with Jesus, but there's a big difference between a pilgrim and a refugee, even when both shlep along the same road. The Christian ideal is to be in this world, but not of it; the Jewish problem, the problem of the Jews in *goles,* is being *of* this world but still not *in* it. We eat, sleep, go to the toilet, and die. We pay taxes and serve in the army and do business, but we're shut out, excluded from all the usual sources of pleasure— we're on Turtle Island, and turtles are *treyf.* The chief sources of Jewish joy, *shabbes* and Torah, aren't part of this world, either. Traditional Jewish culture has everything but *oylem haze,* which means "sensual pleasure" in Yiddish, the today for which hedonists live. Where the gentile world is an endless series of sequential "nows," the Jewish world is nothing but "thens," thens of the past and thens of the future: "then we were . . . then we'll be . . . now we're nothing." Without the Temple, the world is nothing but another *klipe,* a confining husk that cannot be shaken off until the Messiah comes and redeems us.

We've been waiting a long time, though, and he still isn't here; most Yiddish idioms that mention him have something to do with either surprise or disappointment. When your teenager comes into the living room and says spontaneously, "Mom, Dad, I know you're both busy, so I took out the garbage and washed the car. I'm going to make myself a salad and then go mow the lawn," your inevitable response—once you've ascertained that the kid isn't in some kind of horrible trouble—would be, *"Meshiekhs tsaytn,* it's the messianic era!" That is, "I see it, but I don't believe it." If you describe this scene to someone who knows your kid and doesn't believe what you're saying, you can always say, *"Lomir azoy derlebn meshiekhn,* may we live to see the Messiah, the way I have already lived to see my kid mow the lawn without being told." This is a Jewish equivalent of "cross my heart," and would be meaningless if the Messiah were thought to be near.

Me zol nor dermonen meshiekhn, "we should have mentioned the Messiah," has already been encountered as a kind of Yiddish "speak of the devil." Again, the expression would be meaningless if anybody really thought that the Messiah was just around the corner. It's of a piece with *halevay,* an interjection of Hebrew origin which means "if only, would that" (and is sometimes pronounced without the *h* as *alevay*). *Halevay* is one of those Yiddish words and expressions still used by Jewish people who might never have learned Yiddish at all. It expresses a wish that you know will not be fulfilled—at least not while you're here on earth. *Halevay*—it even sounds like a sigh:

BERL: I heard that your son was finishing medical school.
SHMERL: Medical school? *Halevay* he should get his GED.

If you really want to impress someone who asks if you speak Yiddish, you don't say *yo* (yes); you don't say, *a frage!* (some question) or *tsi red ikh yidish* (do *I* speak Yiddish?). No, just say *halevay voltn ale azoy geret,* "if only everybody spoke it the way I do," and you won't have to say anything else. You will have shown that you know not only the words but also the worldview: no one speaks Yiddish like you do and no one ever will. Much as you'd like to be able to converse with your equals-in-Yiddish, it just isn't going to happen on this side of heaven.

The relationship between Yiddish and fulfillment, Yiddish and any sense of satisfaction, is entirely asymptotic: it might occasionally come within shouting distance, but never actually gets there. The more realistic version of "we should have mentioned the Messiah" is *az me reyt fun malekh, kumt der galekh,* "when you talk about an angel, a Catholic priest turns up." You don't get the opposite of what you want—you don't get a devil—you get the usual. "We were talking miracles and in walks Mendel"—Yiddish humor and Yiddish kvetching are both based on this tension between the miraculous and the mundane.

II

Eyn mazl le-yisroel, states the proverb, which is popularly inter-preted as meaning that Jews have no luck. Although *mazl,* as found in *mazl tov,* "congratulations," does mean luck, the luck derives from *mazl*'s original meaning of constellation or sign of the zodiac. There are twelve *mazoles* in the heavens, and if Yiddish papers ran horoscopes, the column would probably be called *Today's Mazl.*

The whole notion of luck is bound up with Judaism's ambiva-lent relationship with astrology. *Eyn mazl le-yisroel* is found—where else?—in the Talmud (*Shabbos* 156a), where it means that even though the destinies of all other peoples and nations are in-deed determined by the stars, the destiny of the Jews is decided by the direct decree of God Himself. Hence the ambiguity of such strictly factual kvetches as *a goy hot mazl,* "a goy is lucky," and *tole hot dos mazl,* "the hanged one is lucky," which is how a Yiddish *Variety* would have reported the box office of Mel Gibson's *The Passion of the Christ.* The hanged one, of course, is Jesus, who is standing in for all Christians. In popular usage, these expressions don't signify much more than that the other guy's grass is always greener. If, however, *mazl* is taken in the astrological sense, these expressions lose any sense of envy and become simple statements of cosmological fact that end up as further digs at the Christian faith: God looks out for us, but lets the stars take care of them.

Jewish destiny's independence of chance or accident sounds very comforting—we're really nestling in the hands of God—until we take a look at what divine providence has in store:

Why is it written, "Behold I have refined you, but not with silver; I have tried you in the furnace of affliction" (Isa. 48:10)? This teaches us that the Holy One, Blessed Be He, reviewed all the good qualities that

He could give to Israel and found nothing so good as poverty. Shmuel said (some say it was Rov Yoysef): "And that's why people say: Poverty becomes the Jews like a red bridle on a white horse" (*Khagigo* 9b).

Rashi comments that the poverty is intended as a means of purification, something to keep the Jews from getting too full of themselves, too self-confident. It's no secret that religious observance tends to decline as wealth and social mobility increase, and people sometimes joke that you can judge the state of the economy by Yom Kippur attendance in non-Orthodox synagogues: the worse the business, the larger the crowd.

Many prominent religious figures once opposed Jewish emancipation on similar grounds. Shneur-Zalmen of Liadi, philosopher, kabbalist, and founder of the Lubavitch Hasidic dynasty, was an outspoken opponent of Napoleon and his social reforms, and prayed for a Russian victory during Napoleon's Russian campaign. Shneur-Zalmen had done time in czarist prisons, and his prayers had nothing to do with patriotism. Anti-Semitism and reactionary politics would help keep the Jews poor and pious, and lack of civil rights was a paradoxically small price to pay for the preservation of that old-time religion.

Shneur-Zalmen's attitude throws an interesting light on a bitter little folk phrase: *Yidishe ashires, mishteyns gezogt—fun taneysim vert men raykh*, "Jewish wealth—if that's what you want to call it: from fasting you get rich" (because of all the money you save by not buying food). It seems that not everyone took this completely ironically.

The idea that suffering is good for the Jews seems to have been embraced by everyone except the Jews who did the suffering. Sholem Aleykhem quotes the red bridle remark in one of the stories on which *Fiddler on the Roof* is based, and provides his own interpretation: "*Got hot faynt a kaptsn.* God hates a pauper, and the proof is that if God loved the pauper, the pauper wouldn't be a pauper."

The fact that *yidish glik,* "Jewish luck," is supposed to be part of a long-range divine plan is of little comfort to people who are alive and suffering. Despite the occasional exceptions—as with snow in March, there were some few Jews who *did* get lucky—life was generally considered to be a wholly owned and operated division of *shlimazl,* which can mean bad luck, a person who has bad luck, a clumsy person—the kind of person who has bad luck *and* embodies it—or a ne'er-do-well in the most literal sense: someone who really fails at anything he or she attempts. The *shlim* in *shlimazl* comes from the German for "bad," and the *shlimazl,* as Albert King would have it, is born under a bad sign; if it wasn't for bad luck, he wouldn't have no luck at all.

Shlimazl can be used of men and women alike. There is a specifically male form, *shlimazlnik,* which means a slovenly man, one who neglects his personal hygiene and probably doesn't smell too good, but it is not encountered nearly as often as its feminine counterpart, *shlimazlnitse,* which means a slovenly woman, but also has the more specific meaning of a bad housekeeper—not because she can't be bothered, but because she just can't seem to get it together enough to look after things the way she's supposed to. This aspect of helplessness distinguishes the *shlimazlnitse* from the *shlumperke,* also known as the *shtinkerke,* who is as close as Yiddish comes to an idea of Jewish trailer trash, although it often means little more than a neighbor whom your mother dislikes.

Dishes piled high in the sink, mold sprouting from the unwashed floor, the *shlumperke* is a working-class Emma Bovary, in love with her own leavings. Everything is too much for her, housework is beneath her; the *shlumperke hot ken mol nisht ken koyekh,* she never has the strength or the energy to do what she's supposed to—despite the fact that not having anything else to do is an essential precondition of true *shlumperkism:* "I have to take the kids to soccer, don't expect me to clean the house!" The *shlimazlnitse* is incompetent; the *shlumperke* just doesn't care.

When *shlimazl* comes, it often comes in spades and we get *shlim-shlimazl.* This is superbad luck of a type that stands out even among Jews. Literally it's "bad bad luck," the kind that jinxes like *Li'l Abner's* Joe Bftsplk, who walked around with a stormcloud over his head, are supposed to bring with them.

You can get *shlimazl durkh tir un toyer,* "bad luck through door and gate"—if *shlimazl* was a liquid, you'd be drowning. *Durkh tir un toyer* is a relatively common Yiddish expression and is roughly equivalent to *af trit un shrit,* "at every step, everywhere you turn." If you say that things are going *durkh tir un toyer* for Mindel, you're saying that Mindel is doing exceedingly well, she's raking it in, whatever "it" might be. In this case, it's disaster that is being reaped, *shlimazl mit esik,* "bad luck with vinegar," misfortune with whipped cream and a cherry on top. Imagine a supermarket of complaint, filled with aisles upon aisles of *shlimazl* and vinaigrette. *Esik,* "vinegar," is sometimes used to convey the idea of something with all the garnishes, all the bells and whistles, on it. You can talk about somebody who is *oysgeputst in esik un honik,* "decked out in vinegar and honey, dressed to the nines." Even better, though, you can say that they're *ayngemarinirt in esik un honik,* "marinated in vinegar and honey." The best-dressed person in Yiddish is the one who most resembles a herring.

The *shlimazl* has *mazl vi a drong,* "the luck of a pole"; once in a while, someone might stick a nail in him. "If he looks into the river, the fish drop dead; *er zol handlen mit takhrikhim, volt men oyfgehert shtarbn,* if he deals in shrouds, people stop dying." He *makht a gesheft vi der feter eysev,* "does business like Uncle Esau," who traded his birthright for a mess of pottage, and *vert ayngezunken vi Koyrekh,* "sinks like Korah," who was swallowed up by the earth for his revolt against Moses.

Korah—whose name means "baldy" in Hebrew—figures prominently in Yiddish phrases having to do with money. There's *raykh vi Koyrekh,* the equivalent of "rich as Croesus"; *Koyrekhs oytsres,* "Korah's treasures," and *momen Koyrekh,* "Korah's lucre." These are all based on a Talmudic legend (*Pesokhim* 119a) in which Korah finds one of the three treasures hidden by Joseph and—as if to vindicate Shneur-Zalmen's support for the czar—wants to stay in Egypt so that he won't have to leave it behind. It's typical of Yiddish that its prime symbol of prosperity ends up quite literally *in dr'erd.*

III

Until the earth swallowed him up, Korah was a big success, the one Jew who managed to make it in Egypt. Similar success stories in later generations—not always with people as unpleasant as Korah—did nothing to alter the fact that poverty was still the basic condition of life for most Yiddish-speaking Jews, and poverty therefore looms large in Yiddish. The main word for poverty is *dales,* from a Hebrew root meaning "to become weak, to be brought low," and there are dozens, maybe even scores of idioms in which *dales* figures.

You can talk about a *dales vi in posek shteyt,* poverty that would fulfill every requirement listed in the Bible, if the Bible listed requirements for poverty. Less scripturally, there is *a dales vi a kurfirsht,* "a poverty like a prince of the Holy Roman Empire," positively regal in the extent of its deprivation, in the degree to which you—the pauper—are nothing but its hereditary tenant. Note how close *dales* comes to being personified, to taking on the traits of a real, living person. Among gentiles, it's puppets like Pinocchio who dream of being real; with us, it's abstractions like Want that yearn to get dressed and act like human beings.

And what does this humanized *dales* do? *Er fayft,* it whistles. *Der dales fayft fun ale zaytn,* poverty whistles from every side, *in yedn vinkl,* in every corner; it makes its presence felt everywhere in a most unpleasant and annoying fashion, coming in with the wind that blows through the chinks of poverty's walls. *Far vos fayft der dales?* Why does it whistle when it could blow the house down? *Vayl er hot nor a dude,* "because a fife is all it has"—i.e., it can't afford a sousaphone, doesn't even have the wherewithal to be as obnoxious as it would like.

Dales doesn't only whistle, though; it can also dance. *Der dales tantst in mitn shtub,* it's dancing in the middle of the house, making itself the center of attention. *Dales* also knocks, makes a lot of noise: *Far vos klapt der dales?* Why does *dales* knock? *Vayl er geyt in klumpes,* because it's wearing wooden shoes.

Among its other effects, *dales* is said to *makhn pasles,* "to create dishonesty," despite the equally current phrase, *dales iz nisht pasles,* "*dales* is *not* dishonesty"—it simply leads to it. Jews were well represented in most forms of criminal endeavor, and seem to have had a particular talent for theft (especially horse theft), smuggling, and—less endearingly—white slavery. As the old saying has it, *vos es tut nisht a yid tsulib parnose,* "what a Jew doesn't do in order to earn a living." Likewise, *noyt brekht ayzn,* "want breaks iron," *dales brekht shleser,* "but *dales* breaks locks." Love and money are also said to break iron, but *dales* seems to have the locks to itself. *Vu dales, dort iz halas,* "where there's poverty, there's an uproar"—that is, there's no peace for the poor. If all this was intended to purify us, I think I'd prefer a good delousing.

Oremkayt is a less emotionally loaded word for poverty, and one who suffers from it is called an *oreman,* a pauper. There are degrees of *oreman: a biterer oreman,* someone who is bitterly poor; *an oreman vi shabbes ha-godl,* "a pauper like the Great Sabbath." This is easy to understand but almost impossible to translate idiomatically. The hook is the word *godl,* Hebrew for "great" or "large"—what the Great Sabbath is to Sabbaths, this pauper is to other paupers: bigger. But *shabbes ha-godl,* the Sabbath before Passover, is also one of two occasions in the year when rabbis in traditional synagogues make a speech: the *oreman's* poverty isn't only big, it also speaks for itself.

There is no lack of proverbs and idioms about *oremelayt* (the plural of *oreman*), most of which seem to concern food. *Dos milkhike tepl baym oreman vert ken mol nisht fleyshik,* "an *oreman's* dairy pot never becomes a meat pot" (because there is no meat to fall into it); *an oreman iz tomid parve,* "an *oreman* is always dietarily neutral"—he never eats dairy and never eats meat. There's a proverb that has also become fairly popular in English: *az an oreman est a hun, iz er krank oder di hun,* "if an *oreman* is eating a chicken, one of them must be sick." Even grimmer: *az an oreman makht khasene,* "when an *oreman* makes a wedding," *loyfn di hint mit gehoybene kep,* "the dogs come running with their heads held high." There are no scraps for them on the floor because the catering consists of a single piece of chicken that is passed from hand to hand—they've got to grab it from the table. To finish with the food motif, we can note that sex is sometimes called *dem oremans ayngemakhts,* "the poor man's jam."

Prominent as *oreman* is, it is far from the most important term for pauper. The quintessential Yiddish word is *kaptsn,* which is probably based on the Hebrew *mekabets nedoves,* "collector of alms," though no one is really sure of this. What is certain is that the word *kaptsn* originated in Yiddish and was later absorbed into Hebrew. It is of surprisingly recent provenance; the first recorded use dates to 1623, which means that Shakespeare, had he written in Yiddish, would not have been able to use it. The *kaptsn's* place in Jewish communal life grew increasingly prominent in the nearly three hundred years leading up to the First World War, so much so that Mendele Moykher Sforim, the father of both modern Yiddish and modern Hebrew literature, invented a whole town called Kaptsansk, "Pauperton," inhabited exclusively by *kaptsonim*.

While almost all of the phrases listed with *oreman* work just as well if you substitute *kaptsn*, there are a few with *kaptsn* that just don't go with *oreman*. The still-popular *kaptsn in zibn poles*—a *pole* is the skirt of a garment—comes gift wrapped in seven layers of rags. He's a *kaptsn vi in posek shteyt*, the fulfillment of the pseudo-Biblical requirements for pauperism, *a kaptsn she-be-kaptsonim*, "a pauper's pauper." There's the fabulous *kaptsn mit ale kheyn-gribelekh*, "a *kaptsn* with all the dimples," all the little adornments that mark the difference between someone who has merely run out of money and someone for whom insufficiency is a way of life. Let's not forget the *draygorndiker kaptsn*, the three-story pauper, whose lack is so great that it reaches up to touch the sky. You can go up to any one of these people and yell out the closest thing that Jewish poverty ever had to a team cheer: *Hulye, kaptsn, drek iz volvl*, "Live it up, *kaptsn*, shit's on sale."

A *kaptsn* can also be called an *oni*, a *loshn-koydesh* word that likewise means "pauper." The proverb *oni khoshev ke-meys*, "a poor person is considered as dead," is based on the Talmudic statement that "Four people are considered as dead: the pauper, the leper, the blind and the childless" (*Nedorim* 64b). Yiddish goes the *gemore* one better and says, *Oni khoshev ke-meys*—"a poor person is considered a corpse": *beyde lozt men nisht in shtub on a shoymer*, "you don't leave either in your house unguarded." You can have an *oni meduke*, an *oni* crushed by his poverty, or an *oni ve-evyen*, one who is both poor and poverty-stricken. This latter is a fairly common biblical phrase (e.g., "Do not oppress your poor and needy employee," Deut. 24:14), a parallelism in which the same thing is said in different ways for rhetorical effect. We saw an example of this in *oysgemutshet un oysgematert*, "run-down and weary," at the end of Chapter One, where the biblical trope is applied to Slavic and Germanic elements.

A poor person can also be called a *dalfen*, which comes from the Biblical name Dalfon. Dalfon was the second son of Haman and was hanged, along with his father and nine brothers, near the end of the Book of Esther. We know nothing else about him; the *dal* with which his name begins is identical to an adjective that means "poor." Nothing else was necessary.

IV

A society in which nobody has anything is a society in which people who have nothing try to make a living by begging from one another. A beggar is a *betler*, a fairly colorless word except in the wonderful old idiom, *der betler iz shoyn in dritn dorf*, "the beggar's on his third village already," which means "hurry up, get a move on." While *shnorer* can sometimes be used interchangeably with *betler*, the *shnorer* is generally considered more of a sponge or a mooch. Begging is often regarded as a profession, and many of its practitioners play music, sing, do physical tricks, wipe the windshields of stopped cars, and engage in other activities designed to pass as services to be rewarded or entertainment to be paid for on a voluntary basis. A *betler* begs; a *shnorer* puts the touch on his victims. A large corporation with annual profits of over $1 billion that seeks subsidies from Washington cannot be called a *betler*, but it's sure as hell a *shnorer*.

A *shleper* can shlep himself from house to house looking for handouts, but he is usually thought of as more of a tramp or hobo than a beggar, as part of the collective known as *orkhe-porkhe*—bums, tramps—*yidishe* bindlestiffs like Stuffy Derma, the tramp on the old *Milton the Monster Show*. The term comes from the Hebrew *oreakh poreakh,* "a flying guest," one who's here today and gone tomorrow. At one time mystically inclined Jews practiced a religious version of this kind of vagrancy called *oprikhtn goles,* "doing exile." They wandered from place to place, suffering along with the exiled *shekhine,* God's indwelling presence, which is in *goles* along with the Jews.

All these people can be said to *lebn fun vint,* "to live on wind," *fun nisim,* "on miracles," and *fun rukhniyes. Rukhniyes* means "spirituality," but this shouldn't be taken to mean that they're subsidized to perform religious works. The idea is that they have no visible means of support; it's a sort of satire of Deuteronomy 8:3: "Man does not live by bread alone, but by everything that proceeds out of the mouth of the Lord does a man live." There's an even more satirical version, a satire of the satire, as it were: *lebn fun shvientem dukhnem,* "to live from the holy spirit, the holy ghost": it isn't only invisible, it doesn't even exist.

The wind, the *rukhniyes,* the holy spirit are all elaborate versions of the much more well known *luftmentsh,* an "air man" full of ideas that never fly. He tends to be busy enough, always rushing hither and yon, never not on his way to a meeting, but no one can figure out just what it is that he does for a living. A little of this, a little of that; and always the hope that something will soon turn up. He tends to be engaged in one *luft-eysek,* "air business, business with no foundation," after another. He's usually portrayed as impractical, but desperate is probably a more accurate description.

You can say that such people *kumen op mit shiye-piye,* "live from hand to mouth," without anybody being quite sure how. The Talmud uses *shiye-piye* as a pejorative acronym for **SH**abbes **HA**-Yom,

Peysakh HA-Yom, "today is the Sabbath, today is Passover"—Jewish holidays used as excuses to get out of work—and puts the phrase into the mouth of Haman. It later came to be applied to Jews for whom every day became a Jewish holiday because there was no work to be had.

People who live this way are sometimes lucky enough to receive *kitsve*, what we'd call welfare or relief, though the word can also mean a pension. It comes from the Hebrew for limit or cut-off point, a determinate measure of something, and doesn't differ very much from the English "fixed income," when that phrase is used as a euphemism for a pension. Interestingly, the Yiddish for butcher, *katsef*, comes from the same root: by cutting up the dead animal, he determines the limits of each separate section and piece.

V

People living on *shiye-piye* who still can't manage to keep themselves in food can be said to *leygn di tseyn af der politse*, "put their teeth on the shelf," or *in baytl*, "in their wallet [or purse]," due to lack of money. Yiddish tended to stand in a *halevay* relationship to money—*halevay* they should only have some—and it's worth having a look at what Yiddish does with the object of so much desire.

Gelt, the basic term for money, appears in various compounds and combinations that usually indicate why it's being paid out. So *dire-gelt*, "dwelling-money," is rent. *Rebbe-gelt*, "teacher-money," was originally equivalent to *skhar limed*, "tuition fee," but the phrase *batsoln rebbe-gelt*, "to pay *rebbe-gelt*," refers to tuition in the school of hard knocks. It means to pay dearly for something, but with bitter experience rather than money. *Kharote-gelt*, "regret-money," refers to what used to be called exemplary damages, money above and beyond the actual loss suffered that is awarded to the plaintiff for the wrong done her by the defendant. *Hobn kharote* means "to regret, to feel sorry for having done (or not done) something." Note the difference, though, between English and Yiddish. In English, the idea is that this extra money will serve as a deterrent to both the present defendant and anybody else considering a similar course of action—an example is being made of his bank account. In Yiddish, if the guy had felt any *kharote,* any real pang of conscience or regret, he wouldn't have done what he did in the first place. The idea here is that the judicially decreed financial loss is the chief source of the *kharote,* but there's no implication that anybody who hasn't yet been forced to pay is going to learn anything from it—*kharote* is only for other people. There is a saying, *kharote iz nisht mayse soykher,* "sorry isn't good for business," i.e., take the money and run. *Mayse,* which we've already met as "story," can also be used in the sense of "like, in the manner of, à la." *Mayse soykher* means "merchantlike behavior."

From *kharote,* "regret," we move on to *kishke-gelt,* "gut money." The *kishkes*—the guts or intestines—in question are your own, and the *gelt* is money that you have saved up by depriving yourself of necessities, money that you can be said to have ripped right out of your guts. *Kishke-gelt* is closely related to *farzetsn di bebekhes,* "to hock your intestines," which also means to do without something necessary or important in order to get the money for something else. There is also *farkrenkn,* one of the greatest words in the entire language, which we saw briefly in Chapter Six. The adjective *farkrenkt* means "weak" or "feeble" and can be used to describe someone just out of the hospital. All that is enfeebled in the verb *farkrenkn,* though, is your bank account: it means to spend your money on your illness (or illnesses). *Zol er farkrenkn dos gelt,* "may he spend the money on doctors and medicines," is the kind of thing you'd say if you heard that the head of the local KKK had just won the lottery.

Another general term for money, though not nearly as common as *gelt*, is *moes*, which comes from the name of a coin in Talmudic times. *Moes* is always plural; the singular, *mo'o* means "a grain, a kernel, a small coin"—but not in Yiddish. *Moes* generally seems stronger, more loaded than *gelt*. If someone asks for spare change and you realize that you've left your wallet at home, you could apologize and say *ikh hob nisht ken gelt*, "I don't have any money," that is, with me or to spare. To say, "I don't have any *moes*," would be to imply that you're just as badly off as the *betler*.

Moes gives us the seasonally important *moes khitim*, wheat money. This is the inevitable name of the fund that provides needy Jews with costly Passover food and supplies. I don't know how it works today, but it used to be done anonymously: bags of Passover supplies would be dropped off in the middle of the night, so as not to embarrass the recipients.

Another term for money is *domim*, which is also the plural of "blood." Although it is not certain that *dam*, "blood," and *domim*, "money," have any real etymological connection, the resemblance is too close to ignore. According to the *gemore*, "*Domim* has two meanings" (*Megillo* 14b). *Domim* is used in modern Hebrew to mean "fee" or "charge."

Much more pleasant is *mamtakim*, which Weinreich's dictionary renders as "dough." It comes from a Hebrew word that means "sweets, candy, sweetmeats," and refers to money only in Yiddish. *Mamtakim* is related to *mesikes*, "sweetness," and to the verb *mamtik zayn*, which means "to sweeten, make pleasant or mitigate." God is often said to *zayn mamtik zayn din*, to mitigate His judgment and ease off on the severity of the punishment. Weinreich's "dough" is a good idiomatic equivalent; for a picture of the psychological dimensions of the term, think of Zero Mostel in *The Producers* saying, "Money is honey, money is honey."

Klingers, which resembles *mamtakim* in having no singular form, is equally idiomatic. It comes from the verb *klingen*, "to ring, jingle," and is roughly equivalent to talking about "coin" in English. *Klingers* has been immortalized in a parody of the *hav-dole* that is thought to have been written by Sholem Aleykhem:

Hamavdil beyn koydesh le-khoyl	"Who divideth the sacred from the profane,"
Ver es hot di klingers, dem iz voyl.	If you've got the money, you feel no pain.

There's also *fodem*, thread, which can be used to mean food as well as money. As with the English "bread" and "dough," a number of Yiddish slang terms for money consist of words describing some kind of food. *Lokshn* (singular, *loksh*) are noodles, and *lokshn* was European Yiddish slang for American dollars. Similarly, *langer loksh*, "a long noodle," which now means only the kind of person who would be called a long drink of water in English, was the equivalent of "the long green." *Unterzupendike lokshn*, "noodles that are slurped up out of the soup," referred to the *lokshn* that you slurped out of the Atlantic after they'd been sent your way by relatives in America. Dollars were also called *yam bletlekh*. *Yam* means "sea"; *bletlekh* is the plural of *bletl*, the diminutive form of *blat*, which usually means "leaf of a tree" or "sheet of paper." But a *blat*—or *bletl*, to use the diminutive—can also mean "a sheet of dough" for making *lokshn*. So once again we get noodles that have come out of the sea.

Money was known as *kez*, "cheese," in thieves' slang. The cheese envisioned isn't hard cheese but *shmir-kez*, "cream cheese," the stuff that you put on bagels—the Yiddish *shmirn*, "to smear or spread," has a slang meaning of "to grease, to bribe." The *kez* here is what is used to *shmir* those who need to be shmorn, it's the grease that goes into the outstretched palm.

Mezumen, "ready money" or "cash," has come into English as "mazooma." In Hebrew the word has a basic meaning of "ready, prepared; something with objectively verifiable existence"—this is money that can be touched and seen and even bitten to make sure that it isn't *linke mezumen,* counterfeit money. *Link,* "left," often has a sense of bad or wrong, a view that Yiddish shares with most, if not all other European languages, and which goes right back to the Latin *sinister.* So *linke zayt,* "the left side," means the wrong side, the bad side. *Oyfshteyn af der linker zayt* is to get up on the wrong side of the bed, and let's not forget that the *akhre* in *sitre akhre,* "the other side," is there as a euphemism for "left." A *linke libe,* "love on the left," is an illicit love affair; *linke skhoyre,* "left-handed merchandise," refers to stolen goods or contraband. *Links* all by itself can also be a synonym for *tarfes,* food that isn't kosher.

VI

There were certainly wealthy people among Europe's Yiddish-speaking Jews and there was also a middle class. They're being given short shrift here for the simple reason that most of the terminology describing them simply is what it is: Yiddish word X is equivalent to English word Y, and that's it. Yiddish speakers certainly needed to discuss other financial states than poverty, but these other states didn't really seem to engage them, probably because it was simply too difficult to maintain a nonnegative conversation for any length of time. Between *keynehores* and spitting and jealousy—hell, it was easier to complain about what you lacked than get too enthusiastic over what others might have had. Why talk about the rich and only imply a complaint when you could talk about yourself and complain to your heart's content?

EIGHT

"Bupkes *Means a Lot of Nothing*":
YIDDISH AND NATURE

I

It's a classic episode of *The Dick Van Dyke Show*, right up there with Buddy's bar mitzvah and Alan Brady's toupee: the break-out hit that's sweeping the nation is actually a song that Rob (Dick Van Dyke) and one of his buddies wrote in the army after being inspired by a Yiddish word: "*Bupkes* means a lot of nothing, and that's what you'll get from me. *Bupkes!*"

The soldier who is supposed to have taught the word to Rob and his writing partner (played by Greg Morris, "the black guy" from the original *Mission Impossible*) spoke either very polite English or fairly rotten Yiddish. *Bupkes* means "nothing," all right, but it's a rather specific kind of nothing, as different from *gornisht*, the dictionary Yiddish for "nothing," as "nothing" itself is from "sweet fuck-all." The basic meaning of *bupkes*, which is spelled and pronounced *bobkes* in official *klal-shprakh*, is dung, specifically the dung of sheep or goats. Like the English "bullshit" or "horseshit," *bupkes* was once fairly widespread as an expression of disbelief. A response of *bupkes* meant that you thought someone was talking nonsense; whatever he was saying, it was crap.

It's easy enough to see how this slang meaning of *bupkes*, which are hard and pelletlike, could be turned around from "Don't give me *bupkes*" into "*Bupkes* is what I'll give you"—just compare the English "I'll give you shit" or "I'll give you sweet fuck-all." Like so much of the Yiddish that has found its way into English, *bupkes* has been downgraded from vulgar to cute; but unless you were discussing barnyard waste, you'd try to avoid the word in polite Yiddish conversation.

As such developments in the slang meaning of *bupkes* indicate, there was a time when the general run of Yiddish speakers knew what goat dung looked like because goats were a part of their daily lives. Expressions like *koolishe tsig*, "community goat," and *koolisher bok*, "community billy goat," could be heard every day from people who felt slighted or unappreciated: "You walk in here and take stuff without even asking? What do I look like, the *koolishe tsig*?"

We have to remember that the supposedly urbanized Eastern European Jews were urbanized only in comparison with the peasants around them. Jews lived in much closer proximity to dirt, dung, and domestic animals than we sometimes care to remember. Indeed, the distinguishing feature of most of the villages and *shtetlekh*—the small, primarily Jewish towns of Eastern Europe— is said to have been *blote*, mud, and *blote* occupies a place in idiomatic Yiddish that is often filled by excrement in English. It took over from *bupkes* as the primary Yiddish exclamation for "bullshit" and is sometimes used where English might use "shit" metaphorically—to show that something is unimportant, that it's nothing. *Gelt iz blote* could be translated as "money is nothing" or even "shit on money" depending on context and tone of voice. "Money? You offer me money? *Gelt iz blote*—it's the music that matters." *Lozn in a blote*, "to leave in a mud" (think of the mud as a mire), means to leave someone in the lurch. *Makhn blote*, "to make mud" of something, is to destroy or debunk an argument or idea; since the idea itself is already *blote*, it doesn't take much effort. *Araynforn in a blote*, "to drive into a mire," is to land yourself in a mess; *araynfirn in a blote* is to land someone else there.

Mud and goat spoors aside, though, there seems to be a widespread belief that Yiddish not only lacks a feel for nature—whatever "a feel for nature" might be—but also lacks the vocabulary necessary to describe it in any but the most cursory manner. This is *blote*. The idea that Yiddish (and thus the Jews who speak it) has no feel for nature seems to be based on the fact that there are few detailed descriptions of nature in preclassical Yiddish literature. The classic triumvirate of Mendele Moykher Sforim, Sholem Aleykhem, and Y. L Peretz, all of whom lived into the second decade of the twentieth century, certainly had no trouble talking about (and identifying) trees, domestic animals, and occasional wildflowers. Most of Sholem Aleykhem's Tevye stories take place out of doors, and Mendele's usual narrator is a traveling book peddler who isn't slow to tell you where he's been:

> The river runs and twists before your eyes, playing hide-and-seek in the meadow, hiding here in the reeds, disappearing, then jumping back out again, appearing before you in all its splendor: diamonds and golden spangles, gifts from its loving relative, the sun, which kisses the water and preens herself in its reflection. The river winks to you, furrows the surface of its brow with a quiet murmur, and you undo your belt and wade in . . . .[3]

Although most Yiddish speakers now live in environments in which the outdoors serves only to indicate where one building ends and the next one begins, Jews in the old days, in the old countries, could recognize and name the flora and fauna of their immediate vicinity no less accurately than the gentiles. Even to

---

3. S. Y. Abramovitsh (Mendele Moykher Sforim). *The Wishing-Ring,* trans. M. Wex. Syracuse: Syracuse University Press, 2003, p. 247.

the non-Jewish farmer in Poland, a birch was a birch, a willow a willow, but a eucalyptus was some kind of tree that he had never seen. It was a name and nothing more, and the same could have been said for far more common species—spruce, ash, and so on—that didn't grow in that particular farmer's neck of the woods: he might have recognized the words, known that they referred to trees, but had no idea what the tree might look like. He might have been able to identify lumber made from spruce without ever having seen a spruce tree on the ground. Before the advent of greenhouses, mass communications, and transportation that allows for the rapid shipment of flowers, the average person of *any* ethnic or religious background could identify only those plants and animals found in his immediate dwelling area or portrayed in such art as he was likely to see. Bible pictures, paintings in churches or synagogues, engravings and reliefs of Jerusalem gave people some idea of palm trees, lions, camels, but firsthand knowledge remained highly local; when my father arrived in Canada from Poland some time before World War II, he had never seen a banana, not even in a photograph, though he claimed to have been familiar with the word.

When it came to day-to-day life, the Jews knew no less than gentiles. Jews were cattle dealers, horse traders, stewards on noble estates. They had vast vocabularies relating to animal parts and agriculture—Yiddish vocabularies that sometimes diverged considerably from the local non-Jewish language. Tailors, shoemakers, and rabbis were treated by folk healers who commonly prescribed herbal specifics—*sgules,* in Yiddish—that the patients (or their wives) were often expected to compound for themselves. This might not be the stuff of *belles lettres,* but that doesn't make it any the less natural.

So why isn't it better reflected in literature? Self-conscious Yiddish literature—literature that knows it's literature—hasn't existed for much more than a hundred fifty years. For all intents and purposes, it went from Chaucer to James Joyce in the space of about sixty years, and didn't have a great deal of time to develop deep-rooted traditions of nature writing or anything else. This lack of literary tradition, especially when coupled with the average Yiddish writer's lack of classical education, has more to do with the "blindness" of Yiddish than you might think. Most European literatures boast a fair amount of nature poetry and plenty of natural description in narrative works. Look at the beginning of Chaucer's *Canterbury Tales:*

> Whan that Aprill with his shoures soote
> The droghte of March hath perced to the roote,
> And bathed every veyne in swich licour
> Of which vertu engendred is the flour;
> Whan Zephirus eek with his sweete breeth
> Inspired hath in every holt and heeth
> The tendre croppes, and the yonge sonne
> Hath in the Ram his halve cours yronne . . .

> (When April with its sweet showers
> Has pierced March's drought to the root
> And bathed every vein of every plant with such liquid
> As produces flowers;
> When the sweet breath of the western wind
> Has also breathed life into the tender shoots
> Of every wood and heath, and the young sun
> Has run half its course in Aries . . .)

It's so beautiful, so invigorating, that readers tend to forget that this description looks as much like an English April as they do. The passage was cribbed from Boccaccio and Guido delle Colonne, and remarkably few English readers seem to care that it's a lovely evocation of springtime in Italy. European literature is undeniably full of nature poetry, most of it based on other nature poetry as much as on nature itself. It's only with the Romantics that it became hep to shlep into field and forest, and Yiddish literature was deeply influenced by such trends. Yiddish spoke plenty about nature when Yiddish was spoken in Poland, Russia, Romania, and Hungary; plants, animals, insects, fish, and agriculture occupy twenty-three closely printed, double-column pages in Nahum Stutchkoff's Yiddish thesaurus. What Yiddish didn't have was enough time to develop a body of nature-writing conventions that could be endlessly copied and redeployed.

Nature cannot be completely divorced from politics, either. Modern Yiddish literature developed more or less simultaneously with the pogrom and racially (rather than religiously) based anti-Semitism. The European landscape wasn't neutral; it belonged to the gentiles, was bound to those gentiles in a way that it could never be to any Jew, who could be forced off it—or even under it—at gentile discretion: a tree is a beautiful thing until you're tied to it by an angry mob. It is surely no accident that many rhapsodic Yiddish descriptions of the European landscape were written by emigrants who had no intention of ever setting foot in those landscapes again. Their full beauty emerged only in memory, after the threat was finally removed—the trees were nice enough, it was the people that you had to look out for.

To be sure, there was some loss of day-to-day nature vocabulary when the language and its speakers moved to places like New York and Chicago, where nature, as the immigrants had known it, had virtually ceased to exist. If there was one tree in six square blocks, the only name it needed was "tree," and that would have been the only name that American-born Yiddish speakers ever heard.

II

Domestic animals didn't change too much from Europe to America, and Yiddish makes plenty of time for cats and dogs. When, for instance, you decide to stop paying attention to someone who is always talking *blote*, you can *hern* [them] *vi dem koter*, "pay as much attention as you would to a tomcat"—if they get too loud, you'll throw a shoe or soak them with a pail of water. Hence the idiom *nas vi a kats*, "wet as a cat," for someone who is dripping wet. If, however, you ask *vi kumt di kats ibern vaser*, "how is the cat going to cross the water," you want to know how a problem is going to be solved or an obstacle overcome: "I've got a great idea for Tom Hanks's next movie, but I can't get him to call me back. *Vi kumt di kats ibern vaser?*" *Koyfn a kats in a zak*, "to buy a cat in a sack," is the same as buying a pig in a poke, while *aroyslozn di kats fun zak* is the literal counterpart of letting the cat out of the bag. A person who can't even do that and is unable to succeed at anything that he might attempt *ken a kats nisht farbinden dem ek*, can't even tie a cat's tail; he is incompetent in any number of fields. If he can't remember what he is unable to do, he also has a *katsn-moyekh*, "a cat's brain"; in English, you'd say a memory like a sieve. *Ketsl, ketsele, ketsenyu*, all of which mean "little cat" or "kitten," are endearments along the lines of "baby," "sweetie pie" or "darling," while the *katsenyomer*, "the feline lament," exists in both Yiddish and German and means "hangover."

Although dogs aren't included in any Yiddish terms of endearment, they still occupy a surprisingly large place in the language of people who are supposed to be terrified of them; peasants used to delight in setting their dogs on passing Jews, and the Jews responded with fear and loathing. Dogs figure in any number of common idioms, almost all of which play upon their homier characteristics. You can talk about *hunts yorn*, "dog's years," which is the same as the English "dog's age": "I haven't seen you in *hunts yorn*." *Hern vi Yurkes hunt* is the same as *hern vi dem koter*. *Yurke* was a common first name that was also used to mean "boor" or "clod"— compare early twentieth-century use of "Reuben" in English—and is here being used as a sort of generic term for peasant. The idea is that the dog barks so much that you no longer notice—imagine Sherlock Holmes discussing the curious incident of *Yurkes hunt* in the nighttime.

There's the very vivid *shnarn vi der hunt nokh tsholnt*, "to snore like a dog after *tsholnt*." *Tsholnt*, for which there is no real English equivalent, is one of those Romance words that Yiddish has never been able to do without. It is related to the modern French *chaud* and *chaleur;* imagine the Spanish *caliente*, "hot," with a *ch* instead of a *c*. *Tsholnt* is a kind of stew, generally heavy on the beans, with some potatoes and bits of cheap or leftover meat tossed in, that is eaten for lunch on Saturdays. Since you're not allowed to cook on the Sabbath, the *tsholnt* is put into the oven sometime on Friday, so that it's had a good twelve or eighteen hours to simmer before it is eaten. It almost always induces a rumbling slumber.

Although you're supposed to rest on *shabbes*, this afternoon nap can prove problematic. In Orthodox circles, the Sabbath is regarded as a particularly good time for husband and wife to fulfill the first *mitsve* in the Torah, "be fruitful and multiply," which is also one of the few recreational activities not prohibited on the Sabbath. Saturday afternoon is the preferred time in many homes; preparations for *shabbes* usually begin on Thursday night, and by the time bedtime rolls around on Friday, the lady of the house is often too tired to do anything. On Saturday afternoon, it's her husband—for whom the *tsholnt* and an alcoholic drink are the first meal of the day—who might be having trouble staying awake long enough to do what needs to be done. But a *mitsve* is a *mitsve*. Whether preceded by sex or not, the Saturday afternoon nap is a time-honored tradition. The image evoked by *shnarn vi der hunt nokh tsholnt* is of a household sunk in a slumber born of satiety, with everything hanging so low and lazy that even the dog, who gets the same food as everybody else, is snoring away as if he's just made love to his wife.

Sleeping dogs who lie long enough can find themselves in trouble. *Do ligt der hunt bagrobn,* "that's where the dog lies buried," is Yiddish for "there's the rub, now you've hit the problematic nail on the head." Rumors abound of Yiddish translations of *Hamlet* in which "To be or not to be" is followed immediately by *do ligt der hunt bagrobn,* but I've never managed to see one of these translations for myself. The Yiddish *Hamlet* on my shelf, translated by the eminent poet I. J. Schwartz in 1918, reads simply, *"ot vos s'iz di frage,"* i.e., *"that* is the question."

Hunt comes from the Germanic component of Yiddish. *Kelev,* the Hebrew word for dog, has also come into Yiddish, but in a less all-purpose way. A *kelev* is a mean, vicious dog, the kind that used to be set onto Jewish passers-by. If "Bad, Bad Leroy Brown" is ever translated into Yiddish, Leroy will probably be described as *"beyzer vi der alter kong"* and meaner than a junkyard *kelev.* The sort of person whom you'd call a *kelev* would be called a son of a bitch or even a mean son of a bitch in English. A *real* SOB can be called a *kelev she-beklovim,* "a dog of dogs" the sort of son of a bitch that even a dog would look down on.

Kelev also has a feminine form in Yiddish, *klafte. Klafte* never refers to anything with four legs; there is another word, *tsoyg,* for that kind of bitch. *Klafte* is so much more unpleasant, so much more offensive than the English "bitch"—I once lost a girlfriend because her father heard me say it one day. I wasn't talking to his daughter or about his daughter—his daughter wasn't even there. I wasn't even talking to him, but the fact that I would use such a word when there was a chance of being overheard meant that I was too low class to be allowed near his daughter ever again.

Barking is *havken* or *biln*, and *biln af der levone*, "to bark at the moon," means to threaten someone whom you can't really hurt, to menace them with threats that they simply can't take seriously. If your lawyer tells you not to worry, the other side is just blowing smoke, he's saying that all they're doing is *biln af der levone*.

When you turn around and hit the *tsad she-ke-neged*, "the other side," with a writ of your own, they will probably start screaming like a *kozak ha-nigzal*, "a Cossack who's feeling aggrieved": a bully who starts whining when one of his victims fights back and breaks the weeping bully's hangnail. The to-do tends to be out of all proportion to the nature of the "injury," and the putative victim always presents himself as having done nothing to provoke it.

Cossacks and other military types might have walked on two legs, but the Jews considered them a separate species. Someone with the manners of a bull in a china shop, the kind of person who interrupts a couple flirting at a party with, "How about them Yankees, eh?" is said to be acting *vi a kozak in sukke*, "like a Cossack in a *sukke*," the temporary dwelling in which Jews eat and sometimes sleep on the festival of Sukkes, or Tabernacles. The Cossack is sometimes replaced in this *sukke* idiom by a *yovn*, a soldier, especially a Russian soldier. *Yovn* comes from *yavan*, Hebrew for Greece or a Greek. Although associations with Antiochus, the villain of the Chanukah story, have given the Greeks a far worse reputation in the Jewish folk mind than they really deserve, *yavan* has no military associations in Hebrew. It came to mean soldier in Yiddish because it sounds very much like Ivan; a *yovn* is basically a czarist GI Joe. *Ale yevonim hobn eyn ponim,* says the proverb; "all soldiers look alike"—you've seen one of them rape and pillage, you've seen all of them rape and pillage. *Yevonish,* the adjective, can mean the Russian language, while *yevonishe toyre,* "Ivan's Torah," is filthy language, especially in Russian.

III

The chicken, the single most prominent "Jewish" animal, has far more in common with us than the Cossack or professional soldier, and we've already seen it used in a variety of idioms, either as a *hon* (a rooster) or a *hun* (a hen). Something said to *shteyn af hinershe fis,* "to stand on chicken legs," is thought to have a shaky foundation, to be built on sand. The *hiner* in *hinerplet,* a fabulous word that means "daze" or "stupor," doesn't actually have anything to do with chickens, but few Yiddish speakers are aware of the fact. "That weed was so good that I spent forty-eight hours in a stoned *hinerplet* thinking about Jerry Garcia," will usually call up images of Deadhead fowl nodding their heads to "Casey Jones." If instead of nodding off, you do the opposite and run around like a chicken with its head cut off, Yiddish has you running *vi a farsamte moyz,* "a poisoned mouse."

Perhaps the most interesting thing about the Yiddish chicken is that the English word has almost completely replaced *hun* in spoken North American Yiddish. Chickens weren't like civil rights—Jewish immigrants had them in Europe, and they went on buying them here. Thanks to *shabbes,* it's likely that most adult Jewish women arriving in the United States in the late nineteenth and early twentieth centuries probably tried to purchase a minimum of one chicken a week, even if they had long since dispensed with any other vestige of Sabbath observance. Yet while a *hunt* stayed a *hunt* and the *kats* remained a *kats,* the no-less-frequently mentioned *hun* was transformed into a chicken almost overnight.

It was a matter of dialect, not nature. Back in the old country, Yiddish-speaking Jews spent most of their time with speakers of a single major dialect. Jews coming to the U.S.A. found themselves mingling with speakers of other dialects in an environment that provided few clues as to which dialect they might be speaking; it wasn't always easy to know when to make mental adjustments or which adjustments to make. *Hon* and *hun* were particularly confusing. The standard language's *hon,* "rooster," is rounded to *hun* by Polish and Galician Jews; but *hun* is also the *klal-shprakh* and *litvish* word for "chicken" (and is pronounced *hin* by Poles and Galicians). Too many people were getting confused; too many may have wound up eating roosters. It must have taken an *alter hiner-freser,* "an old chicken-chomper"—think of James Gleason in *Meet John Doe,* a grizzled old pro who's been all around and knows the score—to come up with the idea of replacing the Yiddish words entirely. The potential for both real and feigned misunderstanding was so great that it became simpler and more convenient to substitute the English, which was completely unambiguous.

Alter hiner-freser isn't a term of great respect. Gruff but lovable Sarge in war movies, the guy who's seen it all and been there a thousand times—*er hot shoyn gepokt un gemozlt,* you'd say, "he's already had smallpox and measles," been through all the childhood diseases, because he's no babe in the woods; he's paid his dues and is as happy to give you advice about dames as he is to lead the platoon safely through a minefield. That's the *hiner-freser*—when he isn't Sarge, he's a Western sidekick.

The image of an *alter hiner-freser,* an old guy eating a young chicken, sometimes leads people to the erroneous belief that the *freser* is always a lecher; he sometimes is, but he doesn't have to be. An incurable womanizer, a lecher who can't seem to control himself, is known as a *khamer-eyzl. Khamer* is the Hebrew for donkey, *eyzl* is the German for the same animal. The man is a donkey-ass. It's a fairly common expression and originates in a kind of schoolroom joke, the humorous *fartaytshn* or translation of a biblical text into Yiddish that was mentioned in connection with *khad gadye* in Chapter Two. Anybody coming across the Hebrew *khamer* would *fartaytsh* it instantly as *eyzl:* "And Abraham arose in the morning and loaded his *eyzl.*"

The joke here is based on the thirty-fourth chapter of Genesis, where Hamor—Khamer in the original—whose son has just raped Jacob's daughter, Dinah, comes to Jacob's sons, and says, "Give us your daughters." Khamer is a randy old man, a real *alter hiner-freser,* but he isn't a donkey. Dumb kids in *kheyder,* though, seeing *khamer,* would unthinkingly translate it as *eyzl:* "And Donkey said, Give us your daughters." Everywhere else in the Torah, *khamer* means *eyzl;* this is the one place where it doesn't.

Khamer-eyzl and the *hun-hon* mix-up both bear witness to the truth of the popular saying that *es vent zikh in vu der khamer shteyt,* "it depends where the *khamer* is standing": the meaning of an equivocal word has to be determined from its context. Based ultimately on a Talmudic joke (*Eruvin* 53a), the saying proceeds from the fact that *khamer*—donkey—has an Aramaic homonym that means "wine." Until you figure out whether the *khamer* is in a bottle or a stall, you can't really be sure that you've understood what's going on.

Lakhn mit yashtsherkes, "to laugh with lizards," is one of those Yiddish phrases that Yiddish speakers themselves seem to think of as quintessentially Yiddish. It means to laugh bitterly, laugh through your pain, laugh to keep from crying; it's the laugh that goes with gallows humor. Imagine lizards walking across your stomach and the feeling that this tickling would call forth. You might be laughing, but there's nothing funny. The same can be said about *lakhn mit kremenes,* where it's flints that induce the mirthless laughter. These idioms are kin to the even more graphic and disgusting *lakhn mit grine verem,* "to laugh with green worms." It might tickle when the maggots start crawling over you, but it sure isn't funny. To do anything *mit grine verem* implies doing it with great difficulty—"I strained so hard that green worms started to come out"—you get the idea. We saw *pishn mit grine verem,* "to piss green worms," in Chapter Six, and none of the other idioms that use the phrase is significantly more pleasant.

Moyshe rabeynus kiyele, "Moses our teacher's little cow," sometimes known as his *beheymele* (which also means "little cow") or his *ferdele* ("little horse"), is the Yiddish name for the ladybug, which is also known as *meshiekhl,* "little Messiah." Remarkably, there is nothing essentially Jewish about these names, no Talmudic background or allusions to biblical exegesis concealed behind the words. Most of the major European vernaculars associate the ladybug with matters of religion. In England, it's still called a ladybird, which is short for "Our Lady's bird," Our Lady being the Virgin Mary. In German, it's *Marienkäfer* ("Mary's beetle"); in French it's *bête à bon dieu* ("the dear Lord's animal/insect"), and its Russian name has the same meaning as the French. Moses and the little *meshiekh* are Jewish substitutes whose names also happen to start with the same letter as Mary.

More surprising than the ladybug's spurious Judaism is the fact that the beaver features prominently in two extremely common idiomatic expressions. *Shvitsn vi a biber,* to sweat like a beaver, seems to allude to the animal's well-known reputation for hard work, most of which is done in water. Someone who *shvitst* like a beaver is dripping with sweat. You can compare the English "sweat like a pig."

In addition to sweating, though, you can also cry like a beaver in Yiddish. Many people have wondered at *tseveynen zikh vi a biber*, "to burst into tears like a beaver." Why of all things a beaver? I'll leave it to Leonardo da Vinci, here echoing centuries of bestiaries, to explain: "Of the beaver one reads that when it is pursued, knowing this to be on account of the virtue of its testicles for medicinal uses and not being able to escape, it stops; and in order to be at peace with its pursuers bites off its testicles with its sharp teeth and leaves them to its enemies."

No wonder it's crying, even though Pliny the Elder had already set the record straight in the first century of this era: "Sextius . . . denies that they cut off their own testicles when they are captured. Rather, the testicles are small; the animal draws them close to its spine and they cannot be removed without killing it."

There's one question that Sextius doesn't seem to consider, which leads us directly to the next stage in our look at animal life: balls or no balls, if we kill that beaver, can we eat it?

NINE

Making a Tsimmes:
FOOD—KOSHER AND TREYF

I

As the voice of a system of thought designed to keep Us Jews from turning into Them Goyim, Yiddish has developed an unusually comprehensive vocabulary of exclusion. Differences between *yidish* and *goyish,* sacred and profane, proper and improper, are built into the structure of the language, nowhere more deeply than when Yiddish deals with food. When you're constantly on guard lest a drop of gravy wind up on a plate used for dairy; when Passover, a major holiday, is based on forbidding more foods than usual, and Yom Kippur, *the* major holiday, forbids any food at all; when food, in other words, becomes a locus of transgression, eating is never too far from your mind. Laconic as Yiddish might sometimes be about nature in the raw, it devotes considerable attention to nature on the plate.

This is the more remarkable in that specifically Yiddish terms for the nonkosher dishes eaten by most of the world can scarcely be said to exist. Yiddish ideas of food are based on the complementary concepts of kosher and not-kosher, and no one shows too much interest in food that they'll never be allowed to eat. *Gebrotn khazerl*—which would be the Yiddish for "roast suckling pig"—is more likely to be interpreted as "roast mumps" ("mumps" is a common colloquial meaning of *khazerl,* "little pig") or a deep tan on somebody you don't like. It's enough to refer to the dish as *treyf*—"unkosher"—or as *khazer*—"pig"; it has no other meaning in a system of values defined by the requirements of *kashres*, "kosherness."

The biblical meaning of kosher is "fit, proper, right." "If the thing seem kosher before the king" (Est. 8:5) has to do with edicts, not eating, and the English use of the word—"a kosher deal," "something isn't kosher here"—fits perfectly with its use in the Bible. "Kosher" was later extended to mean "in accordance with religious law," and people will often talk about kosher *tefillin* or a kosher *mikve*. Kosher food, then, is food that is fit for a Jew to eat, according to the dietary laws laid down in the Torah and elaborated in the Talmud: fish with fins and scales, all birds not specifically forbidden in the Torah, and mammals with cloven hooves that also ruminate, or chew the cud.

This ruminating is called *maalegeyren*, which never means "to think about" or "mull over." Aside from "chew cud," it can mean "to eat noisily with your mouth open," "to mumble, mutter, speak unclearly" or "to chew gum in yeshiva." The Germanic *iberkayen*, which can also mean "to chew cud," has a colloquial meaning of "to parrot someone else" or "repeat something ad nauseam."

In view of the word's history, it isn't surprising that "kosher" should figure in all kinds of idioms that have nothing to do with food. *A kosherer yid*, "a kosher Jew," is exactly what he sounds like—a Jew who does what a Jew's supposed to do. He's honest and trustworthy, esteemed by God and man alike. He is *a yid fun a gants yor*, "an all-year Jew," a day-to-day kind of Jew: John Q. Jew. He isn't a *rosheshonenik*, "a Rosh Hashana Jew," or a Saturdays-and-holidays Jew; he's at shul every day, praying, studying, hanging out, and being a Jew. If a bar mitzvah was a real bar, the *yid fun a gants yor* would be one of the regulars.

A kosherer yid who works hard and attains some measure of

success will undoubtedly earn it in a kosher fashion. Although *kosher fardinen,* "to earn in a kosher way," can mean to obtain a reward by means of honest toil and effort—*Arnold hot kosher fardint Reb Olympia,* "Arnold really deserved his Mr. Olympia title, he won it fair and square"—it is used at least as often to mean "serves them right, they got what was coming to them": "Martha Stewart *hot kosher fardint* her prison sentence," she really deserved it.

Kosher beheymele, "a kosher little cow," and *koshere eygelekh,* "kosher little eyes," introduce a less obvious shade of meaning to *kosher. Beheymele* is the diminutive of *beheyme,* a "cow" or "head of cattle." People used to talk about having five chickens and a *beheyme,* and the phrase *melkn di beheyme,* "to milk the cow," comes up fairly often in Sholem Aleykhem's Tevye stories. In its most general sense, *koshere beheyme* would mean the kind of cloven-hoofed, cud-chewing animal mentioned above: a deer, a buffalo, a cow, or a sheep. Once *beheyme* is shrunk down to *beheymele,* though, the focus shifts from the animal's ritual fitness to the usual fate of the ritually fit. *A kosher beheymele* is a trusting little cow, one that lets itself be led to slaughter; hence, a very naive person, one who, to mix a metaphor, allows himself to be fleeced. *Koshere eygelekh* are likewise naive, trusting little eyes.

Note the implication of youth and inexperience in the diminutives. *Beheymele* is used as Yiddish often uses *kalb,* which can mean both "calf" and "idiot." Shakespeare used calf in a similar way, but without the overtones of *kashres* that make the *kalb* so meaningful to us. *Kalb* gives us the adjective *kelbern,* which in turn gives us the lovely phrase *kelberne hispayles,* "calflike enthusiasm," a foolish enthusiasm or infatuation, the mental state responsible for carnival barkers and infomercials. Spray hair on, vacuum it off, slice, dice, and get six-pack abs—it's *kelberne hispayles* that gets you to reach for your wallet or pick up the phone.

When mothers use *kosher* as an endearment with their infants and toddlers, it occupies a sort of middle ground between "ritually fit," "innocent," and "good enough to eat." "Such kosher little lips! Such a kosher little nose—I could just eat you up." This has been standard mother-Yiddish for a very long time, an endearment of the sort that could never be used between consenting adults.

Kosher returns to the idea of "ritually fit" with *koshere fodem,* "kosher thread," a term virtually never used anymore outside of the wonderfully vicious curse, *kadokhes mit koshere fodem. Kadokhes,* a frequently used imprecation, is a fever, especially a recurrent malarial fever, the kind that always comes back just when you think you're done with it. It's used in curses—*a kadokhes in Saddam Hussein* means "the hell with Saddam Hussein"—and as a nastier stand-in for *bupkes. Kadokhes vel ikh dir gebn,* "Fever is what I'll give you," has nothing to do with Little Willie John; it is equivalent to "I'll give you crap."

Adding *mit koshere fodem* to *kadokhes* takes things into the realm of "fuck-all." In times of trouble and distress, especially in cases of serious illness, women used to go to the cemetery and lay thread around the grave of a notably pious person, as if they were taking its measurements. The thread, known as *koshere fodem,* was used to make wicks for candles that were then donated to the synagogue in an effort to arouse the mercy of heaven. Making such candles was called *leygn kneytlekh,* "laying wicks," and was an organized group activity, a kind of bee, a cross between a tea party and a women's prayer meeting.

In *kadokhes mit koshere fodem,* the heartwarming piety that would normally have suffused a phrase like *koshere fodem* turns into its opposite. The idea is: "All you're going to get from me is a fever so bad that they'll be measuring graves and making candles in a desperate attempt to save your life." It's similar to the equally unpleasant *kadokhes in a kleyn tepele,* "*kadokhes* in a little pot," where you get a fever instead of the hot *kheyder* lunch with which the *tepele,* the "little pot," was usually associated. The *koshere fodem* and the *kleyn tepele* are similar to the English ". . . and the horse you rode in on"—they help make the curse even worse.

II

Whatever isn't kosher is *treyf.* Things that are *treyf* are known as *treyfe* or *tarfes,* but the adjective is sometimes used in place of the noun. *Ikh es nisht ken treyf,* "I don't eat *treyf,*" is heard just as often as *Ikh es nisht ken treyfe, ikh es nisht ken tarfes,* "I don't eat things that aren't kosher." The root meaning of *treyf* (which comes, of course, from *loshn-koydesh*) is something that has been torn apart or trampled, usually by a wild beast: "You shall not eat any flesh that is torn by beasts [*treyfo*] in the field" (Exod. 22:30); "He shall not eat that which has died by natural causes or has been torn by beasts [*treyfo*]" (Lev. 22:8).

As these quotations indicate, *treyfe* originally referred to animals that would otherwise have been kosher, and was the biblical equivalent of "roadkill." It was later extended to all forms of unkosher food, and is the model on which such deliberately ironic terms as *shikse* are based: something attractive but illicit is given a disgusting name in order to make it less alluring. "Thou shalt not eat roadkill" is less of a challenge to your willpower than "Hands off the pork chop" or "Step away from the lobster bisque," and the term *treyf* is a deliberate attempt to change the essence of that T-bone steak.

More than just roadkill, *treyf* comprises all nonkosher animals, birds, and fish; all kosher animals not slaughtered according to the rules of kosher slaughtering; all kosher meat that has been cooked or served with dairy; and all kosher dairy that's been cooked or served with meat. This covers a lot of ground, and *treyf* provides a number of tasty idioms. An SOB can be called a *treyfener beyn*, "a *treyf* bone"; first he sneaks into your throat, then refuses to leave. A *treyfener haldz*, though, an actual unkosher throat (think of it as "a throat that has been rendered unkosher"), is someone who eats anything. Unlike the *treyfnyak*, who simply enjoys a nice piece of *treyf* when one happens to come along, the *treyfener haldz* is a glutton, someone who will eat anything that he can get into his mouth.

Treyfener haldz can also mean a strictly kosher person with a powerful sweet tooth, what Yiddish calls a *nasher* (or *nasherke*, in the case of a woman). In the old country, where food and money were both hard to come by, *nashers* were the equivalent of crackheads, depriving their families of necessities in order to feed their habits. As the proverb has it, *a nasher iz a gonef*, "a *nasher* is a thief." Yiddish-tinged English has removed most of the stigma from being a *nasher;* in a society in which *nashvarg* and *khazeray*, "snack food" and "junk food," is more accessible than food with nutrients, a *nasher* has become a habitual snacker, the sort of person who is always chewing on something. Even so, no Yiddish paper could ever run the kind of personal ads you see in places like *The New York Review of Books:* "Chocolate-loving humanist with Ph.D. . . ."

An omnivorous *treyfener haldz* can also be called a *kal ve-khoymer*, the Talmudic term for an inference that moves from a weaker to a stronger premise or from a lighter to a more weighty example. The classic example is found in the Mishna: "Yosi ben Yokhanan of Jerusalem says . . . 'Do not talk to your wife too much.' If they said this about one's own wife, then it applies, *kal va-khoymer*, to the wife of another" (*Avos* 1:5).

Think of *kal va-khoymer* as equivalent to "how much more"— "How much more does it apply to the wife of another"—then use the same phrase in reaction to another's gluttony: "How much more can one person eat?" *Kal* in Yiddish means "light" or "easy"; it can also mean a "lightheaded or thoughtless person" whose lack of gray matter leads to foolish behavior. *Khoymer* can mean "physical body" or "stomach" in Yiddish, meanings that it doesn't have in Hebrew. A person described as a *kal ve-khoymer* has a head that's always empty and a stomach that's always full; he is a Yiddish Homer Simpson who *shtopt on dem khoymer,* "stuffs his stomach," without bothering to think about what he's putting in there.

Treyfener mazl, "unkosher luck"—i.e., unusually good luck—is the luck of the Irish. Everything always works out for someone who has it, no matter how little she might deserve her success. Things would be very different in a perfectly kosher world, where something very cheap would be *vert vi tarfes,* "cost as much as *treyf,*" when everyone keeps kosher. This is the ritual version of the equally food-oriented *bilik vi borsht,* which has come into English as "cheap like borscht."

Treyf also gives us the *treyf-posl,* the "unkosher null and void," which means a nonreligious or heretical book, especially one in Hebrew or Yiddish. Virtually all nonreligious Yiddish literature consists of *treyf-poslen,* but the term is most meaningfully applied to books that mock or criticize the religious culture and usages of their times.

III

The most prominent forms of irredeemable *treyf* are *shinke,* "ham," and *shpek,* "bacon," but so far as Jewish culture is concerned, the pig exists only to provide gentiles with food and Jews with idioms. We've already seen *khazer* as the primary term for "pig"; as in English, the same word can also denote a slovenly or greedy person. *A kargn ruft men khazer, a shlekhtn—kelev,* "you call a greedy person a *khazer* and a wicked one a dog," a distinction with which English seems to agree. The *khazeray* eaten by a *nasher* has long since become the Yiddish for junk food; it can also mean "filth" or "filthy behavior"—anything associated with pigs—but "junk food" has become the dominant usage.

A *khazernik* can be a not-so-kosher eater of *khazer-fleysh*, "pork," and *khazer-shmalts*, "lard," or he can be someone who buys and sells *khazeyrim* (more than one pig), *khazer-fel* (what footballs are supposed to be made of), and *khazer-hor* (pig bristles—the possibility that such bristles might be used in toothbrushes caused a bit of a social problem a few generations ago). He can engage in such business activities and remain a perfectly kosher Jew. He's likely to tell you that *fun a khazer iz a hor oykh gut*, "a bristle from a pig is just as good as any other." This is the motto of fund-raisers everywhere—as long as it's money, who cares where it comes from?

In English, it's a sow's ear out of which you can't make a silk purse; in Yiddish, *fun a khazershn ek ken men nisht makhn ken shtrayml*, "you can't make a round sable hat worn by Hasidim out of the tail of a pig." If someone assumes an air of unjustified familiarity, you can give them the withering *tsuzamen mit dir khazeyrim gepashet.* "With you I herded pigs?" In other words, "Where do *you* come to *me*? Stick to your place and show some respect."

IV

The major internal divisions of kosher food are *milkhiks, fleyshiks,* and *parve,* "dairy, meat, and in between." Like meat, dairy products have to meet certain criteria to be considered kosher: a trustworthy Jew has to be present at the milking to make sure that the milk is not used as a libation offering to any graven image or deity.

The adjective *milkhik,* "dairy," gives us the really wonderful *blaybn af der milkhiker bank,* "to stay [be left] on the dairy bench." The word *bank,* "bench," was used for what would now be known as a counter or area for food preparation, and every home had a *milkhike* and a *fleyshike bank.* To be left on the dairy bench is to be shut out of something, unjustly excluded on the basis of a very flimsy pretext—when an excuse is offered at all. The image is based on a peculiarity of the dietary laws. The Torah tells us three times that we are not to boil a kid in its mother's milk, and this commandment was quickly expanded to forbid the consumption of milk and meat together. Together on the plate wasn't enough, though. There was some worry about bits and pieces of food coming together inside the mouth, and various customs regarding the length of time that you need to wait to eat dairy after meat and meat after dairy—two entirely different matters—have arisen.

The six-hour wait between meat and dairy that is standard among Jews of Eastern European descent provides an excellent illustration of the real meaning of the proverb, *a mineg brekht a din,* "a custom overrides a law": it doesn't violate it, it makes it more stringent. The whole issue of waiting is based on a couple of short Talmudic passages in folio 105a of tractate *Khulin:*

1) Rov Khisdo says: If someone has just eaten meat, he is forbidden from eating cheese. If he's eaten cheese, though, he can eat meat, but he should wait a little between the cheese and the meat.

2) Mar Ukbo says: With respect to this [waiting], I am as vinegar in comparison with my father, who was like wine. For if my father were to eat meat now, he would not eat cheese for a full twenty-four hours. Whereas if I had meat in this meal, I wouldn't eat cheese; but I would eat it [cheese] at the next meal.

The first passage establishes the principle of a waiting period between meat and cheese; Mar Ukbo's subsequent remarks are used to fix the length of that period—the time between one meal and the next. If lunch is at noon and supper at six, then the waiting time between meat and dairy is six hours.

In a rare instance of leniency, Rabeynu Tam, Rashi's influential and usually stringent grandson, says that Rov Khisdo merely prohibits eating cheese after meat without cleaning the mouth and hands, and that Mar Ukbo is referring only to cases where he hadn't rinsed his mouth. When it comes to making life easier, though, we seem to have as little trouble ignoring Rabeynu Tam as we do in following some of his more difficult rulings. Dutch Jews really do follow him—they say grace, wait an hour, and then rinse their mouths. Even German Jews wait only three hours, the rationale being that the time between meals is shorter in winter (which gives an idea of how old their tradition is), and Jewish law is supposed to follow the least onerous path allowed us. So, if a bunch of Jews of East European descent want to exclude someone of similar background from a social activity, they can make sure that they claim to be going for pizza right after he mentions having just eaten a burger. Everybody's hands are tied and there's nothing to be done about it.

The waiting period after dairy is completely different. With the exception of certain hard cheeses, which require the same waiting period as meat, dairy foods are not thought to leave any residue behind them; you need only rinse your mouth and wash your hands. If you don't want to wait at all, you're supposed to eat some solid *parve* food between cheese and meat, and most people have extended this cheese rule to all dairy foods.

In practice, there is virtually no one who doesn't wait at least half an hour after eating dairy, in accordance with a remark in the

Zohar, the preeminent Jewish mystical text, which says that milk and meat should not be eaten in the same hour.

So to get back to *blaybn af der milkhiker bank,* there's no believable pretext for leaving you out because you're *milkhik*—they just don't like you. Where saying, "We're going for pizza and you're *fleyshik*" has at least the appearance of legitimacy, "We're going for burgers and you're *milkhik*" doesn't even make sense—by the time you got there and ordered the food, it wouldn't be an issue. It's utterly indefensible, except when used against *frimer*-than-thou vipers who sit in judgment of others and find their observance somehow suspect. Such people are always accusing others of eating *kashe mit maslinke,* "kasha with buttermilk." Though the sides of many contemporary kasha packages list recipes that involve little more than water, salt, and the kasha itself, the classic Jewish kasha is made with *shmalts,* and *shmalts* is made of meat. While nobody can *prove* that you put *shmalts* into the kasha that you're eating with buttermilk, no one's going to give you the benefit of the doubt. The phrase is often used of someone suspected of harboring unorthodox ideas, someone considered a little bit "tainted."

Someone who really *is* eating *shmalts*-laced *kashe mit maslinke* just to spite the people who are watching is described as a person who will eat *kheylev mit tshvekes,* "tallow with nails"—not because he wants it, not because it tastes good, but because he's not supposed to. He's a kosher James Dean in *Rebbe without a Cause*—the archetype of the *aftselakhisnik.*

V

Food that is neither *milkhiks* nor *fleyshiks* is *parve,* a word of obscure etymology for an idea that doesn't exist in *loshn-koydesh.* The word seems to come from the Slavic, but the best indication of its meaning is found in an old Western Yiddish word for the same concept, *minikh*. A *minikh* is a monk (compare München—"Monks"—which is German for Munich) and the word was used colloquially in German (and apparently in Yiddish) to mean a gelding, an equine capon, something neither stallion nor mare. *Nisht ahin*, as Yiddish has it, *un nisht aher*, "neither there nor here," no more one thing than the other. Yiddish took hold of the German term and did what it always does—turned a word that means "sexless animal" or "celibate servant of God" into a designation for grains, legumes, fruits, vegetables, fish, water, juice, and alcoholic beverages: things that are neither milk nor meat.

When used of things other than food, *parve* signifies "bland, *phnyeh*, indeterminate." "Everybody said the movie was great, but I thought it was totally *parve*," i.e., nothing special at all. An epicene or androgynous man can be called *parve lokshn*, noodles without enough cheese or meat to tip the balance in either direction.

Parve lokshn can be compared with the *kalter lung-un-leber*, "the cold lung-and-liver," a person so unflappably phlegmatic as to make any sign of life a welcome relief: Calvin Coolidge in a *kupl*. The lung-and-liver in this phrase is a Jewish delicacy that can only be described as *troyerik-barimt*, "notorious, renowned for its bad qualities." As if the two main ingredients weren't bad enough, they were usually covered in a thick red sauce that claimed descent from one or more tomatoes. Now imagine a strong-willed child confronted with such a mess. "You're not leaving this table until you eat it." Ten minutes pass, twenty, an hour; the lung-and-liver is still there, cold now, congealed, unmoving, casting a reddish glow on the poor tyke's face. It's enough to make you uncomfortable even if you like to eat lung-and-liver. The overly phlegmatic person is likewise a *kalter lung-un-leber*; the blood isn't flowing and you can only hope there's no taste.

Lung-un-leber also comes up in the delightful *onhengen a lung-un-leber af der noz*, "to hang a lung and liver from a person's nose"—to dupe them, trick them, leave them with egg (or in this case, something rather colder and slimier) all over their face. With *lung-un-leber* we have moved from *parve* to *fleyshiks*, the meat department of Yiddish life. If simply having a cloven hoof and chewing cud guaranteed the *kashres* of an animal's meat, there'd be a Yiddish-language McDonald's in every Hasidic neighborhood. As things stand, however, the kosher animal must be slaughtered in proper ritual fashion by a person called a *shoykhet*, a ritual slaughterer. In addition to killing the animal, he also checks it to make sure that it has no blemish or ailment that would render it unkosher. His slaughtering is known as *shekhtn*—whence we get the common Jewish surname Schaechter (also spelled Shechter, Shachter, Shecter, etc.)—and the slaughtering itself is called *shkhite*. The extended senses of *shoykhet* and *shekhtn* are fairly predictable and tend to be the same as those that have developed from "slaughter" and "slaughterer" in English.

The more interesting stuff tends to be associated with the verb *koylen*, which also means "to slaughter," but not in kosher fashion: "When he heard that company was coming, the Viking *hot gekoylet an oks*," he slaughtered an ox, plain and simple—there's no pejorative feel to it. All unkosher meat undergoes *kaylung* (the noun formed from *koylen*) rather than *shkhite*. When it isn't being used of meat or murder, *koylen* can mean "to wreck, ruin, do someone in metaphorically." *Er hot mikh mamesh gekoylet*, "he really slaughtered me," means that he might think he's hurt me, but he hasn't even scratched me. He's done nothing but *avekkoylen bay mir di kapote*, "slaughter my capote," my long black coat—the coup de grâce never reached my body. The supremely kvetchy phrase *koylen on a meser*, "to kill without a knife," tends to be used in a pitying, more often than not self-pitying, way: *Me hot mikh gekoylet on a meser,* "they killed me without using a knife," sometimes by slander but more usually by heartbreak: "You show up at your cousin's wedding looking like the lost Jewish Beatle and tell everyone whose son you are!? *Koylest mikh on a meser,* you're killing me without a knife, so promise at least that you'll say Kaddish for me."

Once an animal has been slaughtered and certified as kosher, it is cut up by the *katsef,* the butcher, whom we met briefly in Chapter Seven. The *katsef* usually bought the animal, then took it to the *shoykhet,* who killed it, inspected it, and returned the kosher carcass to the *katsef,* who turned it into steaks, chops, and so on. *Katsovim* (the plural) were the tough guys of European Jewish society, forever threatening *shoykhtim* and rabbis who declared too many animals *treyf,* and often functioning as the first line of defense against both goyim and Jewish undesirables: when it came time to beat up the Jewish pimps, the *katsovim* were usually at the head of the mob. A *katsef*'s shop is called a *yatke,* "a meat shop," and invariably features a *yatke-klots,* a butcher block, for cutting the meat. *Gebn a yatke-klots,* "to give someone a *yatke-klots,*" means to knee them in the butt.

VI

The last category of Jewish food that we need to look at is *khomets,* "leaven," the food that you aren't supposed to eat on Passover. Not eating it is the easy part; a Jew isn't allowed to own or derive benefit from anything leavened, either. The Bible is quite explicit in this regard—"Let no leaven be seen within your borders for seven days" (Deut. 16:4)—and people still go to great pains to hide, get rid of, and sell off leavened food before the start of the holiday. It's thus easy to see how *khomets* also comes to mean "something (or somebody) undesirable"; because it's something that you're not supposed to have and that you need to get rid of, it's also easy to see how it comes to mean "stolen goods" or "contraband." *Khomets-batln,* a slang term for unloading stolen goods, refers to a ceremony in which a symbolic piece of *khomets* is tossed into a fire while the owner renounces any other *khomets* that he has neglected to sell or throw away. He renders the leaven *botl,* "null and void"; the prayer recited during the ceremony describes the *khomets* as "ownerless as the dust of the earth."

Another way of disposing of something that you don't want to have on your hands is called *araynshlayern a khomets,* "veiling a *khomets.*" It means to marry a girl off by means of deception, and is usually done by her father. The image goes back to the Bible, where Laban gave Jacob the daughter whom Jacob didn't want. Veiling the *khomets* implies that the *yold,* "the sap," isn't aware of the kind of bargain he's really getting. If the bride's defects are well-known, though, all the father is doing is *poter vern fun a khomets,* "getting rid of a *khomets*" that he doesn't want and the *hekht,* "the sucker" (literally, "pike," as in "whitefish and pike"), has no one to blame but himself.

These idioms all deal with the fact of *khomets,* but the leavening process itself pops up from time to time. A religious Jew— generally a yeshiva boy—who has strayed into worldly ways of thinking is said to be *niskhomets,* he has fermented and become *khomets.* The Hebrew Bible evinces a peculiar horror at having anything fermented come into contact with anything holy, and the Talmud uses fermentation as an emblem of evil: "Our desire is to do Your will, and what prevents us? The yeast in the dough" (*Brokhos* 17a). Rashi says that the yeast is "the evil inclination in the human heart that makes us *khomets,* causes us to ferment." The fermented yeshiva boy can also be said to be *farfoylt,* "to have gone rotten." Yiddish is quick to note the resemblance between intellectual development and the life cycle of a leftover bagel.

VII

Some foods are more Yiddish than others. *Lokshn*, "noodles," which we've seen a couple of times already, figure in a number of important idioms. Although *loksh* no longer seems to be used as a slightly pejorative term for an Italian (in this sense, it is a calque on the American "spaghetti," which can have the same meaning), you can still hear *brokn ligns vi a yidene lokshn*, "to turn out lies like a housewife turns out *lokshn*," i.e., frequently and well. The verb *brokn* can mean both "to cut into strips" and "to talk a lot" (it can also mean "to crumble"). *Brokn lokshn* describes cutting the *bletlekh*, the sheets of dough, into strips on a *lokshn-bret*, "a *lokshn* board," and it also goes well with *ligns*: "he hacks out lies like a *yidene* hacks out *lokshn*." Note the use of *yidene* for "homemaker"; it's one of the few nonpejorative uses of the word still current in the language.

Lokshn are very closely associated with *kugl*, a kind of pudding made of *lokshn* or potatoes that is eaten on the Sabbath and holidays. A roomful of Jews with ancestors from different parts of Eastern Europe will be able to argue for hours over *lokshn kugl* styles and recipes: sweet or salt-and-pepper; raisins or no raisins; broad noodles or thin. It was, and has remained, one of the Jewish foods par excellence, and has been noted as such in Yiddish. *Der kugl ligt im afn ponim* means that you can see at a glance that he's a real Jew, his very face is redolent of all the *kugl* he's eaten in his time. The literal meaning of the phrase is "the *kugl* is lying on his face," he's got *kugl* all over it. You can also say *mit im iz gut kugl tsu esn*, "he's okay to eat *kugl* with"—and not for anything else. Do not do business or have close personal relations with this no-goodnik.

The phrase is often used in a semijoking way about the Jewish people itself—*mit yidn iz gut kugl tsu esn*—and is of a piece with such self-deprecating folk wisdom as *vos mer yidn, alts mer ganovim,* "the more Jews, the more thieves." The *kugl*'s fundamental Judaism is given a sort of reverse homage in the phrase *kugl mit khazer-shmalts,* "*kugl* with lard," which refers to non-Jewish ideas in Jewish garb. A century ago, this is what most religious Jews thought of Zionism.

The *tsimmes* is as deeply Jewish as the *kugl* and far more likely to glow in the dark. Described by Uriel Weinreich as a "vegetable/fruit stew," the *tsimmes* comes in nearly as many varieties as there are fruits and vegetables for Jews to stew. There is the plum-*tsimmes,* the raisin-*tsimmes,* the apple-*tsimmes,* and the pear-*tsimmes.* There are *tsimmesn* to make kids' hair stand on end: parsnip, garbanzo, green bean, and *farfl.* Although I've never seen one, there is nothing to impede the creation of a lima bean or turnip *tsimmes* or even, God help us, a rutabaga stew. A lychee-*tsimmes* might even taste good. But the classic *tsimmes,* the *tsimmes* of record, as it were, is the carrot *tsimmes.* As the almost inevitable side dish at every Rosh Hashana family dinner—think of it as High Holiday cranberry sauce—the carrot *tsimmes* is familiar even to those who do not make it part of their Friday-night meal: peeled baby carrots; thick, sweet, orange-colored goop; and, in what must surely be a North American innovation, canned pineapple chunks, can after can of pineapple chunks, to assure us of a sweet and happy year and make us yearn to move our exile to Hawaii. There are generations already with us for whom canned pineapple—Del Monte, Dole, or the ultrakosher Festive—is a quintessentially Jewish food.

Makhn a tsimmes, "to make a *tsimmes,*" is a very common idiom meaning to make a fuss, a to-do, a big deal out of something that doesn't deserve it. "Why are you making a *tsimmes* out of it?" That is, "Why are you cutting it into little pieces, setting it to stew for hours, arranging an attractive service, and adding extra pineapple at the end? Why so much ado about nothing?" It's the idea of all the preparation, all the effort that's being wasted, of making a big deal out of small potatoes.

A moyd vi a tsimmes, "a maiden like a vegetable stew," refers to a buxom and robust young woman, the sort also described as *yoderdik*—a *yoder* is a kernel or nucleus, and *yoderdik* also means "nuclear." *A yoderdik meydl*—one with nuclear arms and legs that won't quit—has plenty of kernels with lots of curves in between. A girl with loads of pineapple, she's built like a brick *mikve.*

Yiddish has a wealth of such idioms, food related and extremely Jewish (what else can you call a phrase that makes use of the word *tsimmes*?), but without any specific religious reference. If you call someone a *drel* it's like calling them a jellyfish in English. *Drel,* which puts North American Yiddish speakers of a certain age in mind of Archie Bell and the Drells from Houston, Texas, where " we dance just as good as we walk," is another word for *ptshe* or *ptsha,* the calf's-foot jelly that makes an arugula *tsimmes* as tempting as a chocolate soda. It's shimmery, Jell-O–like, and spineless.

Tsibele trern, "onion tears," are what English calls crocodile tears. You can talk about *veynen mit tsibele trern,* "to cry onion tears," but the more vulgar *pishn mit tsibele trern,* "to piss *tsibele trern,*" gives a far better picture of the kind of hypocrisy involved. *A bitere tsibele,* "a bitter onion," means a wet blanket; imagine the look of someone who's just bit into a bitter onion, then make that face the reaction to others' good times. There is *hefker tsibele* or, more commonly, *hefker petreshke,* "*hefker* parsley," defined by

Weinreich as "anything goes"; the sort of thing you exclaim in amazement when someone tries—let alone manages—to pull off a strikingly brazen piece of *chutzpah*. The basic meaning of *hefker* is "ownerless" or "abandoned"—the *khomets* renounced a few pages ago is declared "*hefker* as the dust of the earth." Kids playing scrambles with their baseball cards used to toss them from the top of the steps at school, yell "*Hefker!*" and then stand back and watch the fun. "Ownerless" developed into "lawless" or "arbitrary." *A velt iz nisht hefker,* "the world is not lawless," means "There's still a God in the world," and the term *hefker-velt* is the rough Yiddish equivalent of Bunyan's Vanity Fair.

So far as *hefker tsibele* and *hefker petreshke* go, all we have to do is recall how cheap onions and parsley were in Jewish Eastern Europe. *Nisht vert ken tsibele,* "not worth an onion," means not worth anything at all, as does *s'iz vert a petreshke,* "it's worth a single sprig of parsley." To *hefker* onions or parsley, to call "scrambles" on what is already growing wild, lets you emphasize the utter senselessness of the world around you even while you pretend to be shocked by it.

Kashe is another deeply Jewish food. In North America, at least, it has come to be identified almost exclusively with *retshene kashe,* "buckwheat groats," but the word itself can refer to any kind of porridge or gruel. *Nisht lozn shpayen in kashe,* "not to let anyone spit in your porridge," means to take no crap. *Farkokhn a kashe,* "to cook up a porridge," is to make a mess of something. "*Host mir nokh a mol farkokht a kashe,*" as Oliver Hardy should have said: "Another fine mess you've got me into."

Klepn vi arbes tsu der vant, "to stick like peas to the wall," means "to have nothing to do with the topic of discussion or the matter at hand; to be completely irrelevant": "We're trying to solve our money problems, and he starts talking a bunch of New Age platitudes that *klepn vi arbes tsu der vant.*" The phrase can also describe an extended argument that doesn't hold water.

Arbes in the narrower sense of "chickpeas" are a fixture of *shaleshides,* the last of the three meals that are supposed to be eaten on the Sabbath. It is usually served in the synagogue between the afternoon and evening services, and generally consists of bread, chickpeas, and leftover herring—nothing very fancy. *A proster shaleshides,* "an ordinary *shaleshides,* an unadorned concluding meal on the Sabbath," is another way of referring to *a yid fun a gants yor* and is often used by such "Jew-in-the-street" types to characterize themselves. While *prost* can mean "vulgar, common, crude," it can also mean "plain, simple," or "ordinary." *Er iz a proster arbeter,* "He's a simple worker." *Prost un poshet* is Yiddish for "plain and simple," and the *proster khay ve-kayem,* "the simple living and existing" is a no-frills human being, a nondenominational version of the *proster shaleshides.*

A busybody, someone who mixes into everyone else's business, is a *kokhlefl,* a dipper or ladle. People who don't speak much Yiddish will sometimes claim the title for themselves. Pay close attention when someone says, "I'm a real *kokhlefl,*" and run, quickly, in the other direction. Anyone clueless enough to say, "I'm a controlling gossip who can't leave well enough alone" is probably telling the truth.

A real *kokhlefl,* the kitchen utensil, might be used to help scrape up the *oyskratsekhts,* the scrapings of leftover dough in a pan or bowl. Idiomatically, though, *oyskratsekhts* means a last-born child, especially one who's come along some years after its next oldest brother or sister.

Kreplekh, "dumplings," pop up in a couple of the most prominent yet baffling idioms in the language. Just about any native speaker can tell you that *kreplekh zolstu esn*, "you should eat *krep-lekh*," means that you're cruising for a bruising, that you've just said something for which you ought to be hit. He or she could probably also tell you that *kreplekh zolstu* nisht *esn*, "you shouldn't eat *kreplekh*," actually means that you *should* eat *kreplekh*—you really *do* deserve to be hit—even though it seems to be saying the opposite. What that native speaker is less likely to know is what *kreplekh* have to do with smart-aleck comments, or why eating them or not eating them should have anything to do with a slap in the face.

It's a matter of Jewish holidays. Although you can have *kreplekh* whenever you're in the mood, it is traditional to eat them three times in the Jewish year: on Purim, the eve of Yom Kippur, and Hoshana Rabba, three holidays associated with the verb *shlogn*, "to beat." On Purim, you *shlog* Haman; he is "beaten," as it were, when the children *klap* with their noisemakers (sometimes called *homen-klappers*, Haman hitters) whenever his name is mentioned during the reading of the Book of Esther. On the eve of Yom Kippur, you *shlog kapores* and on Hoshana Rabba, the *heshaynes*, the willow twigs that we saw in Chapter Two. *Kreplekh* thus come to be associated with beating, and *kreplekh zolstu esn* is a nice oblique way of offering you a kosher knuckle sandwich. *Kreplekh zolstu esn far di reyd*, "you should eat *kreplekh* for saying such things," doesn't need to mention the beating openly; the association between dumplings and drubbings is strong enough to make it unnecessary. "You shouldn't eat *kreplekh*" works just like *geharget zolstu nisht vern*, "don't get killed," with an added sense of warning: Keep on talking and you *will* be eating *kreplekh*.

Shkotsim mit mon, the uncircumcised pastries encountered in Chapter Four, almost find a Jewish counterpart in the *eyer-kugl*, "the egg *kugl*," which is sometimes known as a *zokher-kugl*, "a male *kugl.*" *Eyer,* pronounced *ayer* in many dialects, can mean both eggs and testicles; the word *beytsim* has the same range of meanings in Hebrew, but means only testicles in Yiddish. In order to avoid impropriety and embarrassing double entendres, religious people go out of their way not to use the word *beytso*, "egg." When students or rabbis mention the Talmudic tractate *Beytso*, they don't say *beytso* but *beyo*. An Orthodox scholar with a beard and *payes* who says *beytso* instead of *beyo* would immediately be recognized as an autodidact from a nonobservant family. The substitution comes naturally to anyone raised or educated in the religious world.

So a *kugl* is a *zokher*, "a male," because it has eggs; the phrase is a cute euphemism: "Get me some man-*kugl*." The punning process reverses itself in *beytsimer*, old North American slang for an Irishman, which literally means something like "testicular citizen." It's the *ayer*-sound at the beginning of "Irish" that did the trick.

Finally there is *farfl*, ably defined by Weinreich as "farfl." As food, it is a kind of noodle or a crumb of dough. Colloquially, it means an undersized person, a runt, as with the Murder Incorporated gangster Philip "Little Farfl" Kovolick. *Farfl* is also a dog's name, the Yiddish equivalent of Spot. "See Farfl. See Farfl run." Nestlé's Quik used to run commercials featuring ventriloquist Paul Winchell and his little dog. As the commercial came to an end, Winchell would sing, "N-E-S-T-L-E-S, Nestlé's makes the very best . . . ." At which point the dog would chime in with "chocolate." That dog's name was Farfl.

TEN

A Slap in the Tukhes and Hello:

YIDDISH LIFE FROM BIRTH TO BAR MITZVAH

I

There is almost no phase of human life that Yiddish takes entirely seriously. Not even pregnancy, which might have been expected to remain sacrosanct, is left untouched. The polite terms for pregnant, *trogedik* and *shvanger*—both of which could fairly be rendered as "expecting"—shade all too easily into expressions like *tsushteln a baykhl*, "to provide with a little belly, to knock up," and pregnancy itself is used as a basis for irony in something like *aynredn a kind in boykh*, "to talk a child into someone's belly." A classic Yiddish expression, it means to convince a person of either sex of something patently absurd, which they often go ahead and act on. So far as Yiddish is concerned, the archetypal example of *aynredn a kind in boykh* is the belief that the Holy Spirit entered the Blessed Virgin's ear and made her pregnant. But ears have nothing to do with the process, and any Yiddish speaker can tell you that *fun zogn vert men nisht trogn*, "talk can't make you pregnant."

Such expressions might not make light of pregnancy itself—for that we have to turn to something like *bay ir iz der boykh shoyn af der noz*, "her belly is up to her nose already"—but they show a willingness to treat the idea with a levity that could be considered unseemly in other cultures. The only human condition that Yiddish seems to spare is labor, the actual process of childbirth, which seems to be looked on with genuine reverence and not a little fear.

As soon as a woman's labor pains begin, she is said to *geyn tsu kind*, "to go to child, be in labor," and she immediately enters the state known as *kimpet*, "lying-in" or "confinement." A hastily pronounced version of *kind bet*, "childbed," *kimpet* is taken seriously enough not to have spawned any mocking or ironic idioms. In the old days, a *kimpetorn*, "a woman in labor," lay in a *kimpet* that was already well insulated against several kinds of possible trouble. The *kimpetorn* would often wear a *shternshis*, an eaglestone, to guard against miscarriage. A baker's shovel was sometimes hung on the wall over the bed, along with a couple of loaves of bread, in order to help the baby come out of its mother as smoothly as a bun slides out of an oven, and there was always an amulet, often several, called a *kimpet-brivl*, "a *kimpet* note," or a *yoldes-kvitl*. In this phrase, *yoldes*, another term for a woman in labor, is not to be confused with its etymological cousin, *yold*, "an idiot, a sucker, a mark"; *kvitl* means "note." It can also mean "receipt" or "pawn ticket," and most Jewishly, what can only be described as a prayer note, a slip of paper inscribed with the names of the petitioner and his or her mother (in the form of Mendel ben Jane, Mindel bas Margot; since the soul is believed to descend matrilineally, the mother's name is used instead of the father's). The petitioner also writes down what it is that's being prayed for and takes the *kvitl* to a *rebbe*, a Hasidic leader, who will intercede in heaven for its fulfillment. The *kvitl* can also be left at the grave of a deceased *rebbe* or sage, or taken, either in person or by means of an emissary, and placed between the stones of the Western Wall in Jerusalem. All those little pieces of paper sticking out of the Wall are *kvitelekh* that have been placed there in hopes of an answer.

The *kvitl* hung around a *kimpet* contains the text of Psalm 121, which is widely regarded as having protective powers; one verse reads "May the Lord guard you against all evil," and "all" is taken at face value: my mother's key chain had this psalm engraved on its fob. Because the psalm provides only general coverage, lying-in amulets were also careful to include the names of the patriarchs, along with those of various angels and spirits who do battle with Lilith. For all her recent reclamation by Jewish feminists, Lilith—Eve's predecessor, Adam's legendarily disobedient first wife who was banished and became a demon—was feared more for her habit of killing (or trying to kill) newborn children and their mothers than for her independent womanly spirit.

The child born to the *kimpetorn* can be called a *kimpet-kind*—"a childbed child"—or an *eyfele*. *Eyfele*, "infant," is yet another Yiddish word that seems to have stuck around as an endearment among people who don't much use the language otherwise. It is a diminutive formed from *of*, a word used to denote poultry in general and chickens in particular. *Lekoved shabbes, hob ikh gekoyft an of*, "I bought a chicken in honor of the Sabbath." Calling a baby an *eyfele* is like calling it a "little chick," an image that gives a slightly eerie resonance to such phrases as "kosher little hands and feet" and "I could eat you up." Note that *eyfele* is what's called a second-degree diminutive—if someone's full name is Robert, Bob is a first-degree diminutive and Bobby is the second degree. In the case of the word *of*, the progression should be *of, eyfl, eyfele*—chicken, chick, chickie. Yiddish tends to skip the *eyfl* and go straight to *eyfele; an eyfl*, "a little chick, a baby," sounds exactly like *a neyfl*, "a stillborn child, an aborted fetus." *Eyfl* will appear in compounds—*eyflvayz*, "during babyhood," *eyflshaft*, "infancy"—and a child might even be addressed directly with it—"*Oy, mayn tayer, zis eyfl*, my dear, sweet baby"—but no third-person child will ever be referred to as *an eyfl*, only as *an eyfele*.

One week after its birth, a healthy male *eyfl* is inducted into the Jewish people by means of a *bris mile* ceremony, a ritual devoted to the covenant (*bris*) of circumcision (*mile*). As we saw in Chapter Four, the ceremony of *mal zayn*, circumcising, a child is sometimes called *yidishn dos kind*, "making the child Jewish." The ceremony is performed by the *moyel*, the circumcisor, and concludes with everyone present shouting out, "As he has entered into the *bris*—the covenant—so may he proceed to Torah, the wedding canopy, and good deeds."

A girl gets a slap on the behind to get her breathing and receives a name at some indeterminate later time during a prayer for the health of her mother. Since this prayer is recited by the sexton of the synagogue when the girl's father is called to the Torah, the naming will usually take place on a Monday, Thursday, Saturday, or Jewish holiday. The presence of the baby and her mother is welcome but not required. The father is expected to spring for a *kiddesh*, a postprayer snack; depending on the day, his circumstances, and the practice of the synagogue, this can range from a bottle of whisky to a catered affair.

II

Toddlers don't really form a class of their own in Yiddish ideas of childhood. A child who can walk and do a little talking is often called a *pitsl kind*, "a bit of a child" (you can also talk about a *pitsl broyt*, "a small piece or bit of bread"), or even a *pitsele kind*, "a little bitty child." Its vocabulary might still be quite rudimentary and confined to Yiddish baby talk—*tateshi* (daddy), *mameshi* (mommy), *papa* (bread, food), *koshe* (horsie)—or it might have progressed as far as the finger rhymes mentioned in Chapter Four:

Yidele,	Little Jew,
Shpil fidele,	Fiddle player,
Knak nisele,	Nutcracker,

Puter shisele,	Butter holder,
Grober goy.	Big fat goy.

There is also the very well known "clap-along-with-Mommy":

Patshe, patshe, kikhelekh,	Clap, clap, little cookies,
Di mame geyt koyfn shikhelekh,	Mom is going to buy shoes.
Shikhelekh vet zi koyfn,	Shoes she's going to buy,
Dos kind vet in kheyder loyfn.	The child [or fill in the child's name if it's a boy] will run off to school.

Or one where the mother stretches the child's arms out at the end of the first line:

Vi geyt Shmerele vaksn?	How will Shmerele grow?
Ot azoy geyt Shmerele vaksn.	This is how Shmerele's going to grow.

Boys used to start school at the age of three—no wonder there was no time to toddle—and they spent most of their waking hours there for the next few years. If you can find someone old enough to have attended an Eastern European *kheyder*, as such schools were called, before World War II, you can find out first-hand how the kids left home in the dark and returned in the dark, except on Friday afternoons, carrying paper lanterns to light their way. They used to line up and wait for the *rebbe*, the teacher, to light each boy's lantern at the end of almost every school day be-tween October and May. Most girls were taught the rudiments of reading, writing, and praying, but their education was not as in-tense as that of the boys, who were being groomed to function independently as Jews—i.e., to know the Jewish thing to do in most day-to-day circumstances without having to ask—and to understand at least a little Talmud and rabbinic thought.

Although this goal wasn't reached in every case—not every kid had the ability or inclination, not to mention a family that could afford to keep him in school—it was attained surprisingly often. A boy who left school at ten (well before the norm) had seven years of twelve-hour days behind him.

Entry-level *kheyder* was known as *dardeke-kheyder* and a boy studying there was called a *dardeke-yingl* or a *dardeke-kind*. *Dardeke* comes from the Aramaic *dardak*, "small child." *Kheyder*, which means "room" in Hebrew, was originally short for *kheyder toyre*, "Torah room" or "room of teaching." Quite often, it really was no more than a single room in the home of the teacher, and stories abound of Old Country *khadorim*—that's the plural—in which sheets were hung from a string stretched across the room so that the kids couldn't see their teacher's bed. Until recently, *kheyder* was also standard Jewish-English for "afternoon Hebrew school." Though Yiddish uses either *tsimer* or *shtub* for a regular room in a house, *kheyder* is proper when speaking of a *kheyder meyukhod*, "a private chamber," a famous writer's workroom or an important person's private office; a judge has a *kheyder meyukhod*, just like a Hasidic rebbe.

As schoolroom, *kheyder* figures in the widespread idiom *oyszogn fun kheyder*, which has exactly the meaning of "tell tales out of school." *Geyn in kheyder bay* a person or organization means that you've gone to their *kheyder*, gone to school with them in a figurative sense and learned everything you know there. *Ikh bin gegangen in steks-voltishn kheyder*, "I went to the Stax-Volt *kheyder*," means that you came up on King Curtis and Otis Redding, which explains your unfailing funkiness.

A *dardeke-kheyder* teaches the indisputable: what an *alef* looks like, the sounds of the various vowels, the way letters and vowels come together in Hebrew—where the vowels are a series of dots and dashes that are written above, below, and in between the letters, all of which are consonants. These are matters that a small child can understand, and the *dardeke-yingl* can also be called an *alef-beys yingl,* "an alphabet boy," a boy who is learning the alphabet.

The basic method of *kheyder* instruction has been immortalized in countless folk songs and memoirs, and is still in use in the Hasidic community. Since all Hebrew letters are consonants and all vowels are diacritical marks, the children go through the *alef-beys* over and over again, learning the sound of each letter when paired with each vowel; *komets-alef:o, komets-beys:bo, komets-gimel:go.* This is done in a kind of chant that helps to pave the way for *gemore-nign,* the melody to which the Talmud is intoned. Once a kid has got to *komets-sof:so,* he starts over at the beginning of the alphabet with a different vowel: *pasekh-alef:a, pasekh-beys:ba, pasekh-gimel:ga,* and so on, through all possible combinations. The children are then taught to read letters in sequence, and then go on to read words.

At the same time as they are learning the rudiments of reading Hebrew—Yiddish has never been taught as an independent subject in *khadorim* of this kind—the kids also learn simple prayers and blessings by rote. When it came time to learn to write, it was often by means of a *shure-grizl,* a line that was copied over and over again (often by tracing) until the child got it right. A *shure* is a line or row (but not a queue); *di untershte shure* might well be the original of the English "bottom line."

Shure also provides an important and easily accessible example of Yiddish children's humor. In addition to meaning "line," *shure* can also be a female name. Since a *shure* is a straight line, girls named Shure were always teased by being called *krime*, "crooked, lopsided, crippled." Yiddish-speaking children can be as cruel as any others:

A mol iz geven a mayse;	Once upon a time;
A tsigele a vayse,	A little white kid [baby goat],
A kiyele a royte,	A little red calf,
Mendl iz a shoyte.	Mendl is a moron.

The first two lines echo all kinds of lullabies. The third, with its reminiscence of the *poro adumo*, the red heifer of Numbers 19, hints at redemption. The last line brings us back to Playground Earth, where anybody's name can be substituted for Mendl's. Making fun of other kids' names is an important early step in learning how to kvetch about others, and Yiddish names can be mocked as easily as any. I can still recall plenty of unflattering rhymes: Malke/*halke* (matzoh ball), Dine/*masline* (olive) and Dine/*sline* (spittle), Note (a form of Nosn, Nathan)/*blote* (mud), Sore/*pore* (cow), Shmuel/fool, Shmuel the tool (both are English), Getsl/*petsl* (little *puts*), Itzik/*smitchik* (in this context, penis), Leybl/*shveybl* (match), Mendl/*fendl* (pan—this one I've even seen in books). Around 1966, when our parents would have thought us old enough to know better, my friends and I would sing Shirley Ellis's "The Name Game"—it was new then—with Yiddish names: "Mendl, Mendl, fo *fendl*/Banana *kane* [enema], bo *bendl* [shoelace]" and so on, often on public buses.

Children mean enough to come up with such rhymes in a preradio era had usually left the *dardeke-kheyder* for the regular *kheyder*. No longer *alef-beys yingelekh*, they were now *khumesh-yingelekh*, "Pentateuch boys," put to the twin tasks of learning Hebrew and, along with it, *khumesh mit rashe*, "the Pentateuch with Rashi's commentary." *Khumesh* (plural, *khumoshim*) is used loosely to mean the Torah as printed in a book, with vowels and accents, as distinct from the Torah as read from the parchment scroll, which has no vowels, no accents, no punctuation of any kind. Rashi has come up a number of times already, and as the phrase *khumesh mit rashe* indicates, the biblical text and Rashi's commentary were regarded as inseparable. Any word of the Torah that you knew, you knew along with its accompanying Rashi; anyone who had gone to *kheyder* not only knew some Rashi, he also knew how to think like an eleventh-century intellectual without actually knowing that he was thinking like an eleventh-century intellectual—quite an advantage in a twentieth-century junior high.

A typical piece of *khumesh mit rashe* would look as follows, once we make allowance for the fact that both *khumesh* and Rashi are in Hebrew and that the students would have to *fartaytsh* it into Yiddish. Such Hebrew as is necessary to make sense of the Rashi is included in square brackets; the Rashi itself is in italics.

The verse we're going to look at is Genesis 22:2, where God said to Abraham, "Kill me a son": "Take your son, your only son whom you love—take Isaac and betake yourself to the land of Moriah and offer him up there as an offering on one of the mountains—I will tell you which one."

TAKE [*KAKH NOH*]: Noh *is only used in making a request. God said to Abraham, Please stand up under this test, lest people say that you only withstood the first tests because they had no substance (Sanhedrin 89).*
YOUR SON: *Abraham said to God, "I have two sons." God said, "Your only son." Abraham said, "Each is his mother's only child." God said, "The one whom you love." Abraham said, "I love them both." God said, "Isaac." So why didn't God tell him this to start with? So as not to confound Abraham with its suddenness, so that his reason would not depart and leave him*

tsemisht (disoriented). *Also, to make this mitsve pleasant to him and to give him ever more rewards in proportion to the number of words spoken.*

THE LAND OF MORIAH: *Jerusalem, as it says in 2 Chronicles (Chapter 3), "to build the house of the Lord in Jerusalem on Mount Moriah." And the rabbis say that it is called Moriah because it is from there that* horo'o—*teaching, instruction—goes out to Israel. Onkelos's Aramaic translation refers to the mountain as the place where the Temple incense, which consisted of myrrh, spikenard, and other spices, was burnt.*

AND OFFER HIM UP: *God did not say, "Kill him," because He didn't want him killed. God wanted him brought up to the mountain and treated like an offering. Once Abraham had brought him up onto the altar, God said, "Let him down."*

ONE OF THE MOUNTAINS: *The Holy One, Blessed Be He, makes the righteous wander (or wait) and only reveals things to them afterwards. He does this in order to increase their reward, as it says above "to the land that I shall show you" and in Jonah, "proclaim the message that I will tell you"* [i.e., without letting him know the message first].

It's a lot to say about eight Hebrew words, and this is far from being a difficult passage. In this one selection, we find (in order of appearance): a quotation from tractate *Sanhedrin;* a revamped *medresh* containing a dialogue between God and Abraham; the definition of a biblical word based on its use elsewhere in Scripture; a rabbinic etymology for the same word; corroboration of the proposed definition by an Aramaic translation of the verse; a further dialogue; and an account of two other biblical instances in which God withholds information necessary for the fulfillment of one of His commands.

A ten-year-old encountering this for the first time would have been in the opportunity *kheyder.* Ten-year-olds had usually moved on to Talmud; this stuff was being taught to eight- or nine-year-olds. Such passages were memorized, recited, and translated into a droning Yiddish singsong by kids who often needed help to blow their own noses. No attempt was made to learn *khumesh* without *rashe*. So closely do the two go together that I once overheard the wife of a well-known rabbi telling someone not to be discouraged by his lack of Jewish knowledge. "Even Rabbi Akiva," the Talmudic hero who died in the second century of the current era, "was forty years old before he started learning *khumesh* with *rashe*," she told him.

And in case you should worry that people who stop being religious forget all this stuff, bear in mind that the biblical passage just examined has been incorporated into the liturgy and is recited every day of the year. A man who leaves the religious fold at the age of sixteen will have said it more often than he has said the Pledge of Allegiance. He might come to loathe it, but it's unlikely that he'll ever forget it.

Khumesh mit rashe was also used as a language textbook, a means of teaching the language that the students were already interpreting. The reason underlying the *fartaytshn,* which grew less and less rote as a student progressed, was to be sure that the kids had some idea of what they were really learning. You can't inculcate what they can't understand, and considerable pains were taken to try to teach the students a *tsures alef* or *shaytl ivre,* "the shape of an *alef*" or "a chunk of Hebrew." These phrases are usually used only in the negative: *Nisht kenen ken tsures alef* means "not to recognize even the outline of an *alef*." The *tsures* here should not be confused with the *tsuris* that means "troubles"; this one is the possessive form of *tsure,* a word of Hebrew origin that means "image, face, appearance." If you say that somebody *hot a tsure,* "they have a *tsure,*" you mean that the person is very respectable and highly respected, someone with a good public image. Someone who *shpart in tsure* is stuffing his face, while his opposite number, an otherworldly ascetic who is too spiritual to care for money, is said to *nisht visn ken tsures matbeye,* "not to know what a coin even looks like."

Shaytl is used in much the same way with *ivre,* which means "Hebrew as a language for prayer and study," as distinct from modern spoken Hebrew. You can be an adept in *ivre* without being able to carry on a conversation in Israeli Hebrew; *zogn ivre,* "to say *ivre,*" means to read aloud, not to discourse. The *shaytl* in this phrase is a piece of wood; the idea is that the person who doesn't know a *shaytl ivre* doesn't know a sliver of Hebrew. Poor reading can likewise be called *hiltserne ivre,* "wooden Hebrew," and can lead to the legendary ability to write *noyekh mit zibn grayzn,* "Noah with seven errors": Noah has only two letters in Hebrew and Yiddish.

The New Testament, of all things, provides us with a classic example of *hiltserne ivre* and its consequences. In three of the four gospels, Jesus enters Jerusalem on Palm Sunday on a colt, "the foal of an ass," in apparent fulfillment of the prophecy in the Book of Zechariah:

> Rejoice greatly, O daughter of Zion!
> Shout aloud, O daughter of Jerusalem!
> Lo, your king comes to you;
> triumphant and victorious is he,
> humble and riding on an ass,
> on a colt, the foal of an ass (Zech. 9:9).

The Gospel of Matthew, however, finds Jesus having a bad Hebrew day. Rather than understand "an ass . . . a colt, the foal of an ass" as a parallelism in which one donkey is described in a couple of different ways, Jesus makes a fairly elementary error in *ivre* and says to two of his disciples: "Go into the village opposite you, and immediately you will find an ass tied, and a colt with her; untie them and bring them to me . . . . The disciples went and did as Jesus had directed them; they brought the ass and the colt, and put their garments on them and he sat thereon" (Matt. 21:2, 6–7).

If there were such a thing as a Tetrapygian Heresy, it would have found its origin here, in this unequivocal description of a four-cheeked Jesus, a Jesus with back, a Jesus who looked into the future and beheld the Yiddish proverb, *me ken nisht zitsn af tsvey shtuln mit eyn tukhes*—"you can't sit on two chairs with one rear end"—and set out to contradict it in advance. *And* while moving.

I don't mean any disrespect to Jesus—if I did, I'd be writing in Yiddish—but Hebrew school is not for the meek. Airless and overcrowded, full of preadolescents forced to trudge through steaming jungles of syllogisms, *bobe-mayses,* and kid-eating prohibitions—you can't touch your hair while praying; you can't pet a dog on *shabbes* or go swimming during the hottest three weeks of the year—the *kheyder* had to be run by a combination prison guard, exegete, and child psychologist. But we're in *goles;* we got the *melamed* instead.

III

Not a highly respected member of society—the word *melamed* was sometimes *fartaytsht* as an acronym of *mer lernen, mer dales,* "the more you teach, the less you earn"—the *melamed* was indispensable and expendable in equal measure. In a society so focused on reading, reciting, and interpreting texts, any adult male was theoretically capable of becoming a teacher. There was no such thing as training, no diploma was necessary, and it needed no start-up funds. *Az a bal-agole falt dos ferd,* "When a teamster's horse drops dead," *vert er a melamed,* "he becomes a *melamed*"—not only was the *bal-agole* near the bottom of the Jewish social scale, the word itself continues to carry connotations of boorishness, ignorance, and illiteracy. This was the paradox of a highly literate society: when literacy is valued but widespread, teaching it is left to those who can't put it to better use. The job paid badly, competition for students was fierce, and such tuition fees as there were, often were late or absent. Still, it was, and has remained, an essential service. The *melamed* is called *rebbe* by his students and their parents ("The *rebbe* hit you? Then I'll hit you, too!"). The nascent Hasidic movement adopted the term as a means of conveying the homey and dependent nature of the relationship between the Hasidim and their leader. He was the ideal teacher, a second father. There were undoubtedly pleasant, patient, and devoted *melamdim* who developed real bonds with their students after years of ten- and twelve-hour days, and this was the sort of relationship that *rebbe*-as-charismatic-leader was intended to convey, but those *melamdim* don't figure in Yiddish folklore. For the rest, the indispensable tools of the trade were the *kantshik* and the *baytsh,* the first a knotted leather whip similar to a cat-o'-nine-tails, the second a plain old whip. I don't know if these are still in use anywhere, if *melamdim* in long black coats are sneaking into bondage-and-discipline shops to purchase Hebrew school supplies, but whips seem to have been generally replaced by the *taytl,* "the pointer"—which, being both solid and pointy, can penetrate a nostril or ear for maximum flick value—and the humdrum old yardstick.

Corporal punishment and the fear of corporal punishment were widely regarded as the most effective of all pedagogical tools, and a traditional *kheyder-rebbe* had a whole arsenal of blows at his disposal. These were known collectively as *matnas yad,* "gift of the hand." The basic Yiddish meaning of the phrase is a gift or present that is slipped from one hand into another—a bribe—but it also has the *kheyder* sense of making a "gift" of the hand itself. The term is found in Deuteronomy, and was widely familiar because of its use in the festival liturgy. Every male is commanded to come to the Temple three times a year, "and he shall not appear empty-handed before the Lord. Each according to the gift of his hand [*matnas yodoy*], according to the blessing of the Lord your God" (Deut. 16:16–17). Colloquial Yiddish has so literalized the phrase as almost to make a mockery of its biblical meaning.

There are degrees of *matnas yad,* units of measurement that can be applied to domestic as well as schoolroom discipline. Starting with the *kal,* the light, we'll move toward the real *khoymer,* the more severe degrees of battery, all of which are administered for your good and that of the whole Jewish people.

There is the *knip* or "pinch," favored particularly for huskier students. This can range from the merest pluck at a fold of skin— the *rebbe* walks past and doesn't even break stride, just stretches out a pincerlike hand and gives a squeeze while walking—to a full-bodied grip accompanied by a clockwise twisting motion that can last for up to forty-five seconds.

The particular viciousness of the *knip* resides in its corruption of an act of approbation. The *knip in bekl,* the "pinch in the cheek," administered affectionately, is a standard sign of approval and congratulation. *A knip dir in bekele,* "a pinch in your cheek," a phrase usually *not* accompanied by an actual pinch, means "Good work, well done." It's the power of inversion, the ironic physicality, that gives the *knip* its more lasting sting. A *rebbe* who was a real *knipper* also had the sneaky advantage of being able to get you both coming and going, as it were. If you messed up, you got pinched. If you did well—*nu,* you got the same pinch with different words.

The *shnel,* defined as "fillip" in Yiddish-English dictionaries, involves moving the middle finger along the upper joint of the thumb, whence it takes wing for some part of the hapless youngster's head. Delivered properly, this sort of flick can hurt like the devil, and is never to be used around the eyes. The *shnel* has even deeper traditional roots than the *knip.* The souls of the unborn are supposed to spend their time learning Torah and being schooled in the mysteries of heaven and hell, and there is a *medresh* that describes how an angel comes to each infant just before it is born and gives it such a *shnel* under its nose that it forgets everything that it has learned. Folklore holds that the deeper the cleft over a person's upper lip, the smarter that person is likely to be: the angel had to flick harder in order to knock all that knowledge out.

The *melamed* is the opposite of the angel; he uses the *shnel* to try to knock something *into* an unwilling head, though he doesn't always try from in front. It wasn't unheard of for a teacher to come up behind an unsuspecting kid, who might sometimes have done nothing wrong and might even have delivered a correct answer, and give him a *shnel* in the occipital lobe that'd set the kid's head to bobbing.

A real *knipper* almost never delivered a *shnel;* he would keep his nails long, which could make a *shnel* as uncomfortable for him as for his victim, while the devoted *shneller* tended to prefer the stealth approach to which the *shnel* is so admirably suited. Painful as the *shnel* and the *knip* can be, they were considered more in the nature of constants, things that are always there, and were simply shrugged off as part of the school environment, an occupational hazard of childhood. Real corporal punishment begins with the *patsh.*

A slap or smack, the *patsh* was more a means of focusing attention than an attempt to inflict real harm. Think of it as organic

Ritalin. *Patshn mit di hent* can mean to clap, and the clapping game quoted earlier could take on the air of a threat. When coming from a teacher, *"Vilst shpiln mit mir in patshe kikhelekh?* Want to play *patshe kikhelekh* with me?" meant "Shut up before you get hit." *A patsh in ponim,* "a slap in the face," has the same sense of insult as it does in English: "It was a real *patsh in ponim* when he was denied the lifetime achievement award."

Next up is the *zets,* "the stroke or blow." It is often construed with its destination: *a zets in ponim arayn, in di kishkes arayn, in di krizhes arayn,* "in the face, in the guts, in the small of the back" (*arayn* is an adverb meaning "in, into" and is included here for the sake of proper idiom). The *zets* is a midlevel hit, too strong for a mere attention getter like the *patsh,* but not forceful enough to addle the poor kid completely. With the *zets* we are entering the twin areas of real misbehavior and real lack of understanding on the part of the student. In a system in which study is regarded as the highest moral good, these don't tend to be too finely distinguished: misunderstanding *is* misbehavior and is generally punished in situ, on the kid's empty head.

The *klap* is also a hit or blow, but more intense, more powerful than the *zets.* The defining feature of the *klap,* the thing that distinguishes it from the *zets* even more than its force, is its obliquity. A *zets* is an honest, straightforward, Gary Cooper kind of whack; a *klap* jumps out from the side, or even sneaks up from behind the head so that the victim doesn't see it coming. There's a brief whoosh in the air, and then it's strictly "Incoming!" It's an ambushing varmint, the *klap,* and would have been played by Dan Duryea in a Hollywood western.

Next is the *flem,* the smack that resounds, usually given *in di piskes arayn,* in the face, across the cheeks. Imagine a *patsh* to the power of three; this is a blow to the cheek that causes the victim to do an involuntary double-take. Worse than the *flem* is the *frask*, which even sounds violent. It's a more powerful smack, still open-handed, the *melamed's* answer to the karate chop. Beyond this is the *khmal* or *khmalye*, the all-out, murder-one wallop that makes its victims *zen kroke mit lemberik*, "see Cracow and Lemberg," the Yiddish counterpart to seeing stars. Lemberg is now called L'viv and is in Ukraine; at the time of the Austrian Empire, L'viv was at one end of Galicia, while Cracow, now in Poland, was at the other. The idea behind the expression is that the blow is hard enough to send your head all the way to Cracow, where the recoil snaps your neck back so forcefully that the head that was just in Cracow finally winds up in L'viv, while the rest of your body goes nowhere at all.

The *patsh* becomes truly dangerous when a number of *petsh* (the plural) are combined in an operation known as *oysdreyen a shalsheles*, "to turn or turn out a *shalsheles*." This latter word is Hebrew for "chain," but is also the name of one of the accents printed in *khumoshim* to show how the Torah is to be chanted when it is read aloud in the synagogue. The *shalsheles* is a zigzag line that looks like a hastily scribbled 3 printed over the word to which it applies. *Oysdreyen a shalsheles* involves an ascending series of *petsh* that alternate from cheek to cheek. If you've ever seen the Three Stooges, you've seen many a *shalsheles*. The Stooges did a great deal to transmit classical *kheyder* form to a mass audience, maintaining a proper *shalsheles* while allowing Curly to accompany every *patsh* with a high-pitched "whoo-whoo."

This sort of corporal punishment can also be called *gebn kushn di mezuze*. A *mezuze*, of course, is the tube or little box containing the first two paragraphs of the Shma that is supposed to hang from the right hand side of every doorway (except the bathroom) in a Jewish house. *Kushn di mezuze*, "to kiss the *mezuze*," is what religious people do when they walk past one; they touch the *mezuze* with their fingertips, then kiss the fingers that have touched the *mezuze;* this keeps the cases from getting wet and spreading disease.

The important thing here is the *klap* that the *mezuze* gets as part of the kiss. In *gebn kushn di mezuze, kushn di mezuze* should be thought of as a kind of technical term, perhaps even set off in quotation marks. "I'll give you a 'kiss-the-mezuze,'" i.e., a *klap.* And why? Because you have *azoy fil seykhl vi in kloyster mezuzes,* "as many brains as there are *mezuzes* in a church."

The *klapn* and *kushn* of the *mezuze* have inspired a couple of other interesting idioms. A mother can be called a *mezuze*, because *men klapt zi un men kusht zi,* "you hit her"—mistreat her, that is— "and then you kiss her." Even weirder, in the light of stereotyped notions about the sanctity of the Jewish mother, is that a loose woman or prostitute can also be called a *mezuze* because *yederer leygt on a hant un git ir a kush,* "everybody lays a hand on her and gives her a kiss."

These are all phrases relating to one form or another of bare-knuckle violence. When the *baytsh* or the *kantshik* comes out, the proper verb is *shmaysn,* "to whip," and the usual target, the behind. There are quite a number of words for this beloved Yiddish body part. Among the more refined are *hintn,* "rear"; *hinterkheylek,* "hindpart"; and *unterkheylek,* "underpart." Respectable, slightly jocular terms include: *gezes,* "seat"; *mekhile,* "the you'll-pardon-the-expression"; *der zayts mir moykhl,* "the excuse-me"; and *der vi heyst men es,* "the whatchamacallit." The more common vulgarisms, all of them equivalent to "ass" or "butt," are: *okhor,* "rear, behind"; *akhorayim,* "buttocks, hinder areas"; *morsh,* which simply means what it is; and, best known of all, *tukhes.* From the Hebrew preposition *takhas,* which means "under" or "beneath," *tukhes* is mentioned by Elye Bokher, author of the *Bove Bukh*, in a book called *Seyfer Ha-Tishbi* (composed in 1541–42), where he describes its use as widespread and well established. *Kush mikh in tukhes*, "kiss my ass," is certainly one of the best-known Yiddish imprecations, and its *kheyder* version, *kush mikh vu di yidn hobn gerut*, "kiss me where the Jews reposed," one of its cutest. According to Numbers 33:26, the wandering Israelites "made camp at Tukhes," a place-name rendered as Tahath in standard English translations. Forty years in the desert just to say "kiss my ass."

As a target for armed and irate *melamdim*, the *tukhes* occupies a prominent place in the folklore of the *kheyder*. Indeed, it was customary in many *khadorim* for the *rebbe* to administer a mass thrashing before lunch on Fridays, just as the kids were about to leave for their *shabbes* break. Each boy would be called up and told, "*Gib tukhes un gey varemes*, stick out your can and go have lunch." The idea was to get you for whatever you might have got away with earlier in the week—it was assumed that there was always something—and also to enforce general discipline and esprit de corps:

S'iz fraytik, s'iz fraytik,	It's Friday, it's Friday,
Der tukhes iz tsaytik.	When the *tukhes* does bloom.
Leygt aykh af di kni,	Get down on your knees,
Vel ikh shmaysn on mi.	So my whip can have room.

Kheyder boys tended to classify *rabbeyim* by their preferred disciplinary habits: *knipper, shneller, patsher, zetser, klapper*. Beyond *klapper*, they had only to mention the *melamed's* name because he was already notorious. Perhaps they'd append a *merder*, "murderer," while begging their parents to send them somewhere else.

All these punishments were delivered on the basis of a principle that, empirical evidence to the contrary, was the maxim by which most *melamdim* lived: *eyn shoyte nifgo*, "an idiot is not harmed." The phrase comes from the Talmud (*Shabbos* 13b), and Rashi explains it by saying, "Bad things do not befall him, that is, he doesn't recognize them as bad." In other words, he can't be insulted because he doesn't know that he's being insulted. *Eyn shoyte nifgo* is usually misquoted as *eyn shoyte margish*, "an idiot doesn't feel," by dint of confusion with another statement in the same Talmudic passage: "A corpse doesn't feel [*margish*] a knife, does it?" A *melamed* who said *eyn shoyte margish* just before laying into one of his students would have hit the kid even harder for making the same mistake. And he would probably have killed the kid who dared to ask why he was being hit if he couldn't feel the blows.

At least you knew where you stood, though. You were a *nar*, "a fool"; a *tipesh*, "stupid person"; a *shoyte*, a *sheygets*, a *goy*—the list is practically endless. There's *khokhem*, which is supposed to mean "sage" and usually means "fool," and its cousin from Chapter One, *khokhem be-layle*, "a sage at night," someone who's brilliant when sleeping, smart when nobody sees. There's the *shtik fleysh mit oygn*, "a piece of meat with eyes"; the *shtik fleysh mit tsvey oygn*, "piece of meat with *two* eyes"; *a puts mit oyren, a puts mit a kapelyush*, "a *puts* with ears, a *puts* in a derby" (you wouldn't have heard these from a *melamed*, but he'd have thought them); *a goylem af reder*, "a golem on wheels"; and to return to the natural world, a *shoyte ben pikholts*, "the idiot son of a woodpecker."

Every insult from the *rebbe* gave him a reason to hit you again. This was no sport, though, no mere sadistic game. It was a pedagogical technique designed to cow kids into understanding, a means of *araynleygn a finger in moyl*, "sticking a finger into someone's mouth," prompting them along, spoon-feeding them so that they'll come up with the answer that you want. If you describe a person by saying that nobody needs to *leyg im arayn a finger in moyl*, you're saying that he knows the score and might even be a step or two ahead of you already.

The *rebbe* might also *vayz* something *aroys afn teler*, "show it, lay it out on a plate," demonstrate and explain everything in great detail, starting at the very beginning and going step by step by step. This can be compared with *tseleygn af zibn telerlekh*, "to lay something out"—and it's always just one thing—"on seven saucers or little plates," as if it were a bunch of party sandwiches. It means to make a big show of a tiny bit of fairly common knowledge and to expect plenty of applause at the end.

Not everybody was an idiot, though. A good student could be called a *tayere keyle*, a "precious vessel," while a bad one was a *puste keyle*, "an empty vessel, a good-for-nothing." *Keyle* (plural, *keylim*) means "vessel" or "instrument" and comes from the Hebrew. Dishes can be called *keylim*, as can kitchen utensils. "I'd like to help, but I don't have my *keylim*," means that you haven't brought your tools. *Keyle* is also used to mean "instrument," especially in the operatic sense of "voice." *Pavarotti hot a tayere keyle* means that Pavarotti has a good voice. This use of *keyle* would seem to reflect some influence of the German *Kehle*, "throat," which sounds exactly the same and can also be used to mean "voice." Idiomatically, if somebody is *aroys fun di keylim*, he has lost patience, is beside himself with rage. It is a fine description of the resting metabolism of most of the *rabbeyim* in Yiddish folklore, and helps us to remember the rationale for the old saying, *Ven freyen zikh kheyderyingelekh?* "When do *kheyder* boys rejoice?" *Az der rebbe zitst shive*, "when the *rebbe* sits shiva"—because they're off for a week.

The logic at work here is proof that the *rabbeyim*, for all their faults, must have been getting *something* across. There's no great sense of morality involved in the kids' not wanting the *rebbe* to drop dead. If he drops dead, the kids will be sent to another *kheyder* inside of a day or two; if he's only sitting shiva, though, if all he's doing is observing the seven-day mourning period for a member of his immediate family, everyone knows that he'll soon be back and no one's parents will be worried. The kids' ideal was a healthy *rebbe* with a large and sickly family. A dead *rebbe* meant a new *rebbe;* a *rebbe* in mourning spelled a week's compassionate leave.

IV

With the passage of time, a *kheyder-yingl* is transformed into a *bar-mitsve bokher,* "a youth of bar mitzvah age." In Yiddish, you don't *have* a *bar-mitsve.* No ceremony is necessary, no party need be thrown. Being *bar-mitsve* is most emphatically *not* a confirmation of any sort. At the age of thirteen years and one day, a boy who has managed to live long enough simply becomes *bar-mitsve,* whether he does anything about it or not, whether he knows that he is *bar-mitsve* or not. In this sense, becoming a *bar-mitsve* is similar to attaining the age of majority—no one can make you vote or have a drink, but you'll have a hell of a time if you ask to be tried as a minor. Although the basic meaning of the Aramaic *bar* is "son of," its sense in *bar-mitsve* is that of "vested with" or "subject to." A *bar-mitsve bokher* is a *bokher* who has, as it were, grown into the *mitsves;* they sat in the closet for years, waiting for him to get big enough, and now he's able to put them on, especially if they happen to be a prayer shawl and phylacteries.

The term *bar-mitsve* is already a bit of a euphemism for the synonymous *bar-onshin,* which is so unpleasant that it is rarely used. *Onshin* means "punishments," and *bar-onshin* makes the real meaning of becoming *bar-mitsve* all the more clear. If *bar-mitsve* means "subject to the *mitsves,*" *bar-onshin* means "subject to punishment [for not keeping the *mitsves*]." Not even God can force the kid to observe the commandments, but He can now give the kid hell if he doesn't. And that's the real meaning of *bar-mitsve:* becoming responsible for the consequences of your own actions.

The essence of any bar-mitzvah ceremony consists of giving the boy an *aliye,* calling him up to the Torah. Being called to the Torah is an honor not granted to children under thirteen, and the *aliye* is a sort of public statement that this kid now counts for a minyen and will be seen during the week in phylacteries. Immediately after the *aliye,* his father stands up and makes a blessing: "*Borukh she-ptorani mey-onshoy shel ze,* Blessed be He who has freed me from this one's punishment." Metaphysically, it's time for the boy to start standing on his own two feet. Until today, the father has been a human air bag, shielding the child and taking the impact himself. But now he's cast off the burden of his son's behavior, and is probably waiting to see if his luck might improve for having done so.

In spoken Yiddish, *borukh she-ptorani* is pronounced *borekh she-potrani* and has a colloquial meaning of "good riddance, I'm glad to be rid of something"—or more commonly—"somebody." *Potrani* is related to the verb *poter vern,* "to get rid of," as well as the adjective *poter,* which means "exempt, free from." A boy under the age of thirteen is said to be *poter fun mitsves,* "exempt from performance of the *mitsves*"; he's got official permission not to do them.

The main outward indications that a boy is no longer *poter* from *mitsves* are the *tallis,* the prayer shawl, and *tefillin,* phylacteries. The *technical* sign, should the boy not know the exact date of his birth or some other doubt arise, is the presence of two pubic hairs, a criterion that applies to girls, too. Little seems to be said about who's supposed to do the checking. Of the two less prurient external signs, *tefillin* are the more reliable, but they produce no worthwhile idioms. And the *tallis,* as we'll see, usually belongs to a state well beyond bar-mitzvah.

ELEVEN

More Difficult than Splitting the Red Sea:
COURTSHIP AND MARRIAGE

I

Mitsves might begin at thirteen, but maturity is a matter of marriage. A bar mitzvah ceremony acknowledges developments that it does nothing to bring about; a wedding canopy turns boys and girls into men and women. "A man shall leave his father and mother and cleave to his wife," says the Bible—a man, not a boy: a kid stays a kid until marriage, and the unmarried never really mature. *Bokher,* the Yiddish for bachelor, can also describe a junior high school student; its basic meaning is "male youth, adolescent," someone steaming along to manhood in an engine stoked with hormones. The *alter bokher's* train, the train of the "old adolescent, the confirmed bachelor," never quite arrives, and it's nobody's fault but his. In light of the surprising fact that the Torah's first commandment, "increase and multiply," is incumbent on men but not women, bachelorhood is seen as a deliberate flight from authenticity, a refusal to face up to the fundamental imperative of masculine life. An *alter bokher* of eighty is only a minor on the verge of senility.

The Yiddish spinster doesn't grow up, either. She is a *moyd* or *alte moyd,* a "girl" or "old girl." Like the English "maid," to which it is related, *moyd* originally meant "virgin, girl too young to have known man," but this age-based sense of *moyd* was taken over long ago by its diminutive, *meydl,* and outside of compounds like *kale-moyd,* "a nubile girl, one of marriageable age and estate," *moyd* has become a bit of an insult. *Oy, iz dos a moyd* means that the woman in question is anything but girlish. Strappingly built, loud and ill-tempered, she is a termagant, a virago, a weight-lifting shrew with a flame-thrower mouth.

The *alte moyd,* the "old maid," is usually thought of as someone who has been deprived of the chance to marry. The "confirmed bachelor" makes his own decision to stay single, but the spinster is called *a farzesene alte moyd.* In modern Yiddish, *farzesen* is used only with *alte moyd,* but the root meaning of the word (which is still used in contemporary German) is "to sit around waiting." The Yiddish *farzesene skhoyre* used to mean merchandise that didn't move; it sat in the store and gathered dust on a shelf, just as the *alte moyd* gathers dust on the marriage market.

If the Yiddish-speaking folk mind were to be presented with the concepts of *alter bokher* and *alte moyd,* its immediate reaction would probably be resentment against the former for refusing to marry and pity for the latter, who has to wait to be asked. Where the *alter bokher* is a sort of Peter Pan of phylacteries—now that he's bar mitzvah, he won't grow the rest of the way up—the *alte moyd* doesn't even have a choice: *Bay a yingl makht men borekh she-potrani tsu bar-mitsve, bay a meydl tsu der khasene,* "you say *borekh she-potrani* about a boy at his bar mitzvah; you say it about a girl at her wedding." A woman, traditionally conceived, is supposed to pass from one *reshus,* one jurisdiction or domain, to another. Where a father can be said to get rid of a son at the latter's bar mitzvah, all he can do in the case of a daughter is try to hand her over to somebody else. If nobody takes her, she remains his problem forever.

A woman who never marries is also deprived of the opportunity of fulfilling the major *mitsves* incumbent upon women.

While any male who passed his thirteenth birthday is responsible for such temporally-determined positive commandments as praying with a quorum and putting on *tefillin,* women are exempt from all such *mitsves:* their duties as mothers and caregivers are thought to excuse them from such tightly scheduled activities. With time, this exemption took on the force of a prohibition and women were left with three *mitsves* that were considered their particular province.

The first of these women's *mitsves* is called *hadloke,* lighting candles on the Sabbath and festivals. The second *mitsve* is *nemen khale,* "taking dough." It consists of taking a small amount of dough from every batch of baking and burning it in the oven to commemorate the portion of dough set aside for the priests when the Temple was still standing. If *khale* has not been taken in advance of the baking, a piece of the finished product can be tossed away later, which is why packaged kosher baked goods often have cryptic statements on the boxes that say "challah is taken" or something similar. It's a fancy way of saying that you can eat everything that you've paid for and need have no worries as to the ritual fitness—the *kashres*—of the product inside.

The last of the three *vaybershe mitsves,* "women's commandments," is *nide,* observance of the complicated and multifarious rules concerning menstruation and "family purity." What this comes down to in practice is counting the requisite number of "clean days" after the end of a menstrual period and then going to the *mikve,* the ritual bath. Until she has done so, a woman is effectively no less *treyf*—no less forbidden—than dishes that have become unkosher; until she has returned from the *mikve,* she is not only *treyf* with respect to sexual relations, she can neither touch nor be touched by her husband (let alone any other man), or even pass him the butter; she puts it down and he picks it up. If you describe a woman as *nide*, you're saying that she is "ritually impure": she is either in her menses or has not gone to the *mikve* afterward.

Although men go to the *mikve*, too, they are not obliged to do so. *Nide* is thus the one major *mitsve* that only a woman can fulfill. The woman is not only responsible for figuring out when to go to the *mikve*, she is also charged with making sure that all the corollary prohibitions are observed. Of course, this applies only to married women. Unmarried females who have reached puberty are *nide* by definition; having no husbands, they have no reason to go to the *mikve* and are therefore not to be touched in even the most casual fashion. There is thus no such thing as an Orthodox wedding in which the bride has not been to the *mikve* beforehand, and girls must be careful to schedule their weddings around their menstrual cycles, lest the festivities be severely diminished.

Some dishes can also be koshered in the *mikve*, and typical *mikve* schedules, as posted on the doors, used to read:

Monday, Wednesday, Friday: men
Tuesday and Thursday: women and dishes

While a clever housewife could theoretically take care of everything at once, most *mikve* administrators won't let it happen.

These *mitsves* have had a profound effect on Jewish life. *Khale*, the bread that is usually spelled "challah" or "chala" in English, is eaten on the Sabbath in order to give a woman the opportunity to fulfill all three *mitsves* in one fell swoop. She takes *khale* from the baking; lights the candles; and, assuming that she is "clean," has sex with her husband, in keeping with the Talmudic injunction that a scholar—in this case, any Jewish husband—should lie with his wife on the Sabbath.

The importance of these *mitsves* is brought home to the men-folk every Friday night, when a portion of the Mishnaic tractate Shabbos is read as part of the liturgy: "There are three transgressions that cause women to die during childbirth: laxity with respect to *nide, khale,* and *hadlokas ha-ner*" (*Shabbos* 2:6). These three *mitsves*—*hadloke, khale,* and *nide*—are known collectively as *Khanoh* (i.e., Hannah), which stands for *KHAle, Nide, Hadloke.* Yiddish has a taste for this kind of acronym, and uses it as both a mnemonic device and a vehicle for jokes. It isn't always easy to tell the two apart. *Yaknehoz,* which is formed from the words *yayin, kiddesh, ner, havdole, zman*—wine, kiddush, candle, *havdole,* and occasion—can mean either basic *shabbes* supplies or else the sequence of opening prayers at the seder when the first night of Passover falls on a Saturday. But that's only part one. Old Passover *hagodes* sometimes had pictures of people hunting rabbits at the beginning of the book as a visual reminder of *yaknehoz,* which sounds very similar to *yog 'n hoz,* "hunt the rabbit" (actually, hare). "Be vewy, vewy quiet;" this Passover, we're all Elmer Fudd.

The same technique is also used to comment on absurdities in day-to-day life. Invitations to any function always specify that it will begin at such-and-such a time *bidiyuk. Bidiyuk,* a Hebrew word not much used in spoken Yiddish, means "exactly," but—given the Jewish propensity for lateness and the fact that *'u'* and *'v'* can be represented by the same Hebrew letter—it is taken as an acronym for *BIz DI Yidn Veln Kumen,* "until the Jews turn up." Similarly, you can say that someone who was approached for a donation gave *bitsedek,* which usually means righteously or charitably. Here it stands for *BIz TSu DEr Keshene,* as far as his pocket, i.e., he stopped short of actual money. There's also *shpek yidish,* "bacon Yiddish," the sort of Yiddish spoken by people who only think they speak Yiddish. It stands for *SHmuk, Puts, Kugl*—about as much as such people know.

II

A boy becomes bar mitzvah whether a ceremony is held or not; marriage is a little bit different. According to the Talmud, even God finds arranging suitable marriages to be as difficult as splitting the Red Sea, which might be why He saw fit to pass the job to the *shatkhn,* the so-called "marriage broker." The professional *shatkhn* (or *shatkhnte,* if it's a woman) was the Yiddish world's version of the used car salesman, and was not particularly well thought of. Although amateur *shatkhones,* matchmaking for the sake of helping someone out or simply doing a *mitsve,* was usually regarded as praiseworthy and even pious, making the same matches in order to earn a living was generally felt to be among the jobs of last resort for people who had failed at everything else and weren't too particular about telling the truth: the *shatkhn* received a fee only if the match led to an engagement. As the saying has it, *bay a shatkhn iz nishto ken miyese kale,* "all brides are beautiful to a *shatkhn.*" On the other hand, since the *shatkhn's* deceptions are ultimately for the sake of one of the greatest and most important of all *mitsves*—these little white lies are *good* for the Jewish people—*dem shatkhn shtroft got nisht far zayne ligns,* "God doesn't punish the *shatkhn* for his lies."

When a *shatkhn* notices two youths who *shteyen in shiddukhim,* "are of marriageable age and estate," he seeks to *redn a shidekh,* "propose a match," to the parents of the youths in question. *Redn* means "to talk, to speak"; notice the archaic, prephotographic terminology involved here. By the time anybody laid eyes on anybody else, the deal was usually approaching its final stages, and a good *shatkhn* would already have talked his clients into such a state as to blind them to any but the most glaring discrepancies between objective reality and his own PR—at least until such time as a contract was signed. It was up to the *shatkhn* to paint a picture of each potential partner that was as flattering as possible without straying so far from the truth as to cause one of the parties to back out in disgust.

Redn a shidekh is also a form of moral suasion. Like most other significant activities in traditional Jewish life, it is entirely verbal and appeals to the ear rather than the eye. Intentionally or not, the Christian idea of the Holy Ghost entering Mary through her ear in order to impregnate her is very Jewish in its orientation. We're dealing with people who run their lives according to what they call the Oral Law and who are commanded to have the Written Law read aloud so that all might hear it. With its invisible and image-less God, a Temple in which the Holy of Holies consisted of an empty room, and central texts that are still read aloud and some-times even sung when people study alone, Judaism has always been more of an aural than a visual culture. Where the eye has been the primary sense organ in Western Christian culture since at least the fourteenth century, the most important sights in Jew-ish history—the parting of the Red Sea, the giving of the Torah on Mount Sinai—are known only by dint of hearing about them. There are no pictures, no traditional iconography. The Torah doesn't say, "See, O Israel"; the Torah says, "Hear."

Like so much of Yiddish culture, marriage was more a matter of words than of anything else. It was a matter of conviction, of proof and persuasion as opposed to desire. And bear in mind that it wasn't the future couple whom the *shatkhn* persuaded; it was the parents, the future in-laws, who were the main parties to the ne-gotiations. The *shatkhn* is said to *firn tsunoyf a vant mit a vant*, "to bring one wall together with another," a phrase rooted as much in the Talmud as in the reality of Jewish negotiation. Rashi comments on the Talmudic statement about splitting the Red Sea that "the man is alone [i.e., on one side], the woman is alone [i.e., on the other] and He [God] brings them together and establishes a house." The Yiddish expression seems to be derived from Rashi, with the *shatkhn* replacing the Lord as the agent of togetherness and the couple's fathers replacing the couple. There's a jocular version of this which says that *der shatkhn firt tsunoyf a vant mit a vant,* "the *shatkhn* brings one wall together with another," *un zogt dernokh, shlogt zikh kop in vant,* "and then says, 'Bang your head against the wall.'"

The bond between the two sets of parents is formalized in a set of relationships that have no counterpart in the English-speaking world. When John marries Jane, John's father becomes the *mekhutn* of Jane's mother and father, while John's mother turns into their *mekhuteneste;* and each of Jane's parents stands in a similar relationship to John's. They are not quite in-laws but are more than mere acquaintances. They are like executive board members of a corporation devoted to the production of grandchildren, and the better they get along, the more likely they are to call each other by their titles instead of their names. "Hello, *mekhutn,*" is intimate but not invasive, dignified without being stuffy. It conveys a mixture of affection and respect, and affords the people at either end of the greeting a fair bit of satisfaction.

Mekhutn and *mekhuteneste* can also be used more loosely for any relative by marriage, and people will often refer to their in-laws, as well as any other relatives by marriage, as *mekhutonim.* As such, *mekhutn* develops the less complimentary meaning of "pretender to familiarity" (to borrow Uriel Weinreich's definition), someone who is taking liberties permitted only to members of your inner circle. *Vos far a mekhutn bistu mir,* "what kind of *mekhutn* are you to me," means "Who the hell do you think you are, acting or speaking to me like that?" Hamlet's "What's Hecuba to him, or he to Hecuba/That he should weep for her?" comes out in Yiddish as:

Vos far a mekhutn iz er mit Hecuba,	What kind of *mekhutn* is he to Hecuba,
Er zol veynen af fremde levayes?	That he should weep at funerals that are none of his worry?

If things go wrong between partners or associates, you can say that they are *oys mekhutonim,* "no longer relatives-by-law." Although the image derives from divorce—technically, it could describe John and Jane's parents after the final decree has been issued—it usually means the dissolution of a business partnership, another contractual relationship from which both parties emerge aggrieved and blaming the *shatkhn. Oys mekhutonim* can be compared with the delightful *oys kapelyush-makher,* "no more fancy-hat maker," i.e., no more Mr. Big Shot. *Kapelyush* can mean either "derby" or "fancy woman's hat"; someone who's *oys kapelyush-makher* has "slipped," as they used to say in English. It has a jocular sense, a hint of resignation, and can be used just as easily in the first person as in the third: "So there I am, two days away from my IPO when—bang!—the market caves in, my start-up goes under and I'm *oys kapelyush-makher,* living on unemployment insurance."

III

But we're getting ahead of ourselves. The children have to have a look at each other before anybody can become a *mekhutn.* If either prospective partner refuses to do so or is immediately and absolutely repelled by the other, the potential *mekhutonim* become *oys mekhutonim* right away. The parents can apply pressure, but the formal consent of the people being married is still required before the fathers sign any documents. This is especially important for the girls. There's a saying, *a yidishe tokhter tor men nisht neytn,* "it is forbidden to force a Jewish girl" into marriage, because once she's there, she might not be able to leave. As Jewish law allows a man to divorce a woman but won't let a woman do the same to a man, a woman can be left with no way out of an unpleasant or even dangerous marriage except the consent of someone who probably doesn't like her. The law therefore demands that she at least enter the marriage voluntarily. While the feelings of the young couple are not the decisive factor in marriages of this type, there is nothing that even the most determined set of parents can do against a kid who just says no and refuses to be blackmailed or frightened.

If both kids are willing to proceed, they go on to *bashoyen di kale,* "look over, check out the bride." The boy and his family turn up at the girl's house, where the principals get a chance to have a look at each other and spend a little time together, sometimes even in a separate room—a living room or den where the door has been left open—asking each other questions while their parents talk in the adjoining kitchen or dining room: What kind of schools will they send their kids to? Will the groom go on to learn in *koylel,* the graduate school of the yeshiva world? Will the young wife wear black stockings or brown? Nylon or nice thick cotton? Will the bride have to shave her head? And so on, with the groom all the while imagining what the bride will look like in any of that year's more popular *sheytl* styles.

The *sheytl,* the wig worn to keep a married woman's hair from being seen in public, can be retro in style or relatively up to date, long or short, and can come in any color that you want. A woman can have one for weekdays and another for the Sabbath and holidays. From Sunday to Thursday she might walk around in a mousy chestnut pageboy; Friday night could see blond locks cascading over her shoulders, and Saturday morning—assuming that she has the money—a more restrained, television-mom kind of blond. She might have been gray for the last thirty years, but no one knows for sure except for her husband, the *mikve* lady, and the *sheytl-makhern,* the wig maker.

Although the use of the *sheytl* varies with time and place, the importance attached to concealing the hair of a married woman goes back a very long time. The Jerusalem Talmud talks about a woman named Kimkhis who had seven sons, every one of whom served as high priest. When the sages asked her how she came to merit this, she said, "Never have the beams of my house beheld the hair of my head" (*Yerushalmi Megillo* 1:12).

The problem of covering a woman's hair with a wig that looks *better* has not gone unnoticed, and many Orthodox women don't wear *sheytlekh* at all. They cover their heads with a simple *tikhl,* a kerchief, or else wrap their hair inside turbans and snoods. Many women who do wear *sheytlekh* still take care to cover the *sheytl* with a hat, a style popularized by the late Vishnitzer Rebbitzin.

Sheytlekh are advertised like any other merchandise and each style has a name of its own, always something like "The Britney" or "The Alexis"—never "The Nekhome-Mindl" or "The Sheyndee-Rukhl." There are also spicy, more suggestive names like "Midnight Confession"—as in the old Grass Roots song—or "Silken Whisper," which has nothing to do with what the *sheytl* is made of. Quaint or even corny as these names might seem, the wigs they describe are a welcome change from the old-fashioned *sheytl* that the pope could have spotted from a hundred yards off. When I was in high school, that kind of *sheytl* was called a *mus-het,* with a heavy stress on the *mus.* This was a local innovation, based on talking in false Yiddish accents—while speaking actual Yiddish—and saying, "*Gevalt, zi hot a sheytl vi a mus-het,* she's got a *sheytl* like a moosehead."

IV

If both parties are satisfied with the *bashoy,* the couple usually meets two or three more times, just to assure themselves that the match is really *bashert,* "destined" or "preordained." The person who is *bashert* for you is your predestined mate; he is a *basherter* and she's a *basherte.* The idea of being predestined to spend your life with a particular person comes from a Talmudic passage that has turned into genuine folklore: "Forty days before a human embryo has assumed any shape, a voice calls out from heaven and says, 'The daughter of this one will go to that one, the house of this one to that one, the field of this one to that one.'" The sentence reminds us that love, reproduction, and interfamilial business dealings were all regarded as aspects of one big process.

The initial *bashoy* often marks the first time that the young couple has laid eyes on each other, and is almost always the first time that they've seen each other at close quarters; it is often the first time that either has been alone with someone of the opposite sex who isn't a member of their immediate family. Having been trained from youth never to look at such people, their initial feeling is one of terror. Then they start to stare. Rather than look each other in the face, they're more likely to *gafn in di negl,* "gape at their fingernails," the Yiddish equivalent of staring at your shoes and blushing and saying, "Aw, shucks." They might *oysshteln a por oygn* on each other, "stick out a pair of eyes," stare hard, possibly in bewilderment. If they really can't figure out what the hell is going on or why their parents ever thought that they might want to spend their lives with *this,* they might *shtel oys a por oygn vi der arendar afn ots koytses,* "bug out their eyes like a bumpkin looking at the prayer, *Ots Koytses.*" This is the wholly human version of *kukn vi a hon in bney odem,* "to stare like a penitential chicken at the prayer *Bney Odom.*" The *arendar,* the "bumpkin" here, leased land from a nobleman; he and his family usually lived far from other Jews and were generally a little lacking in Jewish education. They learned basic reading, writing, and praying, but bare literacy is no help against a hymn like *Ots Koytses.* Recited on the Sabbath before Purim—for the sake of which holiday the *arendar* might have come into town—it is a tongue-twister that can leave even well-educated people scratching their heads in bewilderment. It begins: *Ots koytsets ben koytsets, ketsutsay le-katseyts,* "the wicked reaper, scion of the wicked reaper, hastened to cut down those who had been circumcised." In more normal language, Haman really wanted to kill all the Jews. Incomprehensible as it all seems—it looks at first glance like a series of typographical errors—*Ots Koytses* is in the *sidder,* the prayer book; you take it on faith that it's there for a reason, but you can't figure out what that reason could be. This is precisely the way these kids might be feeling: they know that what they're seeing is there, but that doesn't make it any easier to understand or believe.

If shock should cross over to fear, they can *oysshteln a por oygn vi der malekh ha-moves,* "stick out a pair of eyes like the Angel of Death," be wide-eyed and unblinking with anger, stupefaction, or dismay. As we'll soon see, the Angel of Death is made up of nothing but eyes, and his stare is there to make sure that no one should ever escape.

Once the couple has adjusted to their unwonted proximity, they might decide to take a closer peek and look each other in the face. This is called *onponimen—ponim* means "face." If each looks into the other's *ponim* and hears that heavenly voice calling out their names, they'll probably *aynesn zikh mit di oygn,* "cling to each other with their eyes," as if they were joined at the pupils. They might even go so far as to *aynshtshimen zikh mit di oygn,* look at each other with eagerness, literally, "pinch each other with their eyes."

If one gives the other a long, appraising glance, the kind that stops to evaluate each body part in turn, the examination is called *batrakhtn vi an esreg,* "looking something over as if it were an *esreg,*" the citron used on Sukkes, the Feast of Tabernacles. Everybody is supposed to own an *esreg* that is as close to flawless as possible, and a really beautiful one—an *esreg* looks like a lemon and is held in the hand during certain prayers—can cost hundreds of dollars. In order to make sure that the *esreg* that you purchase is the best that you can afford, you consider it from every vantage point, examine it for shape, texture, color, and aroma—this is the *batrakhtn* that precedes the decision about whether or not to buy.

If boy and girl fall in love at first sight, they'll *kukn mit milkhike oygn,* "look [at each other] with milky [i.e., dewy] eyes"—and if they find no fault with each other, they'll go on to *kukn mit glezerne oygn,* "to look with eyes made of glass" (as distinct from glass eyes). There's a well-known saying, *a mame hot glezerne oygn,* which means that a mother sees no fault in her children. *Hobn* or *kukn mit glezerne oygn* is probably best translated as "to be blind to the faults of another"; the defects slide off the glass without penetrating as far as the retina.

Anybody going to meet a potential life partner in such formal circumstances will naturally be dressed in his or her finest, and the idea of dressing up for a *bashoy* gives us the twin idioms *kalen zikh,* "to make oneself like a *kale,*" which actually means "for a woman to dress so that she looks younger than she really is"—an old maid trying to pass for a maiden—and *bokhern zikh,* "to make oneself like a youth or unmarried man," that is, "to dress so as to attract women" (without the reflexive *zikh, bokhern* is tough-guy Yiddish for "to fuck, get laid"). Note the difference in shades of meaning from feminine to masculine. Even though both are trying to draw attention to themselves, the man can get away with simple flash, while the woman feels a need to try to look like a girl.

Duded up as they are, the couple are *oysgeputst* or even *ayngemarinirt in esik un in honik,* idioms that we encountered in Chapter Nine, "dolled up," even "marinated in vinegar and honey." If the girl's taste for jewelry and adornment passes all bounds of restraint and good taste, she can be said to *aroyfshlepn af zikh dem tole,* "to be hoisting the hanged one"—Jesus on a crucifix—"onto herself": she's got so much crap on her that there's probably a cross in there, too. Compare the English, "She's wearing everything but the kitchen sink" and note the difference in terms of reference. Yiddish, which often seems obsessed with food and its preparation, leaps immediately for a religious metaphor, while English—which lacks even the most basic ideas of kosher and *treyf* but can invoke Jesus at the drop of a yarmulke—ends up in the kitchen.

In the similar but less colorful *aroyfshlepn af zikh dem ruekh,* it is pretty clear that the *ruekh,* "the devil," has been brought in to take the place of Jesus, the *tole.* The Jesus image is better; someone might actually wear a crucifix, whereas *ruekh* is best translated here as "the devil only knows what." You can also say that someone is *bahongen mit tsirung vi gots mame,* "as hung down with jewelry as God's mother," or that they *onhengen af zikh vi af der matke-boske,* "are as weighed down with jewelry as the mother of God." The image comes from the gifts and votive offerings that adorn statues of Mary, and is hardly complimentary.

Again, a man who is overdressed for any occasion, let alone the one at which he finds himself, is said to *oyszen vi an almen nokh shloyshim*, "to look like a widower after the thirty days of compulsory mourning." It's not generally realized that official mourning periods for anybody other than your parents last for only one month—this includes siblings, spouses, even your own children, God forbid. According to Jewish religious law, it is also meritorious (though by no means obligatory) for a man to remarry within a year after the death of his wife. The image behind *oyszen vi an almen nokh shloyshim* is of a man who is all duded up and ready to party. Someone who looks like this kind of widower—who is clearly not too disturbed by the loss of his wife—is usually dressed a little too loudly, sporting spats and a rakishly tilted toupee, "a regeleh Casablanca," as they used to say in Yinglish. The female equivalent, *oysgeputst vi Khavele tsum get*, "tarted up like little Evie at her divorce," implies too much makeup and too little cloth—dressed up to get messed up. You can see it all, but you really don't want to. The female phrase is the more pejorative—a divorced woman is supposed to wait ninety-one days before taking another man, but the widower has managed to hold out until the end of the *shloyshim*.

V

If everything is satisfactory after couple's first few meetings, they will move on to *shraybn tnoyim*, "write terms and conditions," draw up an engagement contract. As this is rarely done anymore outside of extremely religious circles, it isn't generally known that these contracts all follow the same fixed form and consist of an agreement made by representatives of the bride and groom, usually the fathers who have been dealing with the *shatkhonim*. The *tnoyim* make all the usual promises; they specify a dowry and fix a fine to be paid in case either party should break the contract.

Although the bride and groom do sign the *tnoyim*, their signatures are primarily a way of indicating that they know that their fathers have arranged for their marriage.

The main thing specified in the *tnoyim* is the *nadn*, the dowry, which these days takes the form of who assumes which wedding expenses and who kicks in what toward the couple's apartment or the minivan when the first child arrives, speedily and in our day. The contract sometimes specifies an attenuated form of the older practice of *kest*—"board" (as in "room and")—in which the bride's family provides or contributes to a stipend that allows the groom to sit and learn in *koylel* for a few years, the number of which is sometimes specified as well. In the old days, *kest* really meant "room and board" and an *eydem af kest*, "a boarding son-in-law," was living with his in-laws, who provided him and his wife with all their material needs while he studied for a given period. Hence the frequent reference to a son-in-law as an *umzister freser*, "a useless consumer of food."

Paying off the dowry—*silekn dem nadn*—or rather, not paying off the dowry, has been a source of problems between *mekhutonim* for centuries. The Talmud already comments that "There is no wedding contract without a quarrel" (*Shabbos* 130a). These fights over money and arrangements are the inspiration for the *beroygez tants*, "the angry dance," that is still performed at traditional weddings: the two *mekhutenestes* start out dancing back to back, then finally come round to face each other, as if to say that all differences have been resolved, all anger has passed, and there are no hard feelings.

In cases of true love or real financial security, the groom might be willing to forgo any *nadn* at all, in which case he is said to *nemen zi in eyn hemd*, "to take her in nothing but her shirt," with nothing but the clothes on her back, or *nemen zi vi zi shteyt un geyt*, "take her as she stands and walks," to take her "as is." Contrary to its romantic appearance, such willingness was often a cause for suspicion—these offers were sometimes made by prosperous older widowers who wanted to buy themselves a hot young wife.

The parents are said to *oysgebn* their children, "marry them off." When not referring to marriage, *oysgebn* means either "to spend money"—a fact that has hardly gone unnoticed in the Yiddish-speaking world—or "inform on, rat out." If the bride is okay, but there is a clear defect on the groom's side that doesn't seem to trouble her father, the latter is said to *oysbaytn a tokhter vi zoyer-milkh*, "to trade his daughter off as if she were sour milk," to take whatever he can get for her. The implication is always that the bride's side could have done a lot better. It is usually used of marriage to classless or unpleasant people as a way of furthering the father of the bride's business interests.

Nevertheless, *in a tsholnt un in a shidekh kukt men nisht tsu fil arayn*, "you don't look too deeply into a *tsholnt* or a *shidekh*"—if you knew what was in either, you wouldn't touch it.

Once the details have been worked out and the contracts are duly signed, the parties proceed to *brekhn teler*, "to break plates." While glass is smashed at a wedding, the vessel smashed at the *tnoyim* has to be earthenware. While the real purpose, once again, seems to be to drive away the demons, the usual explanation for the difference in material is that just as glass can be repaired, so there is a remedy for a bad marriage in the form of a *get*, a divorce. Nothing, though, can undo the loss of self-esteem, the embarrassment and bad publicity for the entire family (who could have other children who need to be married off), of a broken engagement. Many authorities hold that divorce is actually preferable to a broken engagement, but they tend to have lived before the days of custody litigation.

The only recourse in the case of a broken engagement is the *knas,* the fine specified in the contract. So central is this fine to the whole idea of engagement that the process of becoming engaged is usually called simply *farknasn zikh,* "making oneself liable to a penalty." The engagement party at which the *tnoyim* are signed is called a *knasmol,* "a penalty banquet"; the engaged couple is described as *farknast,* "subject to a penalty"; and breaking the plates is sometimes called *knas leygn,* "laying down, stipulating a fine." The verb *derknasn,* which is based on all the goo-goo eyes that go into making an engagement, was criminal slang for "looking closely at something or someone, casing a joint." Jewish criminals might have been thieves, but they spent more time in *kheyder* than Jesus.

Knas is also the origin of the common German word, *Knast,* which has been the major colloquial term for prison since the beginning of the nineteenth century. Drawing on an older Western Yiddish use of *knas* in the sense of "punishment," the German criminals who introduced the word to their language simply applied it to the punishment that they underwent most often—imprisonment. The *'t'* at the end shows us that it was the verb *knasn* on which they were drawing: *Men knast im,* "he is being punished, sent to prison."

VI

Despite its necessity for full-fledged membership in mainstream Jewish society, the wedding ceremony—the *khasene*—has been curiously behindhand in the production of Yiddish idioms and turns of phrase. Most of what it has contributed has been inspired by the elaborate arrangements and concomitant trouble and strife that go into even the simplest wedding. So we get things like *makhn a gantse khasene,* "to make a whole wedding," to make a big deal out of something relatively insignificant. Notice the "whole"—it helps to convey the idea of preparation and worry, negotiation and deliberation out of all proportion to the matter at hand. You don't interview caterers when you feel like ordering a pizza. *Makhn a gantse khasene* is pretty much equivalent to *makhn a tsimmes;* there's been all kinds of pointless effort, all kinds of irrelevant extras tossed in.

Khasene makhn, "to make a wedding, to marry someone off"— *er makht khasene a tokhter,* "he's marrying off his daughter"—can also mean "to destroy," "to get rid of something forever." The idiom depends on a play on words based on the two very different meanings of *kale.* Alongside "engaged girl, fiancée, bride," there is another, unrelated *kale* that looks and sounds exactly the same and means "to be destroyed": *Es iz kale gevorn undzer hofenung,* "our hope has been destroyed." People who know a little Yiddish might be surprised to find out that the much better known *kalye*—"ruined, spoiled, out of order"—comes from this *kale* rather than from the *kalye* found in such Slavic-component words as *kalyeke,* "cripple."

The person who *makht khasene* a person or thing makes it *kale*—and there's the joke. As if this weren't enough, the plural of *kale*—bride—is *kales,* the same as the feminine plural of *kal,* the word that we saw as part of *kal va-khoymer,* an argument that proceeds from a minor premise to a major one. A *kal,* as defined by Alexander Harkavy, is a "loose fellow," a *kale* his female counterpart. Hence the slightly off-color saying, *ale meydlekh zenen kales,* which sounds like it means that they are all potential brides, but is really saying that they are "empty-headed females of questionable moral worth." I once ran across an all-girl klezmer band called *Di Kales* who thought they were "The Brides," but were hip enough to be happy that their younger Yiddish-speaking fans were flocking to see "The Silly Sluts."

If someone complains about *tantsn af tsvey khasenes (mit eyn por fis)*, "dancing at two weddings (with one pair of legs)," they're saying that they can't do two things or be in two places at once. You can talk about *tantsn af fremde khasenes*, "dancing at other people's weddings." This has less to do with party crashing than with devoting yourself to someone who isn't really anything to you, while ignoring your own nearest and dearest: "*Af fremde khasenes tantst er,* but to take his own boy to the father-son banquet, for this he has no time."

The match itself, couplehood as distinct from a wedding ceremony, is called a *ziveg*, which comes from a Hebrew verb meaning "to match, mate." You can talk about your own *ziveg*, though you usually use it—either very formally or somewhat prissily—to refer to someone else's husband or wife. *Dos iz mayn ziveg* is similar to "This is my spouse." Were there a politically correct Yiddish, *ziveg* would be enjoying new life among people who refer to their legal or common-law spouses as "partners." Unlike *khosn-kale* or *man un vayb*, it would also work for same-sex couples.

Ziveg rishon and *ziveg sheyni* refer, respectively, to first and second marriages, while *ziveg min-a-shomayim* has exactly the meaning of its literal translation, "a match made in heaven." A *dybbuk min-a-shomayim*, "a heaven-sent dybbuk," takes the underlying idea of inseparability to an absurd new length: a bad marriage can be dissolved by a *get*, a divorce; a dybbuk isn't quite as easy to get rid of.

A successful *ziveg* is said to be *oyle yofe*, "to go off well, turn out successfully," but Yiddish being Yiddish, *oyle yofe zayn* tends as often as not to be used ironically. A bankrupt business partnership could be described by the expression "*der ziveg hot oyle yofe geven,* the match was a success—they were broke inside of six months." This use of *oyle yofe zayn* can be compared with *tsvey meysim geyen tantsn*, "two corpses go dancing," a phrase used when two failures decide to embark on any kind of joint venture. If you can't get a date for the prom and spend the night in McDonald's with your equally dateless roommate, you could describe the evening's activity as *tsvey meysim geyen tantsn.*

VII

We've already mentioned the *mitsves* to be performed by married women. The main visible change that marriage brings to a man is the *tallis* or prayer shawl. Indeed, the *tallis* was considered the sign par excellence of Jewish burgherhood, so much so that the phrase *vifl taleysim zenen do bay aykh,* "How many *tallises* are there by you," means "How many Jewish families are there in your community?" In virtually all Eastern European communities and among most Orthodox Jews today, the *tallis* is worn only after marriage. An unmarried male wears one only to go up to the Torah or lead prayers, and you can imagine the stigma attached to not wearing one after a certain age. The *bokher's* lack of social standing is evident to all; he counts for a minyen, but not as a *mentsh.*

There are a couple of explanations for this custom. The first is found in the Talmud (*Kiddushin* 29b), where one rabbi asks another why his head isn't covered with a shawl—which, according to Rashi, was the way of married men at the time. The rabbi replies that he isn't married. The commentators all interpret "shawl" as "prayer shawl" and take the question to mean, "Why isn't your head covered with a *tallis?*" Similarly, the fifteenth-century scholar Maharil, one of the most influential figures in Ashkenazic Judaism, points out that the commandment, "You shall make fringes for yourselves" is followed immediately by the proto–Percy Sledge verse, "If a man marries a woman" (Deut. 22:12–13); the proximity is taken as significant, the fringes understood as having something to do with being married.

One of the sweeter customs at a traditional wedding is to use the *tallis* that the groom is about to start wearing as the *khupe*, the canopy, beneath which he and his *kale* are united. The *khupe* is so closely identified with the idea of marriage that it has come to represent the whole ceremony. We've already seen how the guests at a *bris* wish for the baby to enter the *khupe; khupe ve-kiddushin*, "canopy and consecration of one person to another," is a standard rabbinic term for a wedding; and *shteln a khupe*, "to put up a canopy," means to hold a wedding, while *shteln a khupe mit* somebody means simply to marry them (the subject of this idiom is always male).

VIII

Immediately after the wedding, the *khosn* and *kale* become *man un vayb*, man and wife. Yiddish terms for married couples tend to be determined by age. A young couple is a *porl*, a cute "little couple." As the *porl* ages it loses its diminutive *'l'* and becomes just a *por*, "a couple," plain and simple. An older couple is a *porfolk*.

Yiddish has a number of unusual ways of referring to the members of these couples, not all of them as insulting as they might seem at first glance. *Mayn alter* or *mayn alte*, and the even more demonstrative *mayn altitshker* or *altitshke*, are close to the English "my old man, my old lady," but are considerably more affectionate. While "old" can convey the same sense of closeness and affectionate involvement in Yiddish as it does in English (think of such phrases as "good ol' what's-his-name"), there's more to the Yiddish than simple affection. If you recall, one of the extramedical remedies for childhood illnesses was to give the sick child a new name, and that name was often Alter, "old person." Something similar is taking place here. To call your husband or wife old is to give them a sort of surreptitious blessing that they should live a long time—it's a means of trying to trick the Angel of Death into ignoring them. You used to hear people barely into their twenties talking about their *alter*–it's a way of diverting demonic attention from your spouse, of saying "my husband, he should live and be well," in a slightly more amusing way.

This kind of undercover blessing reaches a climax of sorts in a couple of now-archaic ways of referring to one's wife. These are *tsiherste*, "are you listening?" and *her nor*, "listen up," usually pronounced *heno* in Polish Yiddish. Both mean "wife." *Her nor* is a pretty common attention-getting formula—there's a well-known folk song that begins, "*Her nor du sheyn meydele*, Listen up, pretty girl," but that doesn't explain why Yehuda Leib Zlotnick, a prominent rabbi and folklorist who lived until 1962, claims to have thought that his mother's name was Heno until she got sick and his father had a blessing made for her in the synagogue—Zlotnick had never heard her addressed as anything else. There is an old antireligious joke that makes the same point; *Bay di khsidim hot a froy nisht ken eygenem nomen*, "Among Hasidim, a woman has no name of her own"; *ale heysn zey heno*, "they're all called *Heno*."

Heno was not meant to be as crudely insulting as it looks to us. It's against Jewish law to call your parents or teachers by their first names, and this sign of respect is often extended well beyond these two legally mandated categories, as with *mekhutonim* who address each other as *mekhutn* or *mekhuteneste* rather than by name. Real Yiddish politeness involves talking to people in the third person. If you're invited to the house of someone whom you don't really know, they'll refer to you as *der gast*, "the guest," when talking to you. "*Tsi vil der gast a gloz tey*, would the guest care for a cup of tea?" Although you address your parents as *du*, the familiar form of the second-person pronoun, you call a rabbi *der rov*, "the rabbi," even when it's he to whom you're speaking. Likewise with all clergy, social superiors, certain relatives (aunts and uncles, for instance) whom you might not see very often, relatives with whom you've had a falling-out and are now trying to make up, and the general run of strangers on the street, most of whom you'll address as *der yid*, as long as they're men.

This tendency to use third-person grammatical forms as a sign of respect and reverence is taken a step further on the basis of a Talmudic statement attributed to Rabbi Yosi: "I never referred to my wife as 'my wife' or to my ox as 'my ox.' I called my wife 'my house' and my ox 'my field'" (*Shabbos* 118b). It's half the Yiddish mind-set in less than two little lines, and anticipates modern linguistic theory by nearly two thousand years. The explanation is that his wife was the foundation and mainstay of his house, just as his ox was of his livelihood. Of course, the same Rabbi Yosi goes on to say that he had never looked at his penis in his life, but that doesn't affect the basic point—referring to his wife as an inanimate object was a way of showing respect for her.

This idea was picked up by the same Maharil mentioned above in connection with *taleysim*. On the basis of Rabbi Yosi's statement, he began to refer to his wife by the already current term *hausfrau*, "housewife," a word that combines both sides of Rabbi Yosi's equation, and to address her as *hert ir nisht* ("don't you hear?"), a form of address that he used, according to the incredibly important and influential *Minhagey Ha-Maharil* (*The Customs of the Maharil*), "In accordance with the established custom by which couples do not use their names when speaking to each other, so that when the Maharil was speaking to her, he honored her with his words as if he were addressing a multitude."

By avoiding his wife's name and addressing her in the plural, the Maharil—in his own mind, at least—was putting her just slightly behind his parents and teachers, people who occupy the highest rung of respect. Something that appears to us as prima facie evidence of the worst sort of contempt was, in fact, intended as prima facie evidence of reverence and respect. Once the aspect of addressing a multitude started to sound "wrong" because you shouldn't address your wife with the formal pronoun, *hert ir nisht* was transposed into the affectionate singular form and modernized as *tsiherste. Her nor* is just another way of saying the same thing.

This is what people mean when they talk about a lost world—it might not be to our taste, but the people who used such expressions understood what they wanted to say, and it isn't always fair to fault them for our own incomprehension.

Along with *tsiherste* and *heno,* there are other, less ambiguous terms of approbation that might not correspond any more closely with our own ideals. The blue ribbon of female Jewish domesticity is the state of *berye*-hood. A *berye* (not to be confused with Joseph Stalin's homophonous henchman) is the housewife par excellence, the living Yiddish translation of the Peggy Lee hit "I'm a Woman." She cooks, she cleans, she looks after the kids, and has plenty of *koyekh,* plenty of strength, left for lovin', once she's come back from the *mikve.*

The basic Yiddish meaning of *berye* is "someone who is skilled or efficient at any particular activity": *Khanele iz a berye af oysleygn* means that Annie's a real dickens of a speller. Unencumbered by any qualification, however, *berye* means a *gute baleboste,* "a good housewife." *Baleboste* can also mean "female proprietor, woman boss, landlady, hostess," or, in effect, any woman with the power to affect the immediate destiny of someone not part of her immediate family. The feminine form of *balebos*—"a householder, proprietor or boss"—*baleboste* loses nothing by the addition of the feminine suffix. By virtue of her position, she can be said to *trogn di hoyzn,* "to wear the pants," or even the *tsitsis,* the four-cornered fringed ritual undergarment traditionally worn only by men.

Even higher than the *berye* stands the *eyshes khayel,* the woman of valor (from Prov. 31:10–31, recited at every Sabbath dinner). The *eyshes khayel* is more than a mere helpmeet or playmate; she's her husband's very backbone, his mainstay and support, often in the basest pecuniary sense. The verb *eyshes khayelen,* "to act like an *eyshes khayel,*" means to be a businesswoman, quite often the sole support of the family. Less seriously, a strapping, somewhat forbidding woman—a combination of the *gezunt shtik,* "the healthy hunk," and the *zoyere vetshere,* "the sour supper"—is often referred to as an *eyshes khayel*—an Amazon—just as the wife of this year's annual dinner-award honoree is usually acknowledged in a codicil as "his devoted *eyshes khayel.*"

If all this praise goes to the *eyshes khayel*'s head, she might well begin to *goydern zikh,* "to affect a double chin when she doesn't really have one"—to assume the airs of a social station far above the one to which she belongs. This expression harks back to a time when the double chin was considered a sign of beauty, breeding, and prosperity, and men wore their paunches with pride. To say that a woman *goydert zikh* is to convict her of terminal pretentiousness, of condescension to her equals and a fawning attitude to her social superiors. She's Margaret Dumont in a Marx Brothers movie. In extreme cases, she'll even be called *di gotikhe,* "Mrs. God," and her unfortunate domestic servants will probably refer to her—behind her back, of course—as *di madamenyu.*

The *gotikhe* undoubtedly aspires to be known as a *tsadeykes,* "a saint," despite the fact that this latter term, when not being used ironically, isn't thrown around lightly with respect to the living. The *tsadeykes* has all the virtues of the male *tsaddik*—"the righteous man," humble and God-fearing—and probably does windows, too.

The *fausse-tsadeykes,* the female *khnyok* ("sanctimonious religious hypocrite") is known as a *tsitsis shpinern,* "a spinner of ritual fringes." She's *gots straptshe,* "the Lord's district attorney"; she knows what everyone else does wrong.

These designations reflect the mores of an entire society and should not be confused with referring to women in ways that demonstrate real fear and contempt. In some extremely religious communities, it is considered demeaning for a scholar—which means any adult male—even to speak of such a thing as his wife, who serves as a reminder of life below the waist. Certain types of Hasidim do not mention their wives (let alone those of others) in conversation. If you want to talk about your wife, you refer to her as *men* (there's no pun in Yiddish), the impersonal pronoun, similar to the English "one." "*Vos makht men bay dir in shtub?* How's everyone at home?" actually means "How's your wife?" "*Men arbet?* Somebody's working?" equals "Does your wife have a job?"

Zlotnick tells the story of someone who came into a Hasidic synagogue with a message from someone else's wife. The messenger went up to the woman's husband and announced that he had a message from . . . *ayer shvers tokhter,* "your father-in-law's daughter." *Eyshes khayel* and *baleboste* reflect a particular view of family life; *ayer shvers tokhter* is in desperate need of therapy.

TWELVE

Too Good for the Goyim:

SEX IN YIDDISH

I

Ever since comedians like Lenny Bruce realized that words like *shmuk, puts, shlong,* and *shvants* meant absolutely nothing to the goyim in Standards and Practices, Yiddish has been the preferred vehicle for smuggling dirty words past showbiz censors, especially words that mean "penis." Even though these words are as dirty or offensive in their original context as "cock" or "prick" are in English, most non-Yiddish-speakers know them only as innocuous stand-ins for unacceptable English. Still, much of the material in this chapter is as unacceptable as "slut hammer," as powerful as "motherfucker" when "motherfucker" couldn't appear in mainstream print. The basic rule for using them in Yiddish can be summed up as: "no fuck, no *shmuk.*" If you can't get away with saying "fuck" in English, you won't get away with saying *"shmuk"* or *"puts"* in Yiddish. We're looking at a culture in which circumcision is the *only* indispensable ritual, a religion that defines male membership by the state of the male member in the second week of life. Dick jokes are vulgar in any culture, but the Yiddish use of terms for the penis as insults or curses is as close as the language comes to conventionalized blasphemy of the "Jesus H. Christ" type.

Since every Jewish *shmuk* bears witness to its owner's relationship with God, not all the words for it are dirty. *Penis* (rhymes with Dennis) is sometimes encountered in journalism, belles lettres, and books on biology. It is rarely heard in conversation, where the standard polite term for the male member is *eyver,* a word that can also be used for any limb or member of the body. Most people have four *eyvrim,* two arms and two legs, and just as arms and legs can be called "members" in English, so *eyver* means penis only when context makes it plain that it is this *eyver* and not any of the others that is meant. If someone gives voice to the popular kvetch, *"Se tut mir vey yeder eyver,"* loosely, "Every bone in my body aches," nobody thinks that he's talking smut. If, however, the same man goes to the doctor and complains of a burning sensation in his *eyver* while passing water, the doctor isn't going to look at his forearm.

Less formal than *eyver* but just as respectable, the equally Hebraic *mile* smacks less of the textbook and more of the Torah. A *mile*—as in *bris mile*—is a circumcision, and its use for the entire *eyver* is a fine example of using a part of something to represent the whole; it tends to be the preferred term among religious people who need to mention such things.

Bokher and *yung* both mean "youth, young fellow" and occupy roughly the same ground as Johnson, Peter, John Thomas, and other English terms for the penis that rely on proper names. Like the English names, *bokher* and *yung* convey a good-natured vulgarity that stops well short of actual obscenity, as does *kleyner,* "the little fella," who is probably better translated as "Junior." *Der kleyner iz on beyner,* "Junior has no bones," *nor ale beyner kumen fun im aroys,* "but all bones come out of him." *Der kleyner Yankl shtelt zikh oyf,* "little Yankl is standing up," means that Yankl's owner is getting a boner.

None of the terms listed thus far can be used as an insult. You can't call someone whom you don't like an *eyver* and expect him to be upset; if you call him a *bokher,* it's because he's never been married. Things are different with *shvants, veydl,* and *zonef,* three words that all share a primary meaning of "tail." *Shvants* and *veydl* are both Germanic. In German, *Schwanz* means "tail" or "prick," while *Wedel* is a feather duster or an animal's tail. The Yiddish *shvants* is a "cock" or "prick"; applied to a person, it has the same general range as the English "asshole," "dick," or "jerk," but is somewhat more offensive. *Veydl,* which is rarely used of anything *but* people (and animal tails) these days, is a favorite of Yiddish-speaking drivers: the guy who cuts you off because he doesn't notice that you're there is a *veydl,* the one who does it to spite you is a *shvants* (*puts* is also acceptable in such circumstances). *Zonef,* from the Hebrew, also means "tail," "penis," or "jerk." Its relative rarity makes it all the more effective when you use it.

A cuter designation for both the male sex organ or a male you don't like is *vayzuse,* after Haman's youngest son. The great Yiddish poet, Itsik Manger, named the editor in his *Megile Lider* (poems based on the story of Esther) Vayzuse; the creators of the cartoon show *King of the Hill* invented a con-man called Robert Vayzose (*litvish* for Vayzuse). When *vayzuse* is used to mean penis it's a little cutesy, rather like "ding-a-ling" in English; when used of a person, it's vulgar but not obscene, and puts more emphasis on folly or stupidity than *shmuk* and *puts* do.

Neither *shmuk* nor *puts* means anything but "penis" or "jerk." Even a word like *shlong* (*shlang* in most dialects of actual Yiddish) has a respectable meaning of "snake" and is only applied to a person whom you wish to characterize as such. *Shmuk* and *puts* start out meaning "penis" and never advance beyond "unlikable male." The degree of unlikability reaches from "jerk" to "cocksucker" (without the gay-bashing subtext), and both words are considerably more offensive in Yiddish than their frequent use in

English-language media would suggest. Neither is the sort of word you'd use in front of your parents.

Shmuk is related to such well-known Yiddishisms as "Grand Canyon, Shmand Canyon" and "football, shmootball," in which the *shm-* prefix is used to cut something down to size; it has nothing to do with *Schmuck,* the German word for jewelry or decoration. *Shmuk* is a dialect pronunciation of the standard language *shmok,* a word that seems to have been extracted from *shtekele,* "little stick," after *shtekele* became *shmekele* (as in *"shtekele, shmekele"*) in the mouths of boys who wanted to refer to their childish members. Like *petsl* and *petsele,* which come from *puts, shmekl* and *shmekele* start out as baby talk and are equivalent to "pee-wee" or "weenie" in English. But where the *shm-* prefix makes diminutives like *shmekl* and *shmekele* cute and harmless, it turns *shtok*—the full-sized form, an obsolete word for what Yiddish now calls a *shtekn,* "a stick, a walking stick, a club"—into the obscene *shmuk.*

Puts (rhymes with "nuts") has absolutely nothing to do with the German (or Yiddish) *putsn* (where the *puts* rhymes with "toots" in Tootsie Roll), to "clean or shine." The root of the word can be found in the standard medical term for the one thing that a circumcised Jewish *puts* never has: *puts* is basically the "puce" in the English "prepuce," which comes from the Latin *praeputium,* something which is *prae,* "before" or "in front of," the *putium.* In spoken and ecclesiastical Latin, *putium* is pronounced "pootsium" and comes from the same Indo-European root as *puts: put,* "swelling," which has been transferred to the thing that swells.

The basic differences between a *shmuk* and a *puts*—since people are always asking—are pliability and location. You can call someone a "poor *shmuk,*" even feel like a *shmuk* yourself; a *puts* is vicious and always someone else—he's a *shmuk* on Viagra.

In order to call someone a *shmuk* without actually saying the word, people make jocular use of phrases in which the first letter of each word spells out what they really mean: *SHabbes Mikro Koydesh,* "the Sabbath, a holy convocation." The Sabbath isn't demeaned in such a context; the *shmuk* ends up looking worse by being linked to something so utterly unshmuklike. People will also call him a *SHmuel Mordkhe Kalman,* three common first names, or drop the pretence and just spell the word in Hebrew—*SHin Mem Kuf.* You can spell *puts* as well—its constituent letters, *Pey TSadek,* follow each other in the Hebrew alphabet, like *p* and *q* in English.

Perhaps the greatest slang term for penis is the no-longer-as-common-as-it-used-to-be *khalemoyed.* From the Hebrew *khol ha-mo'ed, khalemoyed* is the name for the intermediate days of Passover and Tabernacles. Both of these holidays have two days of official festival at either end, with four intermediate days called *khalemoyed,* "the profane part of the appointed time," that function as semiholidays in between: schools are closed, but driving and watching television are permitted. In the Middle Ages, you could have lit a fire or taken a donkey ride.

As a humorous term for penis, *khalemoyed* is used primarily in a couple of fairly well defined contexts. *Vos geystu mitn khalemoyed in droysn,* "Why are you going around with your *khalemoyed,* 'your intermediate days of Passover and Sukkes,' outside," means: "Your fly is open." But if you say, "And there I was, *mitn khalemoyed in droysn,*" or *"mitn khalemoyed in der hant,"* it's the same as the English "with my dick in my hand": caught short, unprepared, possibly left as the patsy and always looking like a *shmuk.*

Why *khalemoyed,* though? What does the downtime of major religious holidays have to do with male members? Passover and Tabernacles were once pilgrim festivals on which every male in Israel made his way to the Temple in Jerusalem. The Hebrew term for such festivals is *regel,* a word that also means "leg," and popular humor holds that a penis is like *khalemoyed* because it, too, is found *beyn regel le-regel,* "between two festivals," but with a pun here on the more common meaning of *regel,* "between two legs."

Cute as this is, it's a lovely *bubbe-mayse* that isn't really true. *Khalemoyed* moves into penile territory thanks to the Slavic *holomud,* which sounds similar and has a basic meaning of "exposed testicles, balls hanging out." From there it's but a hop, skip, and a jump to the pun on *regel* and the penis. Just think: if Faulkner had written *Light in August* in Yiddish, Joe Christmas might well have been called *Yosl Khalemoyed.*

II

While words like *shmuk, puts, mile,* and *eyver* are used all the time in day-to-day Yiddish, most Yiddish speakers are deeply uncomfortable with even the most polite terms for female genitalia. Traditional Judaism devotes considerable attention to the female sex organs; the rules of family purity give rise to a way of life in which women spend an inordinate amount of time looking out for flux. Indeed, what goes on "down there" is so important to Jewish life that newly established communities are enjoined to set up a *mikve* even before they build a synagogue.

Important as the *mikve* is, though, what goes on there is strictly between a woman and the *mikve* lady, the *tukern* or "dunker," who supervises the immersion and is Yiddish folklore's version of the gossipy hairdresser. Women go to the *mikve* only after dark, and are not supposed to mention that they're going; a woman's trip to the *mikve* is supposed to presage a night of love, and it is considered unseemly to speak of such things. Indeed, the Orthodox version of Freud's primal scene doesn't get as far as walking in on your copulating parents; the *Jewish* version has a married woman run into her mother at the *mikve*. Knowing why her mother is there and knowing that her mother knows why she is there can prove just as traumatic as the Freudian scene.

Such notions of modesty have helped to maintain a centuries-long tradition of reticence. Where a Yiddish-speaking gynecologist might refer to a patient's *vagine* (with a hard *g*) or *mutersheyd*, both of which mean "vagina," the patient herself would be more likely to complain of problems *dortn*, "there," without ever actually naming the site. This reticence was reinforced by the principle known as *khukos-ha-goyim*, "the laws of the gentiles," which helped to keep certain types of curse out of a purely Yiddish linguistic milieu (i.e., if you used these curses at all, you used them in their original language—Polish, Ukrainian, and so on—and did not translate them into Yiddish). The idea of *khukos-ha-goyim* is derived from Leviticus 18:3: "And you shall not walk in their statutes." As Rashi says: "These are the mores that they have legislated for themselves, such as their theaters and [gladiatorial] arenas." More practically, it means that if we have to do something that gentiles also do, we're supposed to do it differently. If their hats have narrow brims, our brims will be wide. If they like the Beatles, we prefer the Dave Clark Five. If their curses and insults focus on mothers and their body parts, then ours won't mention mothers and their organs at all. You can't call a person a "cunt" in Yiddish; words with that meaning refer only to body parts. The Yiddish equivalent, for a woman at least, is *klafte*, which has a literal meaning of "bitch"; the anatomical terms wouldn't make any sense.

Avoidance of such terminology goes back at least as far as the rabbinic period and is crystallized in the single most refined Yiddish term for the female pudenda, a Talmudic phrase that would have reached most women by means of oral and written instruction in the laws of family purity. *Oyse mokem*, literally "that spot, that place," means "the you-know-where." Unlike *mile*, its male counterpart, this term is so refined that it never lets you know what it's talking about. The same construction— *oyse* (which means "that") plus a following noun—appears in another phrase used to denote something unmentionable: *oyse ho-ish*, "that man, Mr. You-Know-Who," as polite a designation for Jesus as Yiddish will ever allow. The *oyse* lets you know that the following noun really means what you thought it might mean, as in this quotation from the *Kitser Shulkhan Orukh:* "It is forbidden [for a man] to look at *oyse mokem*, for whoever does so has no shame and violates the laws of modesty and lacks all compunction."

Oyse mokem would never normally be used in conversation, where the more common colloquial terms for vagina are metaphorical extensions of otherwise innocuous words—faux euphemisms, if you will—and are all considered fairly dirty. *Shpil* usually means "game, show, play" and a *zakh* is a "thing." Used in this context, they're similar to the English "ring-dang-do" and "thing-a-ma-bob" or "thingy." These are pretty crude, as is *yene mayse*, "that story, that act." *Yene* acts as a translation of the Hebrew *oyse* here, and *mayse* has a number of extended senses, ranging from "situation" (*a sheyne mayse*, "another fine mess") to "death" (*zikh onton a mayse*, "commit suicide," where *mayse* stands in for *mise*, "death"). Here, it provides many opportunities for jokes based on the very common idiom, *gekhapt in der mayse*, "caught in the act"; once that which has been *gekhapt* is conceived as a penis, everything else falls right into place.

A *pirge*, a "perogie," is probably the term that you're most likely to hear, either as strict description or else in such phrases as *der kleyner lekhtst nokh a shtikl pirge*, "Junior's dying for a little meat pie." *Pirge* has the same semantic feel as "pussy" does in contemporary English.

III

Moving from one *mayse* to the next, we come to the act itself. As the sole means of fulfilling the Torah's *mitsve* of "be fruitful and multiply," *tashmish ha-mite*, "use of the bed," is considered both pleasant and meritorious when performed in accordance with the rules. Although the *mitsve* of *pru-urvu*, "increase and multiply," is incumbent only upon men, a woman and her *mayse* are considered bottomless wells of desire, and a man is obliged to yield his wife her *oyne*, her "conjugal rights," even though he'd theoretically prefer to be studying Torah. As a religious duty, the payment of conjugal rights has been codified and quantified; a man has to give his wife her due as often as the rigors of his occupation permit:

> Men of strong constitution who enjoy the pleasures of life, who have profitable pursuits at home and are tax exempt, should perform their duty nightly. Laborers employed in the city where they live should perform their marital duty twice weekly, once a week if they're employed in another city. Merchants who travel into villages on donkeys . . . and other such people should perform their marital duty once a week. Those who convey baggage on camels from distant places should have an appointed time every thirty days. [The Mishna adds: Sailors should have an appointed time once in every six months.] The time for scholars is from Sabbath to Sabbath. . . . One should not deprive [his wife] of her rights unless by her consent, and only after he has fulfilled the duty of propagation [*Shulkhan Orukh, Orekh Khayim* 240:1; see also *Kesubos* 61b].

If Congress would only pass a bill obliging all those rich people who don't pay taxes to prove that they "perform their duty nightly," we might be able to raise some money for schools and medical care. Note the statement toward the end about scholars. This is the origin of the *shabbes* sex mentioned earlier: every man is treated as if he were a scholar, an honor that the non-scholar receives on only one other occasion—his wedding. Every *khosn*—every bridegroom—was supposed to give a *droshe,* a speech on some aspect of Torah. Though everybody knew that these were often written by someone else, the fiction has been maintained to such a degree that wedding presents per se are still not given at traditional weddings—it would be like giving you a prize for fulfilling God's *mitsves.* Instead, the *khosn* receives *droshe-geshank,* "*droshe* presents," rewards—payment, as it were—for the Torah that the guests have learned from his speech.

Once the speech has been made, once a week is the minimum expected of a man who comes home from work every night. Like all the numbers quoted above, this minimum applies only to such times as his wife is "clean," about two weeks a month. Still, once a woman is clean, she's clean; and so is anything that a couple might want to do together (so long as the flow of sperm to egg is not impeded; condoms, for example, are strictly forbidden, as is fellatio to the point of orgasm). Just look what happens when someone tries to say otherwise:

Rabbi Yoykhanon ben Dahabai said: The ministering angels said four things to me:

Why are children born lame?

Because their parents overturned their table [had sex with the woman on top].

Mute?

Because the man kissed *oyse mokem.*

Deaf?

Because they talked while doing it.

Blind?

Because the man looked at *oyse mokem*. . . .

Rabbi Yoykhanon [this is a different Yoykhanon] said: That's what Yoykhanon ben Dahabai says, but the sages say that the law does not follow the view of Yoykhanon ben Dahabai. A man can do whatever he wants with his wife. Sex with your wife can be compared with meat from the butcher. If you want it salted, you salt it; roasted, you roast it; boiled, you boil it; fried, you fry it.

And the same goes for fish (*Nedorim* 20 a–b).

It's a rare argument that is so forcefully resolved or that ends with a mention of fish. So why, then, are women so dissatisfied? Why are they presented as constantly horny? A passage from the Talmud concerning the duration of the sex act might help to clear the matter up:

How long does the sex act last?

Rabbi Yishmoel said: As long as it takes to go around a palm tree.

Rabbi Eliezer said: As long as it takes to mix water with a glass of wine.

Rabbi Yehoshua said: As long as it takes to drink a glass of wine.

Ben Azzai said: As long as it takes to fry an egg.

Rabbi Akiva: As long as it takes to swallow an egg.

Rabbi Yehoshua ben Beseyre said: As long as it takes to swallow three eggs in rapid succession.

Rabbi Elazar ben Yirmiye said: As long as it takes to knot a thread.

Hanin ben Pinkhas said: As long as it takes a woman to take a toothpick out of her mouth.

Plemo said: As long as it takes a woman to stretch her hand out and take a bread out of a basket.

And Rashi adds: Each one gives the time that it took him (*Yevomos* 63b).

Pity the wives of these canonical wisenheimers. "Take a toothpick out of her mouth" indeed! It would have been nice if they'd known that the toothpick was in.

The most common vulgarism for intercourse is probably *trenen,* which dictionaries usually define as "to rip," as in ripping a seam, spreading two pieces of cloth apart and separating them from each other. There's a saying about the penis: *a shtumpik meser un trent fort dem vaybershn pelts,* "a dull knife, but it still *trens* the female fur"—that's the kind of "rip" that's meant. *Trenen* is equivalent to the English "screw," vulgar rather than horribly obscene. A mother fighting with a daughter whom she, the mother, considers too "easy," might wonder when her daughter will start *trenen* the boys whom she's dating. Like "screw," *trenen* can be used with male or female subjects; a woman *trent mit*—with—a man; a man *trent* a woman, without any preposition

The much dirtier *yentsn,* "to fuck," far exceeds *trenen* in frequency of use, largely because *yentsn* has been extended to mean "fuck" or "screw" in a nonsexual sense, while *trenen* is restricted to actual intercourse.

Yentsn is a made-up word, invented as a meaningless stand-in for offensive *real* words. *Yentsn* is a verbal form of the pronoun *yents,* which means "that," "the other." Translated very literally, *yentsn* would mean "to that," if "that" were a verb. You can talk about *yents kind* or *yents bukh,* "that child" or "that book" (as distinct from this one), and *yentsn* originally meant "to do *that* thing which I shall refrain from naming, to you-know-what" (compare the substitution of "do" for both "fuck" and "kill" in contemporary English); it now means nothing but "fuck" and, euphemistic as it might once have been, is definitely the y-word of the Yiddish-speaking world. These days, it's used almost exclusively as a metaphor—"I bought a car from that guy and got *yentsed*"—with other words doing duty for the actual sex act.

Dosn (usually pronounced *dusn*, to rhyme with "loosen") comes from the demonstrative pronoun *dos* (pronounced *dus* in some dialects)—"the, this"—and went through a similar "dirtying" process, eventually coming to mean "to shit." Something said to be *dusik*, "this-y," in Yiddish, would be described as "slightly fucked up" in English.

The Yiddish sex word most often used in English is *shtupen*, which is a little closer to "screw" than to "fuck." *Shtupen*, again, is a dialect pronunciation of the *klal-shprakh* word *shtopen*. Its "clean" meanings are "to fill, stuff, fatten up [as with a turkey before Thanksgiving]." *Farshtopt*, the past participle with the prefix *far*, means "constipated," all stuffed up with what ain't coming out. The basic image of *shtupen* a woman is of filling her *pirge* with your juicy sausage.

IV

Chapter Eleven dealt primarily with traditional forms of courtship and marriage. It is now time to have a look at lust and sexual obsession, and there's no better place to start than with the ne plus ultra of can't-live-without-you Yiddish passion, a devotion so intense that one-half of a couple will even *nokhgebn di shmad* of their beloved, "put up with their conversion to Christianity."

This is a mildly humorous way of saying "Put up with anything," despite the fact that *shmad*, "conversion to another religion" (usually Christianity), is one of the most heavily laden words in Yiddish. In a language in which the word for "Jew" is often used to mean "person," there can be no graver insult than *meshumad*—someone who has committed *shmad*, gone over to the enemy and voluntarily relinquished his hold on humanity.

Nokhgebn di shmad, putting up with someone's conversion, means exactly what it says: they could convert to Christianity— change species, as it were—and you'd still stand by them. You'd put up with it, but you wouldn't convert. You'd let them get away with murder. And just as "get away with murder" rarely has anything to do with killing, so *nokhgebn di shmad* has nothing to do with actual apostasy. In idiomatic Yiddish, *shmad* also comes to stand for a certain type of *chutzpah: shmad-shtik* are the "clever tricks" and "wild pranks" played by a *shmad-kop*, "an apostasy head, a cunning blade." His shtik is "totally out there" and crosses all bounds, as remote from day-to-day shtik as ceasing to be Jewish is from day-to-day sinning. Odysseus, for instance, was pulling *shmad-shtik* when he told the Cyclops that his name was Nobody, but Jackie Kennedy was willing to *nokhgebn* J.F.K *di shmad*.

People who *tsien zikh vi tsu an aveyre*, "are drawn to each other as if to a sin," will often *tsufaln* or *tsukhapn zikh vi tsu heyse lokshn*, "fall on or throw themselves at each other as if at hot *lokshn*": "They eyed each other hungrily, a pair of drooling noodles, each with a mind of its own." Each is the other's *gelibte* (feminine) or *gelibter* (masculine)—their lover; their *frayndin* (feminine) or *fraynd*, their "friend"—the quotation marks give the word "friend" the proper tone here; each is the other's *khaver* (masculine) or *khaverte* (feminine), "friend" once again, and again in quotation marks to indicate the sexual relationship—*khaver* can also mean "member of an organization" and even "comrade" in the Communist Party sense.

Whenever two comrades decide to live together without being married, they enter one of the more interesting areas of contemporary non-Hasidic Yiddish: devising appropriate terms for dealing with such a situation. As soon as the news gets out, the woman's older relatives all nod sagely and whisper that they'd always suspected that the girl *shpint nisht ken tsitsis dortn,* "isn't spinning [i.e., knitting, weaving] any *tsitsis* there"; she's leading a less than virtuous life. As recently as a few years ago, *zi shpint nisht ken tsitsis dortn* was a favorite of adult relatives of girls who'd "gone bohemian" in college (especially when the parents and the college were in different cities), and were alleged to be living *vi got in frankraykh,* "like God in France," or, as my mother used to say, *vi um shabbes in holevud,* "like it was *shabbes* in Hollywood."

Back in the days when bohemianism was synonymous with long hair on boys, the girl's parents might have called him a *bitl.* The Beatles's contribution to certain areas of modern Yiddish has never been properly acknowledged or appreciated. Among people who speak English with a Yiddish accent, Beatle and the Yiddish word *bitl* are virtually indistinguishable. *Bitl* means "contempt, scorn"; *kukn mit bitl* is "to look down on, dismiss." In some combinations, *bitl* also means "waste, squandering." So, *bitl zman* is "a waste of time," *bitl toyre,* "a waste of [time better spent learning] Torah." *Er iz a bitl,* "he's a *bitl*/Beatle," could mean so many different things, none of them very nice. And let's not forget that *bitl* can also mean bathtub, the thing that hippies were supposed to sleep in.

The best way I've heard of referring to a "significant other" with whom you might be cohabiting but to whom you are certainly not married is as a *freg-nisht* or *freg-nisht-tse.* The former is a male, the latter female; the phrase is used by the *mekhutonim* manqués to describe the one who isn't their kid. *Freg nisht* means "don't ask"; turned into a noun, it takes on the sense of "the-name-and-character-of-the-person-in-question-so-disgust-me-that-I-can't-bring-myself-to-mention-him-or-her-by-name": "So tell me, Miss Educated-Home-from-College-Who-Has-No-Further-Use-for-

Morals, *vus makht der freg-nisht*, how's the don't-ask?" It means "lover," and were there a choice between two Yiddish translations of the same English novel, *Froy Chatterly's Gelibter* wouldn't stand a chance against *Froy Chatterly's Freg-Nisht*.

Parents can also avoid your lover's name by speaking of *vi heyst er/zi dortn*, "what's his/her name there"—"there" simply underlines the contempt. While *vi heyst er*, with or without the *dortn*, is perfectly legitimate in cases where someone's name really has slipped your mind, it can also be used as a way of showing how insignificant someone really is.

Your mother knows what you're doing—she's your mother, after all—and she can only hope that you guys are using some protection, preferably with rubber products, because God only knows where that *freg-nisht/freg-nisht-tse* of yours has been. The official Yiddish word for condom—the one you'd use in a Yiddish-language pharmacy—is *prezervativ;* less formally, it's a *kapote* or *kapotkele*. This seems ultimately to owe something to the French *capote*, properly, "little hood"; *capote anglaise*, the French version of a "French letter," is a condom, "an English hood." Among Jews, a *kapote* is the long coat still worn by Hasidic men, and the word has an unmistakably traditional resonance. Calling a condom a *kapote* is similar to calling it a tuxedo in English. It can also be called a *kupl*, "a little hat, a cap," i.e., a yarmulke. In some circles it is even known as a *frantsoyzishe yarmulke*, a French yarmulke, or even a *beret*, but back where I come from *frantsoyzishe yarmulke* meant that there were *tefillin* on the end. This sort of yarmulke was also known as a *kitsl-mitsl*, a "tickle cap," and we were convinced that non-Orthodox Jews refused to wear them.

THIRTEEN

It Should Happen to You:
DEATH IN YIDDISH

I

Trust classical Judaism to link sex and death in an entirely novel way two millennia before the development of psychoanalysis. The Talmudic description of the *malekh ha-moves*—the Angel of Death—occurs in the middle of a set of instructions on how to avoid getting an erection in public. We are told that a man should not look at any woman or her brightly colored clothing:

> And not at a male and female donkey, a male and female pig, or even at birds when they are copulating, even if he has as many eyes as the Angel of Death. They said about the Angel of Death that he is all full of eyes. When a sick person's hour has come, he [the Angel] stands over his head, his sword outstretched in his hand, with a drop of gall hanging down from it. When the sick person descries him, he trembles and opens his mouth [in order to scream in terror], and the Angel tosses the drop into his mouth. That's what he dies from, that's what he starts to stink from, that's what makes his face go sallow (*Avodo Zoro* 20b).

The proverbial way in which the Angel's eyes are mentioned— he sees everything and doesn't overlook any living being—makes it clear that the idea of his being "all full of eyes" was an established commonplace long before this passage was written down, long before it gave birth to the idiom *oysshteln a por oygn vi der malekh ha-moves*, "to stick out a pair of eyes like the Angel of Death, to stare without stopping," that we saw in Chapter Eleven. But the angel's eyes aren't the only aspect of this description to have entered the language. This passage is also the source of a far more common Yiddish idiom that no one would ever suspect of having anything to do with death. *Biterer tropn*, "the bitter drop," is a fine example of the way in which Yiddish—which can be unhappy about almost anything—can also be ironic about its unhappiness.

The drop of gall that is said to hang down from the Angel's sword is called *tipo shel moro* in Hebrew; the drop is *tipo*, *shel* is "of," and *moro* means "gall" or "bile." Widespread misreading of *moro* as an adjective instead of a noun led to the loss of *shel* in *tipo shel moro*; the resulting *tipo moro* is perfectly good Hebrew, but means "bitter drop" rather than "drop of gall or bile." "Bitter drop" translates into Yiddish as *biterer tropn*, which became a common idiom for whisky or booze; it's an informal and not unaffectionate term, rather like "the hard stuff" in English. *Er hot lib dem bitern tropn*, "he likes the bitter drop," is a polite way of characterizing a habitual tippler—he enjoys suckling at the sword of the Angel of Death. Bitter as the *tropn* might really be, the image rests on the resemblance between the typical attitude of the Eastern European drinker—head back, mouth wide open, face about to flush and change color—and that of a dead person under the sword of the *malekh ha-moves*.

Although most European cultures characterize whisky as aqua vitae, "the water of life," Yiddish—which loves a drink but hates a drinker—prefers *biterer tropn* to the equally ironic but far less frequent *mayim khayim*, "living water" (and, by analogy with aqua vitae, "water of life"). We're back in the land of *khukos ha-goyim*, "the laws of the gentiles," and days that start at night: if they call it life, we'll call it death but drink it all the same.

Drinking and staring aside, though, the *malekh ha-moves* himself is a little too scary, a little too serious, to figure directly in many idioms. On the rare occasions when he does appear, it's usually in curses that link love with death in no uncertain terms: *der malekh ha-moves zol zikh in dir farlibn*, "the Angel of Death should fall in love with you." He shouldn't only admire you from a distance; he shouldn't confine himself to sending chocolates and never taking any of his thousands of eyes off you. He should overcome any and all obstacles to get to you, then sweep you up in his loving arms and carry you off to his palace, where you'll live with him forever—which in this case really means "forever." And he'll never, ever look at anybody else, so that your death will mean eternal life for the rest of us, which is the least that an SOB like you owes to the rest of the world.

There is the even subtler *zolst mir khasene hobn mitn malekh ha-moveses tokhter*, "you should marry the daughter of the Angel of Death"; not only won't the fruit fall far from the tree, but she'll be sure to want her aged father to come live with you.

II

The Talmud tells us that:

> Nine hundred thirty kinds of death were created in the world. . . . The most difficult of all is diphtheria, the easiest of all is a kiss. Diphtheria is like a thorn pulled all the way through some woolen fleece or like stalks in your gullet. A kiss is as easy as drawing a hair out of milk (*Brokhos* 8a).

The kiss is known as *mise binishike* and is explained elsewhere in the Talmud:

> There were six over whom the Angel of Death held no sway: Abraham, Isaac and Jacob; Moses, Aaron and Miriam . . . [with respect to] Moses, Aaron and Miriam, it is written [Num. 33:38]: "By the mouth of God" (*Bovo Basro* 17a).

The biblical verse actually says, "And Aaron the priest went up Mount Hor at the command of the Lord and died there." The idiom for "at the command of the Lord" is *al pi ha-shem*, literally, "by the mouth of God." According to Rashi, this teaches us "that he died from a kiss," that is, *by the mouth* of God.

The "drawing a hair out of milk" with which the kiss is compared has inspired more than one kosher dairy restaurant and become a well-known Yiddish idiom, *gring vi a hor fun milkh*, "as easy as [drawing] a hair from milk." This image of the hair recurs in a later *medresh* that seems to have influenced subsequent folklore:

> When a person passes from this world, it isn't enough that he should be terrified of the Angel of Death, who's all full of eyes and has his sword unsheathed in his hand, but he is also asked by the Angel, "What, you didn't spend any time on Torah and philanthropy? You didn't pray to your Creator morning and night? You didn't counsel your fellows cheerfully?" If the person has done these things, the Angel tosses a drop into his mouth and his soul departs from him without any trouble, like a hair that is drawn out of some milk. And if he hasn't done them, his soul leaves his body like thorns that are torn out of wool (*Masekhes Khibut Ha-Kever* 4).

Gring vi a hor fun milkh is the Yiddish counterpart of "as easy as falling off a log" and is used to describe anything that's very easy to do. Note the difference between English and Yiddish here: while the English idiom speaks of something that requires no training or skill at all, the Yiddish idea of unsurpassable ease is based on the death of the righteous.

The conceptual opposite of the *mise binishike* is the *mise meshune,* the "strange death"—an unforeseen, unnatural, and usually violent death. You don't die a *mise meshune;* you don't succumb, it isn't visited upon you. No, you "take"—the verb is *aynnemen*—a violent death in the same way as you'd take a spoonful of castor oil. *Aynnemen* can mean to conquer or subdue, but it also means "to swallow, take in," in the sense of taking medicine. If you say that somebody *zol aynnemen a mise meshune,* "they should 'take' a strange death," it's as if the only cure for their existence is a suspension of the rules that normally apply to human life; they shouldn't just die, they should administer themselves an unexpected end.

Mise meshune also provides us with the phrase *mise meshune kolir,* "*mise-meshune* color," a strange, outlandish kind of color that could make you *aynnemen a mise meshune* just looking at it, or—according to some people—is the color of someone in the throes of a *mise meshune.* Though most authorities follow the former interpretation, my parents invoked both of them after noticing the Peter Max poster that appeared in my room one day in 1967.

III

The regular word for ordinary death is *shtarbn,* "to die"; it's related to the English "starve" (which originally had the same meaning and was limited to death from hunger only after the verb "die" was borrowed from Old Norse). Like "die," *shtarbn* is rather cold and colorless, and needs to be qualified if it's to carry any emotional weight. If you're a decent person, the very least you'd like to do is *shtarbn vi a yid*, "die like a Jew," with dignity and at a decent age, rather than *shtarbn in fremde takhrikhim*, "die in somebody else's shrouds," so mired in debt that even a decent death is beyond your means. *Shtarbn in fremde takhrikhim* is among the most baleful expressions in a language full of baleful expressions. *Shtarbn vi a yid*, on the other hand, refers to a death that becomes the deceased; the inevitable is accepted with composure and resignation, with the Shma on your lips if you should pass on while awake. There's nothing really wrong with you. Your time has simply come and you're *ibergegesn mit afikoymens*, you've "eaten too many *afikoymens*," and have died of nothing worse than old age. The *afikoymen* is the piece of matzoh with which the seder meal concludes; it's like describing the cause of death as "one too many Christmases" on a coroner's certificate.

A person can also be said to *shtarbn nokh* something—a drink of water, for instance—"to be dying" for it, just as they would in English. Still, people with any claims to refinement tend to avoid such common terms as *shtarbn* whenever they can. These people would *oysgeyn nokh* the same glass of water instead, in much the same way as similarly "refined" individuals don't "sweat" in English but "perspire." *Oysgeyn*, "to pass away, go out, perish," is also used to describe candles that have gone out and tends to be the preferred verb for portraying the process of dying—Donne's "As virtuous men pass mildly away" can be rendered as *"Azoy vi tsadikim geyen mild oys."* *Oysgeyn* also has the strictly Jewish meaning of taking six little steps—three backwards followed by three forwards—at the conclusion of the *shminesre*, the Eighteen Benedictions, which is recited while standing with the feet together. The double entendre gives us the saying, *dos lebn iz vi a shminesre: me shteyt un me shteyt biz me geyt oys,* "Life is like a *shminesre:* you stand and stand until you go out," until, that is, you die.

While *shtarbn* and *oysgeyn* are used in both the past and present tenses, the Hebrew-derived *nifter vern,* the equivalent of "to pass away, to depart this life," tends to refer only to people who have already passed on: in an access of Damon Runyonism, Uriel Weinreich glosses it with "to become deceased." *Nifter* has become the preferred *frum* way of avoiding the verb "to die" in English: "Just before he was *nifter,* he told me . . . ." Although *nifter vern* has become the term of choice, it stops short of attributing any qualities to the deceased beyond basic human decency; you couldn't use *nifter vern* if you were talking about Ceausescu or Idi Amin. *Ptire,* the noun related to *nifter,* is likewise used only in the most respectable of contexts; it means "passing, decease, demise."

Speaking of somebody who *iz nifter gevorn,* you can say that she *felt zikh.* The verb *feln* means "to be missing, be lacking, be in short supply"; with the reflexive *zikh* it means "not to be here anymore, to have died or passed away." *Feln zikh* has remained a polite and even respectable substitute for *shtarbn,* despite the fact that *feln* appears in all kinds of kvetches and threats. *Dos felt mir!* or *dos felt mir nokh oys!*—"that's what I lack, that's all I need"— means that I don't need it at all, it's the last thing that I need. *Vos felt dir?* is "What's wrong, what's bothering you?" The highly useful *se vet dir mer nisht feln* usually follows a monitory "Keep it up" and means "You're gonna get it!"

Nifter vern and *feln zikh* are prominent as euphemisms of first resort. They are used for relatives, close friends, and respectable individuals. You'd never describe one of your parents as being *geshtorbn* (the past participle of *shtarbn*) or speak of their *toyt,* the most basic word for death. Neither of these is dignified enough. Any idiot can *shtarbn,* and when *shtarbn* is used of respectable people, it's usually in connection with accidents, epidemics, or mass *mise meshunes*. You could say that your great-grandfather *iz nifter gevorn* almost a hundred years ago, but that he was one of those who were *geshtorbn* on the Titanic.

Shtarbn also figures in the culturally definitive *shtarbn al kidesh ha-shem*, "die for the sanctification of the Name, die a martyr's death." While dying on *kidesh ha-shem* referred originally to choosing to die rather than betray the principles of Judaism, it has come to cover any killing committed solely or primarily because the victim was a Jew.

A step up the ladder from *nifter vern, nistalek vern* is used for the passing of someone of exceptional piety or saintliness (with no connotation of martyrdom at all), a Hasidic rebbe, for instance. Unlike *nifter vern, nistalek vern* is susceptible to ironic usage or even laughter if used of the wrong person, no matter how sincerely. If your late father was nothing but an otherwise undistinguished storekeeper or a mild-mannered reporter for a great metropolitan newspaper and you say that he was *nistalek,* you're asking for the smart-ass comments that are sure to follow.

Nistalek comes from a Hebrew root meaning "take out, pay off, send away, dismiss." We saw the same root in *silekn dem nadn,* "to pay off the dowry"; *silekn a khoyv* means to discharge or pay off a debt (there were a lot of bad puns on *silekn* and silicon during the downturn in computer fortunes at the turn of this century). The noun *silek,* "settlement, payment," also has the meaning of "a rebuke, a telling off," somewhat like the English "settle someone's hash." By paying the debt, you've put an end to it. With *nistalek,* we're dealing with the reflexive form of the same Hebrew root. In this form, its basic meaning is "to distance oneself physically, be dismissed, take off." *Nistalek vern* is often associated with the superprissy *oyshoykhn di neshome. Oyshoykhn* means "to breathe out, to exhale." In English you expire, breathe your last, or give up the ghost; in Yiddish you breathe out your *neshome,* your soul.

Neshome also figures in *fokhen mit der neshome,* "to wave or fan the soul," to be on your deathbed, almost literally with one foot in the grave. Someone who *fokhet mit der neshome* is about half a step from *fargeyn in der eybikayt,* "passing on into eternity"—another highfalutin euphemism that scarcely even sounds Jewish.

Peygern, on the other hand, is about as Jewish as you can get. It is the *shtarbn* of the animal world, and there's a well-known Yiddish saying: *a hunt shtarbt nisht, er peygert,* "a dog doesn't *shtarb,* it *peygers,*" a fact that Yiddish teachers are constantly trying to drill into the heads of their students. To say *mayn hunt iz geshtorbn* instead of *mayn hunt hot gepeygert* is to embark on a Yiddish version of the Monty Python dead parrot sketch. *Peygern* can also be used to characterize the death of a wicked person—i.e., anyone with whom you disagree. A member of the Communist Party of Canada once told me that *"Trotsky iz nisht geshtorbn, er hot gepeygert,"* and there are still people who use *peygern* for most gentiles and all Germans. Fundamentally, you can use *peygern* about anybody whom you really don't like. *Peygern vi a hunt,* whether it's a description or a heartfelt wish, is the same as the English "die like a dog"—sometimes it means to die a miserable death unworthy of the person in question and sometimes it means "to die like the dog you are."

Peygern is also used of people who are alive but uncomfortable: "It's so hot in there you could *peyger.*" "I thought I was going to *peyger* from the stench," that is, die after undue suffering. *Ikh peyger nokh a trink vaser,* "I'm dying for a drink of water," is a little stronger than *shtarbn* for the same glass of water. Strangely enough, although I've lived in Canada all my life, I've never heard of anyone *peygering* from cold.

There is also the noun *peyger,* "corpse," the dead body of an animal or of a person about whom you'd use the verb *peygern. Peyger*
has an unpleasantness about it, a sense of gaminess and decay, as
does *neveyle,* which also means "corpse" or "carcass," specifically
the carcass of an animal that has not been slaughtered according
to Jewish law. When used of a human being, *neveyle* is even more
offensive than *peyger,* especially since *neveyle* can also be used to
characterize people who are still alive. A *neveyle* is a person whose
foulness affects her whole being, inside and out. Think of Farley
Granger's wife in *Strangers on a Train*—ugly, venal, adulterous, and
extortionate. Only ugly is optional here: *neveyle* is used of women
more than men and can be used to refer to a well-turned-out but
evil woman, someone like Barbara Stanwyck in *Double Indemnity.*

Turning back to *peyger,* we also get the useful noun *pgire,*
which can mean either "death" or "carcass." In the latter sense, it
came to be applied to a slow or lazy animal, usually a horse.
Mendele Moykher Sforim and Sholem Aleykhem both use *pgire*
frequently in this sense, and I can remember hearing it from
Yiddish-speaking horse players, who never seemed to bet on anything else.

Equally unpleasant, *krapirn* (or *krepirn*) means "to die a
wretched death, to croak." There's a vindictiveness about it when
applied to others, more than a little contempt for the person who
has croaked. *Krapirn* is usually used of people, and still exists in
modern German as *krepieren,* which my German-German dictionary defines as *"platzen."* The Yiddish *platsn*—which means "to
split, to burst, swell up and blow apart"—has become familiar in
Jewish and showbiz English. The patience that you lose in English has *platsed* in Yiddish; you can *plats* with shock, laughter,
envy, or dismay: "I almost *platsed* when I saw what she wore to the
Oscars."

IV

Proper treatment of the deceased is a huge *mitsve* that pays dividends in both this world and the next. *Ton dem mes zayn rekht*, "to give the deceased his due," is a fairly complicated process that starts with preparation of the body by the *khevre kadishe*, "the holy society," and continues through the funeral, burial, and proper observance of all rites of bereavement and mourning. *Khevre kadishes* still exist; in a shtetl, though, the *khevre kadishe* was the equivalent of the volunteer fire department and performed just as necessary a service. The members tended to be prominent and relatively prosperous citizens, and were known—in folklore, at any rate—for their booze-ups and bullying demeanor. They were the only game in town, and they knew it.

The *khevre kadishe's* job is to prepare the *mes* for the *levaye*, the funeral. The literal meaning of *levaye* is "escort, accompaniment;" escorting the coffin to the *besoylem*, "the eternal home" or cemetery, is a *mitsve* of the highest order. *Besoylem* comes from the Book of Ecclesiastes: "Man goes to his *bes oylem*, his eternal home, and mourners go around the streets" (Eccl. 12:5). Since describing a cemetery as a permanent dwelling place could lead demons to think that the speaker never wants to leave, *besoylem* is often replaced with *beys khayim*, "house of life"; *dos gute ort*, "the good place"; *dos heylike ort*, "the holy place"; or simply *dos feld*, "the field," terms that don't leave the demons very much to work with.

Once there, the *mes* is lowered into a *keyver*, "a grave." The process of putting a body into a *keyver* is called *kvure*, "burial." *Kvure* was also thieves' slang for a hideout, and I've been told that it was used in Nazi-occupied Europe by Jews who had gone into hiding. This latter use of *kvure* provides a telling instance of Yiddish irony at its most pointed: hiding in a metaphorical grave in order to keep out of a real one.

Keyver gives us the common *dreyen zikh in keyver,* "to spin, turn over in your grave": a Jewish university student can apply for a scholarship endowed by a well-known anti-Semite simply so that the anti-Semite *zol zikh dreyen in keyver,* "should turn over in his grave" if the student wins. *Dreyen zikh in keyver* can also be used to express dismay or disapproval on behalf of someone who would be expressing it themselves if they weren't already dead. "He sent his kids to school on Yom Kippur? *Gevalt, zayn tate der rov dreyt zikh in keyver,* his father the rabbi must be spinning in his grave."

Like everybody else who is buried in a Jewish cemetery, the spinning rabbi has been brought to *keyver yisroel,* "a Jewish grave, a Jewish burial"—burial among other Jews in an area consecrated to Jewish burial. *Brengen tsu keyver yisroel* can be a simple euphemism for burial, right up there with *brengen tsu zayn eybiker ru,* "to bring him to his eternal resting place," or it can describe the mournful homecoming of remains that had not been given a proper, or at least not a Jewish, burial.

The most famous instance of bringing someone to *keyver yisroel* concerns Rabbi Meir of Rothenburg, whose remains were finally ransomed from the emperor Albrecht fourteen years after Meir's death in prison in 1291—he refused to allow himself to be ransomed while alive, fearing that such easy money would provoke further extortions. Fourteen years of fund-raising against the will of the deceased show the importance attached to the *mitsve* of bringing someone to *keyver yisroel: er zol tsu keyver yisroel nisht kumen,* "may he not come to *keyver yisroel,*" is a well-known and utterly humorless curse. Its real meaning, to use another curse, is that *me zol nisht visn vu zayn gebeyn iz ahingekumen,* "no one should know where his bones have got to," no one should know what has become of him. He should be killed in such a way as to leave no trace; he should *aynnemen a mise meshune.*

While the reverse of *keyver yisroel* is either burial among non-Jews or no burial at all, its obverse is called *kvures khamer,* "a donkey's burial," an ignominious interment. The phrase comes from the Book of Jeremiah: "He shall be buried with the burial of an ass, dragged and thrown out beyond the gates of Jerusalem" (Jer. 22:19), which is pretty close to what really happens. "Sinners in Israel"—informers, collaborators, and the like—are buried in a separate section of their own. This section is usually identical with the area described as *hintern ployt,* "hard by the fence" at the outer edge of the cemetery—a minimum of six feet away from all the other graves—which is also reserved for suicides. While people are said to be brought to *keyver yisroel,* the proper verb for *kvures khamer,* taken likewise from the biblical verse, is *bagrobn,* "buried with the burial of an ass."

To bury or inter someone is *mekaber zayn* or, to cross over to the German component, *ba-erdikn,* which is composed of the same elements as the Latinate "to inter"—*in* plus *terra*—but in Germanic form. These are both "refined" versions of *bagrobn,* which is usually used without any echoes of the *kvures khamer. Bagrobn* is as earthy as the action that it describes and can also be used to mean "to ruin a person or enterprise." Khrushchev, banging his shoe at the United Nations and threatening to bury the West, would have said *bagrobn* if he had been speaking Yiddish. The extremely prissy *bahaltn,* literally, "to hide, conceal," is already a second-generation euphemism, a *fartaytshn* of the Hebrew *nit-man,* which is found in abbreviated form at the top of every old-fashioned Jewish gravestone, or *matseyve.* The letters *pey* and *nun,* stand for the words *po nitman,* "here is concealed [the body of]," which is followed by the name of the deceased—it's easy to see how people with pretensions to culture began to speak of concealing a body instead of burying it.

Visitors to a Jewish cemetery are usually careful to leave a pebble or other small stone on top of the *matseyve* of the person whom they've come to see. The usual explanation for this is that "they [the deceased] will see that someone has been here to visit" or that other visitors to the cemetery will see how beloved the deceased really was.

The truth is that it's a medical procedure. The belief that reading the inscription on a tombstone is bad for the memory dates back to Talmudic times. The only known remedy is another stone. Laying a stone upon the stone that's messing with your mind is some sort of homeopathic trick that nullifies the evil effects of the engraved inscription. One stone can cancel the ill effects of another, but only if there is direct contact between the stones.

V

Each member of the deceased's immediate family is called an *ovel,* "a mourner," and spends the next thirty days (twelve months if it's a parent who has died) in a state of mourning called *aveyles* in which virtually all joyful activities are avoided. The first seven days of mourning, when the mourners are not supposed to leave their homes, is called *shivâ,* from the Hebrew for "seven." You sit *shivâ,* and *zitsn shive* can also be used of any lost cause: "*Me ken zitsn shivâ nokhn gesheft,* you can sit shiva for the business." *Shivâ* leads into *shloyshim,* "thirty," a month of slightly less intense mourning which concludes the mourning period for everyone but parents.

Immediately before the funeral, everyone who will be sitting shiva performs a ritual called *raysn kriye,* "to tear [a] tearing," in which a garment is torn as a sign of mourning. *Raysn kriye* can also mean "to have trouble earning a living," as in *er rayst kriye nokh a shtikl broyt*—getting a piece of bread is as hard for him as *raysn kriye.*

Performing this ritual can also be called *koyreya zayn,* "to tear," which is related to the vaunting *koyreya ke-dag zayn,* "to tear apart like a fish," which is what the champ is going to do to any and all challengers this Sunday night at the title bout. Compare the English "make mincemeat out of"; in Yiddish, you're made into gefilte fish.

At the close of the funeral, the survivors will begin *kadish zogn,* saying Kaddish, the so-called prayer for the dead, which has nothing to do with death. It doesn't mention death, doesn't mention heaven, resurrection, or very much else that isn't God—and all it says about Him is how greatly He deserves to be praised. The message of the Mourners' Kaddish is that God's in His heaven and all's right with the world, because everything that happens, happens according to His will. As with sitting shiva, you can also say Kaddish for relationships, businesses, hopes and dreams, whatever has up and died on you: "The day the music died, we all said Kaddish for rock 'n' roll."

The idea of saying Kaddish struck a real chord with the Yiddish-speaking masses, to the point where it became a positive pleasure to daydream about your son saying Kaddish for you after your death. It isn't that anybody *wanted* to die, but everybody knew that it was coming. The idea that someone would be saying Kaddish, that you would not vanish from the world without a trace, was indeed "beyond all blessings and songs, praises and consolations in the world," as it says in the Kaddish itself. A man or woman who had daughters but no sons would have Kaddish said by a son-in-law. A man or woman who had no children now had one more reason to be miserable; siblings have a thirty-day obligation, but are far less likely to survive you than your children and are within their rights to stop when the month is over.

The best thing for the childless is a *gedungener kadish*, a "hired Kaddish," in which someone is paid to say it. The phrase itself has an air of woe and abandonment, of loneliness and a life lived in vain, that is difficult to fathom from outside. The only thing worse is a *gedungener kadish* when the deceased *has* left eligible offspring (or offspring-in-law—none of this applies to unmarried daughters) who are too lazy, self-centered, alienated, or uncaring to be bothered to go to shul every day for nearly a year. Or worse, they have abandoned the religion entirely and possibly even converted; in which case it is *kool*, "the community," that pays for the *gedungener kadish*. In such cases, *gedungener kadish* also takes on a dollop—a large dollop—of contempt for the worthless children. Whether the parent was actually worth remembering varies from case to case, but there is no excuse for the kids: mother and father are mother and father and it isn't a matter of sentiment. Colloquially, *gedungener kadish* can be used for any sort of ringer or hired gun, whether it's yourself or somebody else—*Mrs., ikh bin nor a gedungener kadish. Zayt azoy gut un red mit der farvaltung.* "Lady, I just work here. Please speak to management."

Calling a son *mayn kadish, kadish mayner, kadishl*—"my Kaddish, Kaddish of mine, little Kaddish"—is quite common in Yiddish, and little boys are often introduced to adults in just such a way. "*Mendel, kum-zhe aher un baken zikh mit mayn kadish.* Come on over here and meet my mourner." In addition to the reasons just adduced, which are cause enough for some amount of pride and satisfaction, calling your son your Kaddish is another one of those disguised blessings in which Yiddish seems to specialize. By saying that your son is going to say Kaddish after you die, you're really saying, "This is my son, he should live and be well and survive me and say Kaddish in my memory for a hundred and twenty years, amen." It's another way of showing love without ever having to admit what you're doing.

VI

As soon as the funeral is over and the body has been laid in the ground, the owner of that body begins to undergo *khibet ha-keyver*, "the beating of the grave," or as Alexander Harkavy puts it in his dictionary, "the percussion of the grave." It's Duke Ellington's "Caravan" with the drum solo, only you're the drum. Harkavy, who definitely had a way with English, goes on to say, "Punishment inflicted on the defunct at the grave." This punishment is described in a *medresh:*

> The *malekh ha-moves* comes and sits on the grave, gives the occupant a whack with his hand and tells him to get up and tell the *malekh* his name. The deceased has forgotten his name and says, "It is known and revealed before the Creator of the Universe that I do not know my name." The *malekh* brings the body back to life and has it submit to judgment; it is found guilty of lying. In his hand, the *malekh* holds a chain, half fire and half iron. He hits the body with it once and the limbs fall apart; a second time, the bones fall apart. Then the ministering angels come and gather up the bones and make the deceased stand up again. And the *malekh ha-moves* beats him for a third time. The deceased is then asked to give an account of himself, and he is judged according to his deserts. He is judged for two days, and on the third they start to beat him—the eyes, ears, lips, tongue and teeth (*Masekhes Khibut Ha-Kever* 2).

There is a peculiarly Yiddish feel to all this. No matter what the question, you know in advance that there's no right answer—it's the sort of thing that helped make Kafka Kafka. *Khibet ha-keyver* appears in *er vet shoyn nisht hobn ken khibet ha-keyver,* "he won't have to undergo *khibet ha-keyver,*" because he has already suffered enough in life. This is the Yiddish equivalent of the jackets that Vietnam vets used to wear: "When I die I'm going to heaven, 'cause I've done my time in hell."

Just as death marks a new stage in Jewish suffering—the one for which death itself offers no hope of release—so the coming of the Messiah, when everything is supposed to be rosy, brings its own unique sort of pain, called *gilgel mekhiles,* "cave rolling":

> "Rabbi Elazar said in the name of Rabbi Simon: The Holy One, Blessed Be He, makes caves for them [the dead] in the ground and they travel by rolling through them until they come to the land of Israel, and when they get to the land of Israel the Holy One, Blessed Be He, puts the spirit of life into them and they stand up, as it is said: 'And I will put my spirit within you and you shall live' (Ezek. 37:14)" [*Bereyshis Rabbo* 28].

Originally intended to answer one of the great *klots-kashes* of all time—how would all the Jews who died in exile get to the land of Israel to be resurrected?—this *medresh* was later elaborated into yet another description of tortures and torments, including demons who beat you with hot metal rods from one end of the earth to the other. Avoiding such treatment was a powerful inducement to die in the land of Israel, and over the centuries many Jews went there for precisely that reason—not to live but to die, and thus avoid the underground caves and their tormenting demons. The custom of placing a bag of *erets-yisroel erd,* "dirt from the land of Israel," in the casket is usually portrayed as a naive yearning for Zion rather than the sophisticated trick that it really is. With that dirt in your grave, you can stand up before the demons and say in all truthfulness, "Sorry, guys, but I *was* buried in the soil of Israel, my dust has already joined itself with the dust of the Holy Land and there's nothing you can do about it."

The *gilgel* in *gilgel mekhiles* comes from a Hebrew verb that means "to roll, knead, bring to pass." Used on its own in Yiddish, *gilgel* means "metamorphosis," "transmigration of the soul," or "(re)incarnation." Shirley MacLaine is always talking about her different *gilgulim;* a dybbuk is the *gilgel* of a dead creature that has taken up residence in a living one, and so on. The verbal form is *megulgl vern:* "And the handsome prince was *megulgl gevorn in* an ugly, croaking frog." There is a folk belief that kosher butchers who knowingly sell *treyf* to their customers *vern megulgl in* dogs after they die. This meaning is illustrated perfectly in the famous curse, *Zolst mir megulgl vern in a henglaykhter:* "You should be reincarnated as a chandelier": *Bay tog zolstu hengen un bay nakht zolstu brenen,* "You should hang by day and burn by night."

Megulgl vern can also be used to express surprise at seeing someone in a particular place: *Gib nor a kuk ver s'iz megulgl gevorn,* "Look who's here," as if the rabbi to whom you're speaking didn't walk into the burlesque house on his own two feet but was unwittingly transmigrated there by occult forces beyond his comprehension.

Megulgl's meaning of "to be transformed, to turn into" is related to the Germanically rooted Yiddish verb *farvarfn,* which can also mean "transform." But *farvarfn* can also mean "to throw, toss," as in *farvarfn mitn kop,* "to turn your head away, shake your head, be unwilling to do something." *Farvarfn mit di fis,* "to shake a leg," has nothing to do with making haste; it's the Yiddish way of kicking off or kicking the bucket. Similarly, there is *oystsien di fis,* "to stretch your legs" (like a corpse, that is), and even to do so *af der langer bank,* "on the long bench." The bench is the ground, the longest bench of all, where a corpse is laid out immediately after death. There is also *oystsien di potkeves,* "to stretch out your horseshoes"; you're a horse, you've fallen, and you'll never get up.

A dead person is said to *lign mit di fis tsu der tir,* "to lie with his feet toward the door," in the halakhically mandated position for a corpse, or *avekgeyn a borveser tsu got,* "go barefoot to God." You can *lign mitn pupik aroyf,* "navel side up"; compare the English "belly-up," but the Yiddish is not restricted to bankruptcy and business failure. You can also *geyn a gang,* "go off on an errand." *Er iz gegangen a gang,* "he's stepped out for a moment"—yes, because a thousand years are as a yesterday's day to the Lord. This is an ironic version of being summoned to the yeshiva in heaven.

Someone can be said to *opzogn di kapote,* "to give up or bequeath his capote" so that someone else can wear it—he won't be needing it where he's going (compare the English, "hang up his guns" and the Yiddish *opzogn di etlekhe gildn,* "bequeath his pocket change"—a *gildn* was worth fifteen kopecks), and you can say *men geyt shoyn in zayne shikh,* "someone else is already wearing his shoes," which isn't very nice but also doesn't flinch from the truth. Not nice and probably not even true, *men est shoyn ire beygl,* "someone else is eating her bagels," not only takes us all the way back to *lign in dr'erd un bakn beygl,* it also reminds us of the poverty at the root of so much Yiddish life for so many hundreds of years.

Finally, there's *makhn a siyem,* "to make an end," but with a bit of a twist that brings it closer to "go to graduation." Someone who *makht a siyem* brings a project of some sort to an end. The word *siyem* has never lost its Talmudic associations, though, and has come to be applied to the celebration held to mark the completion—the *siyem*—of a course of Talmudic study, whether that course consists of the entire Talmud, one of its six orders, or an individual tractate. It celebrates the attainment of a goal and is often attended by a sizable *kiddesh*.

Even people who didn't learn at all were aware of the annual *siyem* held on *tunis bekhoyres*, the Fast of the Firstborn that takes place on the eve of Passover. Firstborn Jewish men are supposed to fast as a way of showing their appreciation for the fact that they would have been spared when all the firstborn in Egypt were killed on this date, the eve of Passover. As this is a minor fast, not prescribed by the Torah and not incumbent on the entire people, it can be canceled if there's a good reason, and a community celebration is always a good reason in such cases—especially on Passover eve, when there's always a ton of work to be done and supper won't be served much earlier than nine or ten that night. So the rabbi of each congregation studies something, generally a very small tractate, and times its completion to coincide with the morning service on the eve of Passover. He finishes the tractate in public, makes the appropriate blessing, and invites everybody to the *kiddesh* to celebrate the *siyem*. It would be unseemly to refuse, and firstborn males who do not attend the *siyem* are still obliged to fast.

Everybody knew about the *siyem*, everybody knew that the word means "conclusion, the end of what you've been doing," and everybody noticed that a funeral, which also marks an end, is also followed by a meal at the shiva house. Everybody also knew that part of the *siyem* ritual consists of saying Kaddish. *Makhn a siyem* is descriptive and ironic at the same time, like so much of Yiddish, like so much of life.

GLOSSARY

The glossary is designed for quick reference. It lists basic nouns and verbs; representative expressions from each chapter; words and phrases that recur throughout the book; and weird stuff that readers might want to find quickly.

afikoymen—piece of *matse* eaten to end the seder meal; *ibergegesn mit afikoymens*—"to have eaten too many *afikoymens*," to die of old age

aftselakhis—to spite (someone), in spite of

akhtsn un draytsn—eighteen plus thirteen; *redn fun akhtsn un draytsn*—to talk about a delicate subject, to talk about money

aliye—being called up to the reading of the Torah in the synagogue

alt—old

amkho—the common people, the not-so-silent Jewish majority

asher yotser—"He who has created," blessing said after relieving oneself; *asher yotser papir*—toilet paper

ashires—wealth

avekleygn dem tatn—"to lay your daddy down," sign your name

ayngemarinirt—marinated; *ayngemarinirt in esik un honik*—"marinated in vinegar and honey," dressed to the nines

aynredn a kind in boykh—"talk a child into someone's belly," to convince someone of something ridiculous

azoy—so, thus

bagegenish—meeting, encounter

bagrobn—to bury

baleboste—hausfrau, female boss, proprietress

bankes—cups (for healing); *helfn vi a toytn bankes*—to help like cups on a corpse

barmenen—corpse

barot—care, custody; *af gots barot*—abandoned, forsaken; left to God's care

bashert—destined, preordained; *basherte(r)*—predestined mate

batsoln—to pay; *batsoln rebbe-gelt*—"to pay tuition," learn from experience

beheyme—animal, beast; cow

berye—person who is very good at a particular activity; a good *baleboste*

bes-medresh—small synagogue; chapel in a larger synagogue

besoylem—cemetery

betn—to ask; to pray

beyz—evil, bad, angry

biter—bitter; *biterer tropn*—"bitter drop," hard liquor

blintse—blintz

blote—mud, mire

bobe—grandmother; *bobe-mayse*—cock and bull story

bobkes—goat turds; sweet fuck-all

bokher—adolescent male; bachelor

borekh dayan emes—"blessed be the righteous judge"; said on hearing of a person's death

borekh ha-shem—blessed be God

boykh—belly

bris—circumcision

bube—see *bobe*

bupkes—see *bobkes*

Chanuka gelt—money given as a Chanukah present

dakhtn—to seem, mention

dales—poverty

darfn—ought, to have to, to need; *darfn vi a lokh in kop*—to need like a hole in the head *davenen*—to pray (used only of Jewish prayer)

derlebn—to live to see

dermanen/dermonen—to mention, remind

dibek (plu., *dibukim*)—demon or soul of a dead person that has taken over the body of a living person

dover akher—"something else," a pig

dreyen—to spin, turn, twist

dybbuk—see *dibek*

efsher—maybe, perhaps

epes—something, somewhat

esn—to eat

eyfele—infant

eyver—member of the body; penis

fardinen—to earn, deserve, merit

fargesn—to forget; *got zol in dir fargesn*—may God forget about you

farkrenken—to spend money on an illness

fartaytshn—interpret; translate from Hebrew into Yiddish

fayer—fire

fayfn—to whistle; have contempt for someone

feln zikh—to be deceased

fir kashes—the four questions recited at the Passover seder

fleyshik—having to do with meat

foter—father

frage—question

fregn—to ask; *freg nisht*—don't ask

frimer—comparative form of *frum*

frum—religious, pious

fus—foot, leg

galekh—Catholic priest

galitsiyaner—native of Galicia

ganeydn—paradise, the Garden of Eden

gants—whole; *in gantsn*—completely, totally

gedakht—*nisht far aykh/ken yidn gedakht*—it shouldn't happen to you/to a Jew

gelt—money

gesheft—business

geshmat—see *shmadn zikh*

get—divorce

gevis—certain

gey in dr'erd—"go into the ground"; drop dead

gezogt: af ale yidishe kinder gezogt—all the Jews should be so lucky

gezunt—health; healthy

gikh—quick

glik—good luck, happiness

glomp—stalk of a cabbage or lettuce; stupid person

goles—exile

gonef—thief

gornisht—nothing

got—God

goy (adj., *goyishe*)—non-Jewish man

goye—non-Jewish woman

groys—big, large, great

gut/git—good

hadloke—lighting candles on the Sabbath and *yontef*

hagode—"narrative," the collection of prayers, songs, and stories recited at the Passover seder

hakn a tshaynik—"to knock a teapot," rattle on at great and pointless length

hakn—to chop, knock; (vulg.) to fuck

halevay—"would that . . ."; "if only . . ."

halokhe—Jewish law

ha-moytse—blessing made over bread

havdole—division; ceremony marking the end of the Sabbath or Jewish holiday

haynt—today

hefker—ownerless, lawless

hekht—pike (fish); sucker

helfn—to help

heshayne—willow twig used on the holiday of Sukkes

heysn—to be called, named

hon—rooster

Hoshana Rabba—seventh day of Sukkes when *heshaynes* are beaten against the floor and benches of the synagogue

hundert un tsvantsik—one hundred twenty, the optimal human life span

hun—hen, chicken

hunt—dog

inyen—subject, matter, topic

itst—now

ivre—Hebrew as a language of study and prayer; *ivre be-loy*—using Hebrew words in the presence of a *goy* who understands Yiddish

Kaddish—prayer recited in memory of a deceased relative; also used to refer to your son

kadokhes—ague, fever

kal ve-khoymer—argument that proceeds from a minor to a major premise

kale—engaged girl; bride

kaporenik—gentile

kaporenitse—chicken

kapores; shlogn kapores—a penitential ritual in which poultry is waved around the head on the eve of Yom Kippur; *a sheyne reyne kapore*—good riddance

kaptsn—pauper

kashe—1) a difficult question; 2) gruel, porridge; a dish made with buckwheat groats *kashres*—kosherness

katsef—butcher

kazarme—barracks; *a kazarme zol af dir aynfaln*—may a barracks collapse on you

ketsele/ketsenyu/ketsl—"pussycat," darling

keyle—vessel, instrument

keyn yirbu—"so may they increase"

keynehore—"no evil eye"

keyver—grave

khad gadye—song with which the Passover seder ends; jail

khale—egg bread; *nemen khale*—to take *khale*, throw a piece of dough into the fire when baking

khalemoyed—intermediate days of Passover and Sukkes; penis

khapn—to grab, snatch

khasene—wedding

khateysim—Boers

khazer-fisl—pig's foot; *aroysshteln a kosher khazer-fisl*—to show only the kosher-looking part of an unkosher activity or proposition

khazer—pig

khet—sin

kheyder—traditional elementary school

kheylek—portion, section

khitsoynim—demons, evil spirits

khokhem—sage, idiot; *khokhem be-layle*—"a sage at night," idiot

khomets—leavened or fermented food that cannot be eaten on Passover; contraband

khosn—engaged man; bridegroom

khotsh—although, at least

khoydesh—month

khumesh—the Pentateuch

khupe—canopy

khutspe—chutzpah, overweening gall

kidesh ha-shem—sanctification of the Name; *shtarbn af kidesh ha-shem*—
to be martyred for being Jewish

kimpet—childbed, lying-in

kishke—stuffed derma

kishkes—guts, innards

klafte—bitch

klal—rule, standard; community; *klal yisroel*—the Jewish people as a
whole; *klal-shprakh*—standard language

klap—stroke, blow

kleyner; der kleyner—junior, the little guy, the penis

klipe—"husk," evil spirit, shrew, troublesome child

klole—curse

klots—wooden beam; klutz

klots-kashe—stupid question

knip—pinch

koyekh—strength, power

koyfn—to buy

koylen—to slaughter (nonkosher)

krank—sick, ill

krapirn—to croak

krekhts—moan, groan

krenk—disease, illness

krepl (plu., *kreplekh*)—dumpling

krikhn—to crawl

kugl/kigl—noodle or potato pudding

kukn—to look; *kukn vi a hon in bney-odem*—to stare like a chicken at the
kapores ritual

kumen—to come, arrive

kupern—of brass, brazen; *kuperner yeytser hore*—fetishistic sexual desire

kupl—yarmulke

kushn—to kiss

kvetshn—to squeeze, press, urge, complain

kvure—burial

lakhn mit yashtsherkes—"to laugh with lizards," to laugh through one's pain

layt—people, respectable people

lehavdl—"you should excuse me, you should pardon the expression"; used to separate sacred and profane people or things that are mentioned immediately after each other

levaye—funeral

levone—moon

leygn—to lay, place

leynen—to read

lign—falsehood, lie; *lign in dr'erd un bakn beygl*—to lie in the ground, baking bagels; be up a creek

link—left

litvak—Lithuanian

litvish—Lithuanian and White Russian Yiddish

lokshn—noodles

loshn—language; *loshn sgey-nehoyr*—euphemism; *loshn-koydesh*—the holy tongue; Hebrew; the Hebrew and Aramaic component of Yiddish

loy aleykhem—may it not befall you

loy oleynu—may it not befall us

maalegeyren—to ruminate, chew cud

make—plague, blow

makhle—sickness

malekh—angel; *malekh ha-moves*—Angel of Death

mame-loshn—mother tongue; Yiddish

mamoshes—substance, substantiality

mark-yidene—market woman

matse—unleavened bread

matseyve—gravestone

mayse—story, deed; (vulg.) cunt

mazik (plu., *mazikim*)—demon

mazl—constellation, luck; *mazl tov*—congratulations

mehume—riot, turmoil

mekhitse—divider between men and women in a synagogue

mekhutn (m.), *mekhuteneste* (f.)—father and mother of your son- or daughter-in-law

melamed—*kheyder* teacher

mentsh—person, human being; decent, upstanding person

mer—more; carrot

mern zikh—to increase

mes—dead person, dead body

meshiekh—the Messiah; *meshiekhs tsaytn*—the messianic era

meshuge/meshige—crazy

meshugener/meshigener—crazy person

meshumad—apostate, Jew who has converted to another religion

meydl—girl

mikve—ritual bath

milkhik—dairy; *milkhike oygn*—milky eyes, dewy eyes

minyen—quorum of ten men for prayer

mise-meshune—"strange death," violent death

mitsve—positive commandment; good deed

miyes—ugly

moyd—maid, termagant; *alte moyd*—spinster, old maid

moyel—circumcisor

moykhl zayn—to pardon, forgive, excuse; *der zayts mir moykhl*—rear end

moyshe ve-arendlekh—little Moses-and-Aarons; *sheyne moyshe ve-arendlekh*—nice boobs

nakhes—pleasure, satisfaction

nakht—night

nar—fool

nekhtiker tog—"a yesterday's day"; bullshit

nekhtn—yesterday

neshome—soul; *oyshoykhn di neshome*—to breathe one's last

neveyle—carrion, improperly slaughtered animal; vicious person

nide—menstruation; a woman having her period

nifter vern—to pass away

nikhpe—epilepsy

nishkoshe—okay, pretty good, tolerable

nisht geshtoygn un nisht gefloygn—"it didn't climb up and it didn't fly"; unbelievable story or excuse

nitl—Christmas

nitsn—to use

nokh—after, even, still

nomen—name

nopl—navel

nudnik—persistent bore

olehasholem/olevhasholem—may she rest in peace/may he rest in peace

opgesheyt zol er/zi zayn—may he/she be separated from us (because they're dead)

orel (plu., *areylim*)—uncircumcised man; gentile

oreman—pauper

oremkayt—poverty

ovel—bereaved person, mourner

oyg—eye

oylem habe—the next world

oylem haze—"this world," sensual pleasure

oysgematert—exhausted

oysgemutshet—exhausted

oysgeputst in esik un honik—"decked out in vinegar and honey," dressed to kill

oysgeyn—to perish

oyssheygetsn—to bawl out

oyszen—to look (like), appear, resemble

oyszen vi a hon nokh tashmish—to look like a rooster who's just finished having sex; appear exhausted

oyszen vi an opgeshlogene heshayne—look like a willow twig that's been beaten on the floor; look the worse for wear

oytser—treasure

parnose—livelihood, occupation

parve—neutral, neither dairy nor meat

patsh—slap

pempik—short, squat person

petreshke—parsley

*peye (*plu.*, peyes)*—sidelock

peygern—to die (used of animals; contemptuous if used of a person)

peysakh—Passover

pgire—animal carcass; death of an animal

pintele—dot, Hebrew vowel sign; *pintele yid*—one's Jewish essence

pirge—perogie; (vulg.) pussy, cunt

pisher—pisser, small child, young or inexperienced person

pishn—to piss

platsn—to burst

pleytses—shoulders, back

ployneste—"the missus"

polyakn—Poles; Polish Jews

ponim—face

porets—nobleman, aristocrat

posek—biblical verse; *vi in posek shteyt*—as it is written in the Bible; par excellence

poter vern—to get rid of

poyer—peasant

poyersher kop—"peasant head," stupid person

poylish—Polish

prost—simple, common, vulgar

ptire—decease, passing

pupik/pipik—belly button

rakhmone litslan—heaven forfend

rashe—Rashi, the preeminent commentator on the Bible and Talmud

reb—mister

rebbe—*kheyder* teacher; leader of a Hasidic group

redn—to speak

refue—remedy, cure

rekht—right

reyn—pure, clean

ruekh (plu., *rukhes*)—devil, demon, evil spirit

ruf -nomen—Hebrew name by which a man is summoned to the Torah; always in the form of "X ben [son of] Y"

seyfer toyre—Torah scroll

seykhl—reason, intelligence

shabbes—the Sabbath, Saturday

shaleshides—third meal on the Sabbath

shammes—sexton

shatkhn—marriage broker, matchmaker

shed (plu., *sheydim*)—demon

shekhine—divine presence

shekhtn—to slaughter according to Jewish law

sheltn—to curse

sheygets—young gentile male

sheyn—beautiful, pretty

sheytl—wig worn by married Orthodox women

shidekh—match

shikker—drunk

shikn—to send

shikse—non-Jewish girl

shive—seven days of mourning following the death of a family member

shkhite—kosher slaughtering

shkots—mischievous Jewish youth

shlekht—bad

shlepn—to drag, draw, pull

shlimazl—bad luck; someone who has bad luck

shlimazlnitse—bad housekeeper

shlogn—to hit, strike, beat

shloyshim—thirty-day mourning period following the death of a family member

shlumperke—sloven, bad housekeeper

shmad—conversion, apostasy

shmadn zikh—to apostatize

shmalts—animal fat

shminesre—Eighteen Blessings, central prayer of all services

sho—hour; *in a guter sho*—in an auspicious hour

shoykhet—ritual slaughterer

shoyn—already, right away

shprakh—language

shraybn—to write

shrayen—to scream, yell

shtarbn—to die

shtark—strong; very

shtendik—always

shtern—star; forehead

shteyen—to stand

shtinkerke—see *shlumperke*

shtupn/shtopn—to stuff; to fuck, to screw;

shul—synagogue

shvanger—pregnant

shvarts-yor—the devil

shver—hard, difficult; father-in-law

shvitsn—to sweat

shvues—Festival of Pentecost

sibe—reason, cause; accident

sidder—prayer book

sitre akhre—"the other side," the collective designation for evil spirits

siyem—conclusion; end of a course of study; celebration of such a completion

skhoyre—merchandise, wares

sof—end, conclusion

sonim (sing., *soyne*)—enemies; *af mayne sonim gezogt*—it should happen to my enemies

strakhovke—insurance; *zolst brenen on strakhovke*—you should have a fire and be uninsured

sude—feast, banquet; meal

sukke—a hut erected for the festival of Sukkes

sukkes—Festival of Tabernacles

takhles—point, purpose, result; "brass tacks," business

takhrikhim—shrouds; *shtarbn in fremde takhrikhim*—"to die in someone else's shrouds," die deeply in debt

tallis—prayer shawl

tantsn—to dance

tarfes—unkosher food

tashlikh—Rosh Hashana ritual in which Jews stand by a river and turn their pockets inside out, as if casting their sins into the depths of the sea

tashmish (short for *tashmish ha-mite*, use of the bed)—sexual intercourse

tate—father, dad

taytsh—translation, interpretation

tayvl—devil

tefillin—phylacteries

tishe b'ov—the Ninth of Av, the anniversary of the destruction of both Temples; the saddest day on the Jewish calendar

tnoyim—"conditions," an engagement contract

tokhter—daughter

toygn—to suit, be fit (for); be good for

toykhekhe—reproof, esp. "chapters of reproof" in the Bible (Lev. 26 and Deut. 28); *oyslozn di gantse toykhekhe (af)*—to pile curse after curse onto someone

toyt—dead; *toyte kloles*—vehement curses

trefn—to happen, befall; to meet, encounter

treyf—not kosher; forbidden; illegitimate

trinkn—to drink

trogedik—pregnant

tsebrokhn—broken

tseveynen zikh—to burst into tears

tshatshke—knickknack, ornament, trinket

tshaynik—teapot; *hakn a tshaynik*—to prattle on pointlessly; *hak mir nisht ken tshaynik*—enough with the chin music, knock it off; talk about something else for a change

tsholnt—stew eaten on the Sabbath

tsibele—onion; *zolst vaksn vi a tsibele, mitn kop in dr'erd*—may you grow like an onion, with your head in the ground

tsimmes—fruit or vegetable stew; fuss, commotion, big deal

tsitsis—fringed ritual undergarment

tsore—standard language pronunciation of *tsure*

tsure (plu., *tsuris*)—trouble, affliction

tukhes—ass, butt

umglik—misfortune, calamity

vayzuse—penis; jerk

ver—imperative of *vern*, to become; *ver dershokhtn*—get stabbed; *ver dershtikt*—get suffocated; *ver dervorgn*—get choked; *ver geharget*—"get killed"; drop dead; *ver tsezest*—blow up

veynen—to cry, weep

veynik—few, not enough

vintshn—to wish

visn—to know

vist—dismal, desolate

voynen—to live, dwell

yandes—nerve, gall

yemakh shmoy—may his name be blotted out; *yemakh-shmoynik/yemakh-shmoynitse*—scoundrel, evildoer, SOB

yene velt—the other world, the next world

yenike, di—"those others," demons

yentsn—(vulg.) to fuck

yeytser hore—the evil inclination; *yeytser hore bleterl*—hickey; *yeytser tov*—the good inclination

yid—Jew, anonymous male

yidene—(pej.) Jewish woman

yidish—Jewish

yidishkayt—Judaism; Jewishness; Jewish culture

yidishn—to circumcise

yingl—boy

yold—sap (i.e., a person)

yontef (plu., *yontoyvim*)—Jewish religious festival; holiday; special occasion

yor—year; *aykh tsu lengere yor*—may you live for many years

yortsayt—anniversary of a person's death

yoyz—crucifix; sourpuss

yung—young

zakh—a thing; (vulg.) vagina

zayn—to be

zets—blow

zingen—to sing

zitsn—to sit

zogn—to say

zokhn—(pej.) to be ill

zol lebn—may he/she live

zoln—should